ANCIENT FAITH *for the* CHURCH'S FUTURE

EDITED BY

Mark Husbands AND Jeffrey P. Greenman

IVP Academic

An imprint of InterVarsity Press
Downers Grove, Illinois

InterVarsity Press
P.O. Box 1400, Downers Grove, IL 60515-1426
World Wide Web: www.ivpress.com
E-mail: email@ivpress.com

InterVarsity Press® is the book-publishing division of InterVarsity Christian Fellowship/USA®, a student movement active on campus at hundreds of universities, colleges and schools of nursing in the United States of America, and a member movement of the International Fellowship of Evangelical Students. For information about local and regional activities, write Public Relations Dept., InterVarsity Christian Fellowship/USA, 6400 Schroeder Rd., P.O. Box 7895, Madison, WI 53707-7895, or visit the IVCF website at <www.intervarsity.org>.

Unless otherwise noted, the Scripture quotations quoted herein are from the New Revised Standard Version of the Bible, *copyright 1989 by the Division of Christian Education of the National Council of the Churches of Christ in the U.S.A. Used by permission. All rights reserved.*

Design: Cindy Kiple
Images: church: Jim Pruitt/iStockphoto
        open door: Ugur Evirgen/iStockphoto

ISBN 978-0-8308-2881-4

Printed in the United States of America ∞

Library of Congress Cataloging-in-Publication Data

Ancient faith for the church's future / edited by Mark Husbands and
Jeffrey P. Greenman.
     p. cm.
 Includes bibliographical references and index.
 ISBN 978-0-8308-2881-4 (pbk.: alk. paper)
 1. Evangelicalism—Congresses. 2. Church renewal—Congresses. 3.
Church history—Primitive and early church, ca. 30-600—Congresses.
I. Husbands, Mark, 1961- II. Greenman, Jeffrey P.
BR1640.A2A53 2008
230—dc22

                                                                      2008002176

P	21	20	19	18	17	16	15	14	13	12	11	10	9	8	7	6	5	4	3	2	1
Y	26	25	24	23	22	21	20	19	18	17	16	15	14	13	12	11	10	09	08			

In memory of
Robert E. Webber
(1933-2007)
Teacher, scholar, mentor, colleague and friend

Contents

Introduction

Mark Husbands

We do not presume to come to this thy Table, O merciful Lord, trusting in our own righteousness, but in thy manifold and great mercies. We are not worthy so much as to gather up the crumbs under thy Table. But thou art the same Lord, whose property is always to have mercy: Grant us therefore, gracious Lord, so to eat the flesh of thy dear Son Jesus Christ, and to drink his blood, that our sinful bodies may be made clean by his body, and our souls washed through his most precious blood, and that we may evermore dwell in him, and he in us. Amen.

Cranmer's dramatic and arresting "Prayer of Humble Access" brings to mind a crucial facet of the Christian life: the church exists at the hand of a gracious and merciful Lord. As evangelical Christians, our love of Scripture arises out of God's use of the Word in our lives. We aim not only to hear God's Word but also to put it into practice. Thus, we should be eager to hear the witness of Christians throughout the history of the church who likewise have been moved by God's Word. When the content of the church's confession coheres with the witness of Scripture, and when Scripture is regarded as the ground of the church's tradition, respect for the place of tradition is a matter of considerable importance. Notice Paul's appeals to tradition: "Be imitators of me, as I am of Christ. I commend you because you remember me in everything and maintain the traditions just as I handed them on to you" (1 Cor 11:1-2) and "Now we command you, beloved, in the name of our Lord Jesus Christ, to keep away from believers who are living in idleness and not according to the tradition that they received from us" (2 Thess 3:6). We should take from this the claim that when a given tradition is consonant with God's self-revelation, it is to be upheld and honored by the church. On this count, the early confessions, creeds, hymns, commentaries, sermons and works of theology constitute a deposit or treasury of ancient witnesses.

In May 2006, Robert Webber and Phil Kenyon published "A Call to an Ancient Evangelical Future." The prologue to this document declares, "In every age the Holy Spirit calls the Church to examine its faithfulness to God's revelation in Jesus Christ, authoritatively recorded in Scripture and handed down through the Church." Aware of the striking challenges posed to Christianity by competing narratives, the "Call" exhorts evangelical Christians to "restore the priority of the divinely inspired biblical story of God's acts in history" in order that "the Church will be strengthened to address the issues of our day." Given the precise focus of our edited volume, article 3 of the Call is germane:

> We call for the Church's reflection to remain anchored in the Scriptures in continuity with the theological interpretation learned from the early Fathers. Thus, we call Evangelicals to turn away from methods that separate theological reflection from the common traditions of the Church. These modern methods compartmentalize God's story by analyzing its separate parts, while ignoring God's entire redemptive work as recapitulated in Christ. Anti-historical attitudes also disregard the common biblical and theological legacy of the ancient Church.

The Call stands in a much larger tradition than one might imagine. Perhaps without being fully aware of the fact, the Call represents a long overdue summons to learn from arguably one of the most significant theological developments of the twentieth century: *ressourcement* theology.

In the middle of the twentieth century, a group of French theologians, including Henri de Lubac, Jean Daniélou, Henri Bouillard, Yves Congar, Louis Bouyer and Marie-Dominique Chenu, and the Swiss Hans Urs von Balthasar inaugurated a remarkable theological movement termed *ressourcement* theology. While far from being a unified school of thought, these figures shared a common belief that the writings of the early church constitute an incomparable source for the contemporary renewal of the church. Facing a post-Christian Europe, *ressourcement* theologians turned to the work of great patristic and medieval theologians such as Origen, Ignatius of Antioch, Cyprian, Chrysostom, Cyril of Alexandria, Augustine, John of Damascus and Thomas Aquinas. In so doing, they essentially rediscovered crucial sources for the revitalization of contemporary theology and pastoral life. These forward-looking theologians sought creative and faithful ways of moving beyond the rigid neo-Scholasticism represented in Pope Leo XIII's 1879 promulgation of *Aeterni Patris*.

A number of intriguing parallels can be drawn between the challenges faced by Roman Catholic theologians leading up to Vatican II and the contemporary state of evangelical theology. Maurice Blondel, for instance, saw that neo-Scholasticism bore a stronger family resemblance to Aristotle than it did to Augustine. Blondel and Lubac observed that when neo-Scholasticism drew a sharp distinction between the natural and supernatural, it unwittingly helped to usher in the very secularism that marks a contemporary post-Christian Europe. Similarly, when evangelical Protestants aim to secure the meaning of the biblical text by relying on a theory of authorial intention, we need to wonder about the long-term effects of such a move. Evaluating the conservative theological response to Hans-Georg Gadamer and E. D. Hirsch, Roger Lundin perceptively argues that by openly embracing Hirsch, many conservative critics of Gadamer have unknowingly "appropriated a theory of intentionality directly connected to Friedrich Schleiermacher's heterodox views of Christ" when ironically "Gadamer's understanding of interpretation issues in good part from Lutheran theology and Trinitarian reflection."[1] Although conservative critics of Gadamer might not immediately recognize this, Gadamer stands much closer to Augustine than does Hirsch. Those familiar with Augustine's remarkable work *De Doctrina Christiana* recognize that the patristic period saw a necessary correspondence between reading and growth in Christian formation. In contrast, the modern period approaches reading in

---

[1]Roger Lundin, *From Nature to Experience* (New York: Rowman & Littlefield, 2005), p. 158.

ways that are self-consciously devoid of prayer for God's grace and illumination. The Jesuit theologian George Schner writes, "The modern call to methodological virtue carries with it demands such as 'be critical,' 'be inventive,' 'be accommodating,' 'be authentic.' Faith, hope and charity are present in the modern metaphors, but decidedly on modern grounds." To this he adds, "The chastened modern faith of Kant saves doctrine and Scripture by purging them of what in patristic practice gave them their content and power, namely revelation."[2] Given all of this, it is evident that if contemporary evangelical theology aspires to help the church engage the contemporary world in a faithful and persuasive fashion, it would do well to recover the best conversation partners it can find, even if this means reaching back a thousand or more years. As we have indicated, "A Call to an Ancient Evangelical Future" is an indispensable invitation to recover the kind of approach to the early church that we find so powerfully on display in Roman Catholic *ressourcement* theology.

The 2007 Wheaton Theology Conference sought to demonstrate the viability and promise of an evangelical engagement with the early church. This volume includes a number of the most constructive and perceptive examples of evangelical Protestant *ressourcement* theology. Standing in the shadow of Lubac, we believe that Christianity cannot meet the challenges of modernity and postmodernity without returning to the tradition of the early church.

This volume is divided into four parts, each with a particular focus. The first portion of this work is dedicated to providing the underlying rationale and attendant challenges of an evangelical *ressourcement* theology. Christopher Hall offered a keynote address at the conference, and his work, "Tradition, Authority, Magisterium: Dead End or New Horizon?" leads off this volume. Charting a path through the thicket of concerns voiced by evangelicals regarding the appeal to tradition, Hall offers a winsome apologetic arguing that evangelical Protestants must pay serious attention to the church fathers. Showing the substantial difference between the doc-

---

[2]George Schner, "Scripture, Modernity and Patristic Principles," in *Essays Catholic and Critical*, ed. Philip G. Ziegler and Mark Husbands (Burlington: Ashgate, 2003), p. 184.

trine of *sola Scriptura* and a common yet confused appeal to *nuda Scriptura* (a view of the Bible in which no ecclesial context is thought to bear on the meaning of the text), Hall prompts a vital consideration of reading Scripture with the church fathers. Standing with the patristic tradition, one of the most important contributions of Hall's work lies in his judgment that genuine discipleship requires "a lengthy apprenticeship to Jesus under the tutelage of those who have known him well."[3] Beyond acknowledging that theologians such as Athanasius, Gregory of Nazianzus, Irenaeus, Basil the Great, John Chrysostom and Augustine were able to properly discern the voice of the Good Shepherd, Hall argues that the contemporary church will be impoverished if we fail to follow the pattern set by the church fathers in seeking the ongoing guidance and protection of the Holy Spirit for the church.

The annual Wheaton theology conference has often been an ecumenical affair. Given the precedent of Roman Catholic *ressourcement* theology, it was crucial to have Father Brian Daley participate in the conference. Documenting the guiding theological and spiritual convictions of Roman Catholic *ressourcement* theologians, Daley shows that Scripture and the theological interpretations of the early church constitute a necessary basis for the renewal of theology and the church. In conversation with Irenaeus, Origen and Augustine, Daley argues that it is only within a "worshiping, discerning, interpreting, preaching church that Scripture becomes Scripture—is received as a canon and generates the rule of faith."[4] This positive depiction of the relationship between scriptural interpretation and the community's rule of faith is followed by an exhortation to read "old books" (the theology of the church fathers), for they form us with irreplaceable vitality and promise into Christ and his church.

Turning to D. H. Williams's contribution, "*Similis et Dissimilis:* Gauging Our Expectations of the Early Fathers," we encounter an appropriate yet cautionary note. Recognizing that evangelicals are susceptible to offering a romantic version of the church fathers, Williams is alert to the telling

---

[3]Christopher A. Hall, "Tradition, Authority, Magisterium: Dead End or New Horizon?" p. 34.
[4]Brian E. Daley, S.J., "Old Books and Contemporary Faith: The Bible, Tradition and the Renewal of Theology," p. 66.

dissimilarities between the ancient church and contemporary church. He insists on the claim that an evangelical *ressourcement* of the faith of the early church must be established on an honest and true assessment of the period. Williams claims, "The early church was truly engaged in a search—sometimes haphazardly—for a Christian doctrine of God, rather than slowly unveiling what it knew implicitly all along."[5] As such, naive depictions of the work of church fathers must be set aside in view of the historical evidence showing that while the early church was often engaged in a defense of the faith against heterodox views, the battle lines of doctrinal controversy more often than not divided one Christian community from another. Notwithstanding, Williams shows that there is much to be gained from patient attention to the witness of the early church. Finally, one of the most decisive contributions made by Williams lies in his account of the relationship between intellectual virtue and Christian *paideia*.

The encyclical *Dei Verbum*, "Dogmatic Constitution on Divine Revelation," carries with it a clear representation of the fruit of *ressourcement* theology. Arguing that *Dei Verbum* is the most fundamental document to emerge from the Second Vatican Council, George Schner accounts for its significance believing that "the text requires that the Word of God, as expressed in the Scriptures, becomes normative for theological construction," to which he adds, "what Vatican II strongly recommended was, in many ways what Trent had been interested in: a rediscovery of the Word of God as the norm for Church life and teaching. After 400 years, the Church has returned to the importance of the Scriptures."[6] Given all of this, it is fitting that this volume briefly examines the setting and promise of patristic exegesis, for it was this material that led to *Dei Verbum*.

Beginning our extended consideration of the challenge and promise of patristic exegesis is the contribution by Michael Graves. His chapter, "The 'Pagan' Background of Patristic Exegetical Methods," counters overly simplistic criticism of the influence of Hellenism on the early church. Those familiar with Tertullian's query, "What has Athens to do with Jerusalem?"

[5]D. H. Williams, "*Similis et Dissimilis*: Gauging Our Expectations of the Early Fathers," p. 77-78.
[6]George Schner, "A Commentary on the Dogmatic Constitution on Divine Revelation," in *Essays Catholic and Critical*, ed. Philip G. Ziegler and Mark Husbands (Burlington: Ashgate, 2003), pp. 41-42.

quickly recognize the significance of the question of whether or not there is a uniquely Christian method of interpretation. Noting that one of the most pressing hermeneutical disputes of the early church had to do with the split between literal and allegorical interpretation, Graves demonstrates that the frame of reference for this dispute often demanded that one show how indebted one's interlocutor was to pagan learning. This fact makes Origen's and Theodore of Mopsuestia's scholarship all the more impressive, for as representatives of the competing Alexandrian and Antiochene schools, they both used pagan learning to great effect, preserving the scriptural literary tradition and demonstrating its significance. All of this raises the question of what evaluative tools are needed to discriminate among good and poor uses of pagan wisdom. Graves proposes that the questions that any interpreter of Scripture (ancient or contemporary) must pose are (1) how successfully does the borrowed method achieve the goals toward which it is inherently directed, and (2) how compatible is this appropriation with the gospel? Graves's analysis shows that by these measures, Origen and Theodore appear to do commendably well.

Peter Leithart's contribution, "The Quadriga or Something Like It: A Biblical and Pastoral Defense," is a nuanced response to the issues raised by Michael Graves. With a view toward encouraging a more confidently christological preaching of God's Word, Leithart offers concrete examples of how patristic and medieval exegetical practices challenge contemporary approaches to biblical exegesis. Reflecting on the work of Augustine, John Cassian, Aquinas and Lubac, Leithart offers a measured assessment of the fourfold sense of Scripture (literal, allegorical, tropological and anagogical). Leithart provocatively characterizes the exegetical and hermeneutical approaches of modern biblical scholarship as a "ruse." As readers will see, he arrives at this judgment on the basis of the observation that modern biblical scholarship "pries apart theological inquiry from religious devotion in an effort to conform biblical study to the standards of objective scientific pursuit."[7] More positively, one of the most appealing facets of the quadriga lies in its self-consciously theological nature. Leithart argues that

---

[7]Peter J. Leithart, "The Quadriga or Something Like It: A Biblical and Pastoral Defense," p. 116.

far from offering a neutral or scientifically objective method, the quadriga enables a "theological interpretation of the Old Testament shaped by the theology of the New and by the New Testament's interpretive example."[8] While perhaps this is a foreign claim to many moderns, the history of interpretation shows that Scripture and tradition belong together. Consequently, the kind of biblical reading informed by the inner logic of the quadriga—effectively on display in Leithart's work—faithfully extends Augustine's commitment to reading Scripture in light of "the whole Christ" *(totus Christus)*, such that members of Christ's body share in the paschal mystery "grow[ing] up in every way into him who is the head, into Christ" (Eph 4:15). The fact that the exegetical practices of the early church point us toward this most glorious mystery is itself a gift of God.

One of the principle aims of *ressourcement* theology is to examine the ancient sources of the Christian faith in order to draw out their significance for revitalization of the contemporary church. Nicholas Perrin's chapter, "Irenaeus and Lyotard Against Heresies, Ancient and Modern," is a fine example of this project. The point of departure for Perrin is Irenaeus's contention that "the Gospels could not possibly be either more or less in number than they are" (*Against Heresies* 3.11.8). While recognizing that normative authority should be accorded to the biblical witness, the early church also saw that biblical authority and witness was in fact mediated through the development of biblical interpretation and doctrine. Quite apart from the question of how John 16 has been read to warrant a given understanding of the authority of the church, a Christian doctrine of revelation is one that is open to the view that the development of tradition may indeed follow the leading and work of the Spirit, particularly when one has in place the kind of criteria set out by Graves. Perrin's work draws out the implications of a Christian doctrine of revelation. In the course of sketching the guiding principles of Irenaeus's critique of ancient Gnosticism and Jean-François Lyotard's assault on the pretensions of modernity, Perrin displays the force of a Christian doctrine of revelation. Alert to the many ways in which a modern confidence in the objectivity of science

---

[8]Ibid., p. 122.

comes at the expense of failing to recognize the hidden political, social and moral features of neutral/objective claims, Perrin finds an alarming parallel in the way in which both Gnosticism and modern science overly circumscribe the question of truth. By way of contrast, Irenaeus insists that the Word made flesh is the visible, tangible light and life of God with humanity. Perrin shows that according to Irenaeus, the reason why there are four Gospels follows from what God has done. Perrin is correct to see that Irenaeus proceeds abductively: "Because Christ is the recapitulation of Adam, it is only fitting that Christ, the embodiment of new creation is constituted by the four world zones."[9] In saying this, Perrin draws the contemporary significance of Irenaeus's work by reminding us that the "storyline *(regula)* does not spring out of numbers, but numbers from a storyline" (*Against Heresies* 2.25.1). In short, Perrin's work offers us a sophisticated treatment of how Irenaeus allowed theological judgments regarding the centrality of Christ to stand as the measure of exegetical conclusions.

The third section of this book focuses on the social ethics and practices of the early church. With a view toward uncovering the connection between patristic exegesis and the moral life of the early church, three scholars reflect on the concrete ways in which the early church sought to live out the gospel.

Christine Pohl begins "Hospitality: Ancient Resources and Contemporary Challenges" by offering a brief narrative of her journey from a formal consideration of political and social theory in the context of doctoral studies to her discovery of the life-giving and theologically rich engagement with Scripture found among the early church fathers. One of the central claims of Pohl's argument is that it is no small matter to find that in the New Testament issues of justice, love and social acceptance arise in the context of gathering together for meals. With the help of Lactantius, Jerome, Chrysostom and Augustine, Pohl contrasts hospitality in the Greek and Roman traditions (where it is imbedded in a system of merit and patronage) with the practice of the early church. Far from offering a romantic or naive picture of hospitality, Pohl's examination of the tradition repre-

---

[9]Nicholas Perrin, "Irenaeus and Lyotard Against Heresies, Ancient and Modern," p. 130.

sents a moral challenge to seek the justice of God's kingdom and rule in the practice of breaking bread with one another. In short, the early church lived out the peace of Christ in such a manner as to extend hospitality to the abject, lowly and needy, people regarded as the undeserving poor.

In "Crumbs from the Table: Lazarus, the Eucharist and the Banquet of the Poor in the Homilies of John Chrysostom," George Kalantzis further extends the consideration of moral theology in the early church. Whereas Pohl granted pride of place to the question of hospitality, Kalantzis turns to Chrysostom's treatment of wealth and poverty. Chrysostom's homiletical cycle on Luke 16:14-31 forms the centerpiece of Kalantzis's essay. The strength of his interpretation lies in his command of the overarching moral claims of Chrysostom's homiletics. In the course of learning that Chrysostom reminded wealthy Christians of God's judgment upon self-indulgence, we immediately realize that we are to look upon ourselves as the rich man in the pericope. Kalantzis documents a dramatic shift among early Christians from understanding moral acts as patronage to regarding them as gifts consonant with *philia*. In this context, he draws our attention to perhaps one of the most beautiful images of moral witness in the Christian tradition: namely, Chrysostom's image of the almsgiver as a harbor for those in need: "a harbor receives all who have encountered shipwreck, and frees them from danger. . . . So you likewise, when you see on earth the man who has encountered the shipwreck of poverty, do not judge him, do not seek an account of his life, but free him from his misfortune."[10]

Why did Christianity flourish in the midst of intense persecution? Addressing this question Tertullian famously announced, "The blood of the martyrs is the seed of the Church" (*Apologeticus* 50). While not disputing Tertullian's claim, Alan Kreider's chapter, " 'They Alone Know the Right Way to Live': The Early Church and Evangelism," offers us a rather different analysis of why the early church grew. Kreider successfully shows that in the absence of short-term mission programs, day camps or seeker-

---

[10]George Kalantzis, "Crumbs from the Table: Lazarus, the Eucharist and the Banquet of the Poor in the Homilies of John Chrysostom," p. 164.

sensitive worship services, the reason for the success of the Christian witness of the early church has to do with the quality of its common life. Kreider argues that the Christian life was shown to be so compelling that nonbelievers were drawn to a community of mercy and justice. According to Kreider, the vital witness of pre-Constantinian Christianity represents a substantial challenge to contemporary Christians. This challenge is one of setting aside the love of money and power in order to live out the gospel from a position of weakness and vulnerability. Evidently, this is one of the most significant moral lessons to be learned from the early church: how to share in a life of worship and witness in the hope that others might come to faith in the God of the gospel.

The final portion of this volume examines early Christianity in terms of its theology of worship, understanding of Christ and the theology of political life.

In John Witvliet's chapter, "Embodying the Wisdom of Ancient Liturgical Practices: Some Old-Fashioned Rudimentary Euchology for the Contemporary Church," we are given a renewed appreciation for the liturgical and confessional documents of the ancient church. Revisiting Webber's pedagogical distinction between content, form and style of worship, Witvliet notes that while evangelical worship comprises many different and distinct forms—perhaps due to a suspicion of ritual or habit—evangelicals are seldom aware of this aspect of their worship. This becomes even more telling when we recognize how much form reveals what Christians understand about God and humanity. Attending to the form of intercessory prayer litanies, the collect and Eucharistic prayers, Witvliet aims to recover the wisdom hidden within the structure of ancient patterns of invocation. Witvliet alerts us to the grand scale of a Christian vision of history and God's acts embedded in the prayers of the early church. By comparison, *our* worship is often somewhat sparse and uninteresting, perhaps to the point of conveying our indecision concerning the redemptive work of the triune God. As Witvliet indicates, the fourth-century Eucharistic prayers present "a theological vision of space, time, good, evil, personhood, salvation, creation and final redemption—all compressed into a prayer that is open to eternity and to the mystery and beauty of God's being."[11] Surely, prayers of this kind are worthy of extended theological reflection and genuine Christian practice.

Paul Kim's contribution, "*Apatheia* and Atonement: The Christology of Cyril of Alexandria and the Contemporary Grammar of Salvation," confirms the significance of an evangelical *ressourcement* theology. Kim offers an example of how close attention to the theological work of the early church may challenge or even correct contemporary dogmatic claims. Recognizing that theologians such as Alister McGrath, Jürgen Moltmann, Eberhard Jüngel, Kazoh Kitamori and Andrew Sung Park affirm the belief that God suffers, Kim returns to patristic sources in order to show why the majority opinion on divine suffering is mistaken. Documenting the crucial role that the question of divine *apatheia* played in the trinitarian and christological controversies of the early church, Kim shows why the early church thought it necessary to construct a dynamic understanding of divine impassability. In the course of returning to the work of Cyril of Alexandria, Kim offers an elegant depiction of the mystery of the impassable suffering of the Son. Working out the full implications of a Word-flesh Christology, Cyril maintains that "united with a humanity like ours, he suffered human things impassibly."[12] Well aware of the recent debate surrounding this issue, Kim argues "it is a grave mistake for contemporary theologians to posit that making God passible would alleviate human suffering."[13] Simply put, we need far more than a God who merely identifies with our vale of tears. Cyril expresses this in even more definitive terms: the "Word becoming flesh is the undoing and the abolition of all that fell upon human nature as our curse and punishment."[14]

When looking at the title of the penultimate chapter of this volume, "Two Augustinianisms: Augustinian Realism and the Other City," one

---

[11]John Witvliet, "Embodying the Wisdom of Ancient Liturgical Practices: Some Old-Fashioned Rudimentary Euchology for the Contemporary Church," p. 211.

[12]Cyril of Alexandria *On the Right Faith* 163, trans. Rowan A. Greer (unpublished), *Patrologia Graeca* 76:1393B, cited by Paul I. Kim, "*Apatheia* and Atonement: Cyril of Alexandria and the Contemporary Grammar of Salvation," p. 221.

[13]Kim, "*Apatheia* and Atonement," p. 229.

[14]Cyril of Alexandria, *On the Unity of Christ*, trans. John Anthony McGuckin (New York: St. Vladimir's Seminary Press, 1995), p. 60.

might reasonably question whether or not anything new can be found in a field that has been worked over for such a long time; surely its fruitfulness must be wearing thin. Put differently, if the aim of an evangelical *ressourcement* is that of mining ancient sources for new ways of engaging the contemporary world, is Augustine the right place to begin? Of all the patristic figures, Augustine seems to the one with whom we are most familiar, and haven't we learned all that we can from such a recognizable figure? For those in particular who might harbor such suspicions, Stephen Long's essay offers an unexpected surprise.

Reminiscent of Lubac's retrieval of Thomas Aquinas, Long offers a fresh reading of Augustine, one that shows how mistaken we have been in imagining that he would endorse the claim that nature, the secular or the political could be properly understood apart from Christ. At the center of Long's argument is the judgment that "Augustine's importance for the emerging, future church lies in his development of a city that is other than our earthly cities."[15] Insisting on a reading of Augustine that refuses to allow the operative values of the earthly city to set the terms of Christian political engagement, Long challenges evangelicals to reimagine political life in such a way as to regard the common good as a subset of the peace of Christ rather than a good that may be secured only through a process of incremental and negotiated gains won against those committed to deceit, compromise, violence and power. In short, Long's reading of Augustine underscores the need to rediscover an ecclesiology in which penitential practices and common life (what, on occasion, Long terms "transnational unity") stands as a bold countercultural challenge. While evangelical Protestants are likely to persist in refusing Rome's invitation to "return home," Long's analysis presents us with an acute dilemma. How may we faithfully embody a moral and political life grounded in the peace of Christ when the very structures of doctrinal, liturgical and moral accountability continue to elude our grasp? Given that *City of God* was written to counter the *Republics* of Plato and Cicero, Augustine was well aware of the fact that the loudest cheerleaders for social order were the rich, whose self-interest created

---

[15]D. Stephen Long, "Two Augustinianisms: Augustinian Realism and the Other City," p. 233.

dependency and profound inequity (*City of God* 2:20). It is here where Long's essay demonstrates the genuine force of Augustine's moral argument: far from recommending that Christians acquiesce or make common cause with the dominant players in the earthly city (for this is how Augustine is customarily interpreted), Augustine's *City of God* countenances agreement with political forces "so long as no hindrance to the worship of the one supreme and true god is thus introduced."[16] Evidently, Augustine's theology of politics demands prior allegiance to Christ, thereby refusing to imagine that principal alliances are determined by the state. In short, political life and moral order arises, for Augustine, by sharing in a life formed by the Word and Eucharist.

Finally, given that this volume represents a number of the most promising examples of evangelical *ressourcement* theology, we thought that it was helpful to address one of the most prominent ways in which contemporary Protestantism seeks to appropriate the heritage of early Christianity. The Emergent movement—commonly identified with figures such as Brian McLaren, Dan Kimball and Tony Jones (who gave a thought-provoking plenary address at the conference)—has been eager to explore the ancient practices of the church, especially in order to enrich corporate worship and revitalize contemporary discipleship. Given how relatively young the Emergent conversation is, it is too soon to measure the lasting influence of this loosely affiliated movement of Christians focusing upon postmodern culture(s), worship and the missional witness of the church. The Wheaton Theology Conference benefited immensely from Jason Byassee's thoughtful analysis of this movement, and his contribution forms the epilogue to this volume. Combining a rare balance of generous praise and measured criticism, Byassee offers an account of the best practices of the Emergent movement. As the epilogue shows, as soon as one moves beyond the disarmingly unfortunate rhetoric of "rediscovering Christianity" (heard among the many voices of this conversation), one can readily find a moral witness that is often genuinely faithful to the gospel.

The elegance of Byassee's sketch is striking. Taking the example of new

---

[16]Augustine *City of God* 19.17, cited by Long, "Two Augustinianisms," p. 237.

monasticism, for instance, he is quick to contrast this movement with the Mennonites, an established Christian tradition that is "much less interested in what is culturally relevant and much more interested in pursuing the form of life laid out for us in the New Testament, including Jesus' call to nonviolence, love of enemies and peace making."[17] Byassee's open-handed examination of the Emergent conversation demonstrates the need for the church to evaluate contemporary ecclesial practice in the light of a preceding tradition. For that reason, we hope that an evangelical *ressourcement* theology may truly share in the rediscovery of ancient sources for the revitalization of contemporary theology and pastoral life.

This volume is dedicated to the memory of Robert Webber, longtime faculty member at Wheaton College, who finished his teaching career at Northern Seminary in Lombard, Illinois. The Wheaton conference on this topic probably would not likely have happened apart from his influence on the evangelical movement in North America and beyond. His many books and extensive public speaking ministry have done more to inspire evangelical students, teachers and pastors to seriously reengage the life and witness of the early church than has the work of any other single figure. He was scheduled to give a plenary address at the conference. However, due to deteriorating health, he was unable to participate. Our event's annual banquet featured a moving tribute to Bob's life and ministry given by three of his friends and colleagues: John Witvliet, Andrew Hill and Tom Schwanda. Within two weeks of the conference, Bob died of pancreatic cancer, leaving behind a marvelous legacy that will continue to challenge and inspire God's people.

In the end, this volume represents first fruits of what we hope will prove to be a vital and life-giving harvest of evangelical *ressourcement* theology. We offer this work to Christ in the prayer that it may have a share in encouraging others to join with us in what promises to be an exciting and positive field of scholarship and ministry.

---

[17]Jason Byassee, "Emerging from What, Going Where? Emerging Churches and Ancient Christianity," p. 258.

PART ONE

Evangelical *Ressourcement*

Retrieving the Past
with Integrity

1

Tradition, Authority, Magisterium

Dead End or New Horizon?

Christopher A. Hall

Brian McLaren, one of the leading thinkers and voices of the emergent church movement, has written an interesting, stimulating book titled *A Generous Orthodoxy*. In McLaren's book he proposes the laudable goal of "seeking to find a way to embrace the good in many traditions and historic streams of Christian faith, and to integrate them, yielding a new, generous, emergent approach that is greater than the sum of its parts. This approach is both ancient/historical and avant-garde innovative." Leonard Sweet, McLaren notes,

> uses the image of a swing to capture this simultaneous kicking-back/lean-ing-forward, kicking-forward/leaning-back. He also uses the image of a pole vaulter, who, in order to move forward and fly upward, begins by going backward to get a running start. He calls this an *ancient-future* approach, as does Robert Webber, another wise Christian thinker looking for ways ahead for the Christian faith by reaching back at the same time.[1]

McLaren, Sweet and Webber seemingly agree that the ancient tradition of the church, reflected and grounded to a great extent in the writings and

---

[1]Brian McLaren, *A Generous Orthodoxy* (Grand Rapids, Mich.: Zondervan, 2004), p. 18.

behaviors of the church fathers, is a valuable resource that we neglect to our detriment and, yes, even peril. A key question then poses itself: how can we best "embrace the good in many traditions and historic streams of Christian faith," as McLaren encourages us to do? More particularly, how can we move safely, sanely and effectively into the world of the church fathers, where in many ways the great tradition of the church was birthed? What are the best practices for drawing on the Fathers' insights? How can evangelicals best approach the patristic period honestly and openly? Other questions quickly emerge as we ponder the past and future. Why should we pay attention to the Fathers? More broadly, how do we wisely harvest and digest historical and theological sources from another time? Or, to stick with the metaphors Sweet and Webber propose, as we kick our swing backward, how do we reach what lies behind us? As we move backward to get a running start, how do we plant our feet firmly to get an energetic and powerful running start?

Let us begin by exploring the question at least some must be pondering: Why bother about church tradition? Why do we need any authorities or authority outside of the Bible? Can we not simply affirm *sola Scriptura* and be done with it? Many Christians, including a vast number of evangelicals, would affirm yes. We have our Bible and the inner illumination of the Holy Spirit, and we attend an excellent church where our pastor interprets the Bible thoroughly, faithfully and insightfully. What need for more?

Of course a question immediately poses itself: How do we know our pastor is interpreting the biblical text thoroughly, faithfully and insightfully? Is our confidence in the veracity of the pastor's reading and interpretation of the Bible based solely on the illumination of the Holy Spirit within us corresponding to and confirming the illumination of the Spirit within the pastor as we both read the Bible and interpret its meaning? What if an individual within the congregation disagrees with pastor's teaching and is convinced that his disagreement is from the illumination of the Holy Spirit? The fundamental questions are these: Are the illumination of the Holy Spirit and the interpretation of holy Scripture individual or communal experiences and practices? May they be a mixture of the two?

We face a significant problem if we define and practice *sola Scriptura* as confidence in an inspired, inerrant text that is then to be interpreted by individuals illumined by the Holy Spirit: many of the great heretics of the church, especially in its earliest period, were committed to the authority of Scripture. All were convinced the Holy Spirit guided them in their interpretation of the Bible, and many were willing to suffer significantly for their beliefs. Heretics such as Arius and Sabellius had few if any doubts concerning the inspiration and authority of the Scripture. Indeed, among other reasons, Arius refused to affirm the deity of the Son because he was convinced that an affirmation of Christ's deity clearly contradicted key biblical texts. After all, Arius and his followers asked, how could Jesus increase "in wisdom and stature, and in favor with God and man" if he were consubstantial with the Father? If Christ possessed all wisdom and knowledge, a necessary predicate of deity, why would Jesus ask the disciples how many loaves they possessed at the time of the miracle of the feeding of the five thousand? Why would Jesus cry out on the cross, "My God, my God, why have you forsaken me?" Can God be separated from God? Why, in response to the question of the disciples concerning the signs of the end times, would Jesus respond, "But about that day or hour no one knows, neither the angels in heaven, nor the Son, but only the Father" (Mk 13:32)? How could there possibly be this division of knowledge within the Godhead, the Father knowing all things and the Son only some things, if the Son was God as the Father was God?[2]

Arius had not only exegetical but also philosophical and theological problems with the possibility of an incarnate God. Was God a composite being made up of parts? How could the divine essence be divided between Father, Son and Spirit? How could God, a spiritual being, possibly become a human being? "How could the Immaterial bear a body?" Whereas Jesus' adversaries had asked, How can a human being be God? Arius asked, How could God become a human being? "How can He be Word or God who slept as man, and wept, and inquired?"[3]

---

[2]Drawing on material from Christopher A. Hall, *Reading Scripture with the Church Fathers* (Downers Grove, Ill.: InterVarsity Press, 1998), p. 62.

[3]Arius, as quoted by Athanasius in *Four Discourses Against the Arians,* Nicene and Post-Nicene Fathers 4 (Peabody, Mass.: Hendrickson, 1994), p. 408.

Most readers of this book would assert that Arius was not interpreting the Scripture well. I too think we are right to question Arius's biblical exegesis and the model of God he proposed. Yet the resolution of biblical and theological conflict is particularly difficult for evangelicals if we make the Bible the only authoritative source we draw on for guidance. Thomas Howard highlights the difficulty evangelicals face in resolving theological questions, issues and practices on the basis of the Bible alone:

> The great difficulty here is that Eutychius and Sabellius and Arius got their notions straight out of the Bible as well. Who will arbitrate these things for us? Who will speak with authority for us faithful, all of us rushing about flapping the pages of our well-thumbed New Testaments locked in shrill contests over the two natures of Christ or baptism or the Lord's Supper or the mystery of predestination? . . . When a crucial issue arises—say, what we should teach about sexuality—who will speak to us with a finally authoritative voice? The best we can do is to get *Christianity Today* to run a symposium, with one article by J. I. Packer plumping for traditional morality, and one article by one of our lesbian feminist evangelicals (there are some), showing that we have all been wrong for the entire 3,500 years since Sinai, and that what the Bible really teaches is that indeed homosexuals may enjoy a fully expressed sexual life. The trouble here is that J. I. Packer has no more authority than our lesbian friend, so the message to the faithful is "Take your pick."[4]

What I want to explore is the rationale behind the church's rejection of the Arian position and the methodology the church employed in reaching its decision. As I do so, we will consider together the implications of the ancient church's methodology for resolving the problem posed by Arius for how we interpret the Bible today and how evangelicals may wish to interact more deeply with the church's tradition.

In the time of Arius—the great age of the church fathers—Athanasius, the archbishop of Alexandria, was the key leader in opposing the Arian position. Athanasius contended that Arius did not understand the "scope

---

[4]Thomas Howard, "Recognizing the Church: A Personal Pilgrimage and the Discovery of the Five Marks of the Church," in *Ancient and Postmodern Christianity*, ed. Kenneth Tanner and Christopher A. Hall (Downers Grove, Ill.: InterVarsity Press, 2002), pp. 133-34.

and character" of Scripture. Scripture contained, Athanasius argued, a "double account of the Savior." The Bible, that is, affirmed both the deity and humanity of Jesus. As the eternal Son, Christ existed as "the Father's Word and Radiance and Wisdom"; in the wonder and mystery of the incarnation the Son willingly and lovingly took on human flesh "of a Virgin, Mary Bearer of God, and was made man."[5] Thus, Athanasius taught, when we encounter biblical texts speaking of Christ as weary, anxious in the garden of Gethsemane, ignorant concerning how many loaves the disciples possessed at the feeding of the five thousand and so on, these texts are referring to characteristics and conditions manifesting Jesus' genuine humanity. Christ possesses every characteristic of a human being apart from sin: a body, a mind, a will, a soul, though Athanasius centered his attention on the body the eternal Word joined himself to in the womb of the Virgin Mary.

We must acknowledge, however, that Athanasius's exegesis is not self-evidently correct in and of itself, if we make the Bible and the Bible alone the sole criterion for judging between Athanasius and Arius. Both Arius and Athanasius produced coherent interpretations of the biblical text; both believed that they were guided and illumined by the Holy Spirit as they interpreted Scripture. And yet Arius's interpretation was rejected by the church as heretical while, after years of debate and conflict, the church recognized Athanasius's exegesis as orthodox. Why?

We can better understand the acceptance and success of Athanasius's exegesis—and the theological model he proposed based on his interpretation—by looking beyond Scripture itself to the practices, habits, theological intuitions, insights and understandings engendered within Athanasius as he lived and worshiped within the community of the church. In a word, Athanasius did not approach the Bible as though the text could be understood as standing alone apart from the practices of the church as it communally interpreted and incarnated the meaning of the Scripture in the church's daily life.

Athanasius did not approach the text as *scriptura nuda*, a naked text to

---

[5] Athanasius, *Four Discourses Against the Arians*, p. 409.

be interpreted by autonomous individuals, illumined though they may believe themselves to be by the Holy Spirit. Nor did he or other church fathers believe that Scripture could be fully understood if interpreted strictly in terms of its historical context, authorial intent, grammatical syntax, cultural background and so on.

None of the church fathers ignored entirely what evangelicals understand as the grammatical-historical method. Yet the interpretive grid or lens through which the Fathers read the Scripture was broader and deeper than issues of background, grammar and authorial intent. Athanasius, for instance, employed the church's rule of faith *(regula fidei)* and tradition as interpretive tools to help him expose the hairline fractures in the Arian model of Christ. Athanasius utilized the practices of the church in worship and the theology the church's worship embodied to criticize Arius's refusal to acknowledge Christ as God. That is to say, if Athanasius worshiped Christ as God on a daily basis within the community of the church—praying to Christ, feeding on Christ in the Eucharist—as also did many Arian Christians, how could Arius possibly be correct in his reading of Scripture? The communal practices of the church as it met in worship clearly guided Athanasius as he made key interpretive moves. In addition, the ancient church was convinced that its theology as incarnated in its communal practices, habits and disciplines was grounded on the apostolic testimony and practices contained in Scripture.

Irenaeus, Tertullian, Novatian, Augustine and Vincent of Lerins affirmed and utilized authoritative summaries of the apostles' teaching that had shaped and guided the church across the years as it interpreted the meaning of the Bible's apostolic testimony. These summaries, based on Scripture itself and key practices of the church, aided them in combating distorted views of the Christian faith.

Irenaeus, writing in the late second century A.D., writes:

> The church, though dispersed throughout the whole world, even to the ends of the earth, has received from the apostles and their disciples this faith: she believes in one God, the Father Almighty, Maker of heaven and earth, and the sea, and all things that are in them; and in one Christ Jesus, the Son of God, who became incarnate for our salvation; and in the Holy Spirit . . . *The*

Rule of Truth which we hold, is, that there is one God Almighty, who made all things by His Word, and fashioned and formed, out of that which had no existence, all things that exist.[6]

When Tertullian turns to the rule of faith in his disagreement with Gnostic teachers, he insists it "was taught by Christ."[7]

Athanasius trusted, I think rightly, that as the Holy Spirit had guided the apostles as they remembered, reflected on and interpreted in their writings the meaning of Christ's person and work, so the Holy Spirit had providentially guided the church in its preservation, transmission and understanding of the apostles' teaching and in the formulation of doctrine based on apostolic testimony. R. R. Reno comments:

> The principle of apostolic legitimacy motivates this close correspondence between doctrine and scripture. The logic is transparent. If the Bible teaches x and the church teaches not x, then either the Bible teaches the truth or the church teaches the truth. But since the true church of Christ teaches the gospel, and since the Bible is the sacred and canonical witness to the gospel, such a disjunction is intolerable. Therefore, any church claiming apostolic legitimacy must assert that her public doctrine is in accord with the content of scripture.[8]

The church's great tradition is larger and more extensive than summaries such as the rule of faith. My colleague Phillip Cary describes the content and dynamic of tradition this way:

> Tradition is more than a repository of doctrinal propositions. It is a way of being educated, trained and formed in the virtues necessary for Christian life and good theologizing. Along with these virtues come various skills, patterns of experience and habits of perception as well as pieces of knowledge. It's like learning to be a musician or scientist: you don't just learn a

---

[6]Irenaeus *Against Heresies* 1.10.1; 1.22.1, Ante-Nicene Fathers (Peabody, Mass.: Hendrickson, 1994) 1:330, 347, slightly modified and emphasis added; cited in *Tradition, Scripture and Interpretation,* ed. D. H. Williams (Grand Rapids, Mich.: Baker Academic, 2006), pp. 68-69.

[7]Tertullian *On the Prescriptions of Heretics* 13, Ante-Nicene Fathers 3:249, slightly modified; cited in *Tradition, Scripture and Interpretation,* ed. D. H. Williams (Grand Rapids, Mich.: Baker Academic, 2006), p. 71.

[8]R. R. Reno, quoted in the newsletter of the Center for Catholic and Evangelical Theology (fall 2006), p. 4.

bunch of theories; you learn to become a kind of practitioner; as a result you perceive the world differently, make different kinds of judgments and live differently from someone who is unmusical or scientifically illiterate.[9]

In a nutshell, orthodoxy and orthopraxy are married in ancient Christianity. The thought that they might somehow be separated—a situation in which a Christian would be more concerned with orthopraxis than orthodoxy, as though practice could be elevated above doctrine in importance—would have made little sense to the Fathers. It was the ecclesial practices they encountered each week, often in the context of worship, that informed how they thought about the gospel. For the Fathers, the ability to perceive a doctrine's truthfulness is predicated on cultivating orthopraxis in a variety of settings. In a word, how a person lives out the gospel shapes her ability to believe well in terms of the content of the faith. To practice the way of Jesus in the postmodern world entails a lengthy apprenticeship to Jesus under the tutelage of those who have known him well.

Robert Wilken makes a similar point.

In many fields of creative work, immersion in tradition is the presupposition for excellence and originality. Think, for example, of music. On Saturday mornings, I often listen to a jazz show on National Public Radio that features interviews with famous and not-so-famous jazz pianists, saxophonists, drummers, trumpeters, etc., and I am regularly struck at how they speak with such respect of teachers and masters, and how to a person they learned to play the piano by first playing in someone else's style or learned to blow the trumpet by imitating Louis Armstrong or someone else. Similarly, one is impressed with how often a performer like folk singer Jean Redpath speaks about tradition as the necessary condition for making and singing folk music. How often we are admonished not to let the old traditions be forgotten. Why? Surely not for historical or archaeological reasons, but because musicians, like painters and writers and sculptors, know in their fingertips or vocal cords or ears that imitation is the way to excellence and originality.[10]

---

[9]Phillip Cary, private e-mail, February 27, 2007.
[10]Robert Wilken, *Remembering the Christian Past* (Grand Rapids, Mich.: Eerdmans, 1995), pp. 170-71.

Rodney Clapp reiterates Wilken's insight: "We can no more become and grow as Christians apart from the church than we can become accomplished painters and sculptors apart from the guild and ongoing history of painters and sculptors."[11]

Learning to enter into the church's tradition in a wise, loving, discerning manner is a Spirit-shaped skill developed through the acquisition of key habits of thought, behavior and devotion. Again I turn to Wilken:

> Without tradition, learning is arduous at best, impossible at worst. In most things in life—learning to speak, making cabinets, playing the violin—the only way to learn is by imitation, by letting someone else guide our movements until we learn to do the thing on our own . . . Reason, it seems, is found within rather than outside of things; it is not an abstract quality that exists independently in the human mind—which means, of course, that it is *reasonable* to allow one's hands to be guided by a master, and foolish to go it alone, as though one could learn to play the violin or sculpt a statue by studying a set of instructions. In this context, the ideal of the autonomous individual is glaringly inappropriate; for we recognize that here the true mark of rationality is to apprentice oneself to another rather than to strike out on one's own. To paraphrase Kenny Rogers, "There'll be time enough 'for originality when the apprenticeship is done.'"[12]

The imitation involved in apprenticeship entails training that is both intellectual and behavioral in nature. Athanasius insisted that to understand Scripture demands

> a good life and a pure soul. . . . One cannot possibly understand the teaching of the saints unless one has a pure mind and is trying to imitate their life. . . . Anyone who wants to look at sunlight naturally wipes his eye clear first, in order to make, at any rate, some approximation to the purity of that on which he looks; and a person wishing to see a city or country goes to the place in order to do so. Similarly, anyone who wishes to understand the mind of the sacred writers must first cleanse his own life, and approach the saints by copying their deeds. Thus united to them in the fellowship of life, he will both understand the things revealed to them by God and, thence-

---

[11]Rodney Clapp, *Tortured Wonders* (Grand Rapids, Mich.: Brazos Press, 2004), p. 87.
[12]Wilken, *Remembering the Christian Past*, pp. 171-72.

forth escaping the peril that threatens sinners in the judgment, will receive that which is laid up for the saints in the kingdom of heaven.[13]

Rather than tradition undercutting or enervating Athanasius's ability to interpret the Bible, it provided a milieu for the cultivation of insights, skills, habits of perception and virtues within Athanasius that aided him as he faced key hermeneutical choices earlier generations of Christians had not been forced to explore thoroughly. Though the church from its earliest days had worshiped Christ as God, it had not explored thoroughly the implications of its practice. It took a specific hermeneutical challenge, in this case that of Arius, to force the church to examine carefully what it was fundamentally asserting theologically as it worshiped Christ.

Gregory of Nazianzus, one of the greatest theologians in the history of the church, in a manner similar to Athanasius, continually reiterates and reinforces the habits of mind and heart theologians must develop and practice if they are to interpret the Scripture well and faithfully preserve and pass on its meaning to succeeding generations of believers. "Not to everyone, my friends, does it belong to philosophize about God . . . not to everyone; the Subject is not so cheap and low; and I will add, not before every audience, nor at all times, nor on all points; but on certain occasions, and before certain persons, and within certain limits."[14]

They who speak and write of God on behalf of the church must be "those who have been examined, and are passed masters in meditation, and who have been previously purified in soul and body, or at the very least are being purified." For Gregory, personal holiness, a holiness cultivated within the communal practices and disciplines of the church itself, is the gateway to the knowledge of God, an emphasis with which Athanasius would have agreed. "For the impure to touch the pure is, we may safely say, not safe, just as it is unsafe to fix weak eyes upon the sun's rays."[15]

Gregory lists a variety of vices that can infect exegetes and theologians who fail to cultivate the habits of mind and behavior birthed and nourished

---

[13]Athanasius, *On the Incarnation* (Crestwood, N.Y.: St. Vladimir's Seminary Press, 1982), p. 96.
[14]Gregory of Nazianzus, *The First Theological Oration*, Nicene and Post-Nicene Fathers, 2:285.
[15]Ibid.

from the church's tradition as the church has reflected on the meaning of the gospel: the practice of theology as a competitive sport; an insatiable knowledge for God that refuses to accept the boundaries and limitations God has placed on theological reflection; endless, empty talking about God; speech concerning God that is hollow and brittle; undisciplined lives in which the "passions" reign; anger that "swells and rages." Vice breeds in the human personality left to its own devices, Gregory teaches, and the devil exploits cracks in human character for his own purposes and ends.[16]

If these vices remain unacknowledged or unchecked in theologians' lives, the very knowledge they seek to understand and explicate on behalf of the church will blow up in their faces. Gregory insists that unless one simultaneously engages in the arduous task of perceptual and behavioral habit formation within the tradition of the church as one attempts to understand and speak of God, it is best to leave God alone and to dwell on lesser subjects. The exegetical and theological work of the church, Gregory emphasizes, possesses an inherent *gravitas*. It is for persons "to whom the subject is of real concern, [and not for those] who make it a matter of pleasant gossip, like any other thing, after the races, or the theater, or a concert, or a dinner, or still lower employments. To people such as these, idle jests and pretty contradictions about these subjects are a part of their amusement."

Avoid undisciplined, frivolous, "unseasonable," immoderate speech about God, Gregory advises. Continual prayer, meditation and mindfulness of God's holiness married to the theologian's personal call to purity are the antidotes to immodest, proud speculation. "For," Gregory writes,

> we ought to think of God even more than we draw our breath; and if the expression is permissible, we ought to do nothing else. Yes, I am one of those who entirely approve that Word which bids us meditate day and night (Psalm 1:2) . . . or to use Moses' words, whether one lie down, or rise up, or walk in the way, or whatever else he be doing—by this recollection we are to be molded to purity (cf. Deuteronomy 6:6-10).[17]

---

[16]Ibid., p. 287.
[17]Ibid., p. 286.

Overarching our entire discussion thus far is what I have coined the pneumatological arc of the Holy Spirit. The Holy Spirit inspired the apostles to interpret authoritatively the meaning of Christ's work and person. We now possess this authoritative interpretation in the canonical documents of the New Testament. The guidance, protection and enlivening of the Spirit did not cease, however, with the passing away of the apostolic generation. The Holy Spirit has continued to guide the church as it interprets and incarnates the meaning of these unique texts, a process that now spans hundreds of years and is grounded in the cluster of practices and beliefs contained in the church's rule of faith *(regula fidei)* and great tradition.

Reno comments:

> Irenaeus, Origen, and the great cloud of premodern biblical interpreters assumed that puzzling out the mosaic of Scripture must be a communal project. The Bible is vast, heterogeneous, full of confusing passages and obscure words, and difficult to understand. Only a fool would imagine that he or she could work out solutions alone. The way forward must rely upon a tradition of reading that Irenaeus reports has been passed on as the rule or canon of truth that functions as a confession of faith.[18]

The church's rule of faith and broader tradition inculcated in ancient Christians "virtues, skills, patterns of experience, portions of knowledge and habits of perception"[19] that enabled them to detect false hermeneutical moves or faulty theological models. As the years passed the unique authority of the canon was recognized. Key creeds were formulated at Nicaea, Constantinople and Chalcedon to aid the church in its understanding of God, Christ and a host of other issues.

The Orthodox, Roman Catholic, Anglican and many Protestant communions recognize these developments as occurring under the guidance of the Holy Spirit. If so, then the tradition of the church possesses a pneumatologically based authority. The issue for evangelicals—and for the broader

---

[18]Quoted in Brian E. Daley, S.J., "The Acts and Christian Confessions: Finding the Start of the Dogmatic Tradition," *Pro Ecclesia* 14, no. 1 (2005): 19.
[19]Cary, private e-mail.

Christian community—is the nature and extent of the church's tradition.

A musical metaphor may help us grasp the nature of tradition's authority. Picture the church's tradition as a symphony made up of different, complementary movements, with the Bible providing the central thematic element.

A gifted composer—I have the Holy Spirit in mind—discerns the possibilities inherent in a symphony's main theme and develops them as the symphony unfolds. The genius of master composers such as Mozart and Beethoven manifests itself in their ability to see possibilities in a simple phrase to which other composers remain tone-deaf.

Yet the risk exists that the conductor of the composer's work may distort the symphony's core thematic element in a fashion that results in dissonance rather than harmony. In a similar fashion, the church's tradition in its best moments represents the music the Holy Spirit is singing to the church, the musical notes, if you will, of the divine symphony of the gospel. In its worst moments, the tradition may fail to interpret the divine composer's musical score well, and dissonance and discord is produced.

William Abraham writes that "the music of salvation" emerges from the "different elements" of the church's "varied canonical traditions."

> The music which results . . . naturally transposes itself into hymns of praise. Some of the canonical traditions, like the water, oil, bread, and wine of the sacraments, represent various instruments in the orchestra of the Church. Some, like Fathers and bishops, represent various players. Some, like liturgical material, represent the scores, which are best followed according to the program notes which accompany them. Everyone involved in the orchestra must approach his or her role in a spirit of humility and dependence, of joy and praise. Most important of all, everyone must heed and be open to the leading of the great conductor, the Holy Spirit, who, through the use of the canonical traditions of the Church, creates within the participants the melody of Christ the Savior, a music which leads ineluctably into the unfathomable, unspeakable mystery of the living God.[20]

---

[20]William J. Abraham, *Canon and Criterion in Christian Theology* (New York: Oxford University Press, 2002), p. 55.

To affirm the pneumatological grounding and empowering of the church's tradition is to trust that the Holy Spirit has continued to guide the church as it has sought to understand and embody the gospel ever more fully in its communal life and mission to the world. It is my contention that ancient Christian interpretation and reflection were especially astute and gifted in the ability to hear and sing the music of the gospel.

Irenaeus, for example, insists on the priority of ancient ecclesial voices in aiding the church in comprehending the gospel's meaning and in resolving disagreements when they arise over the meaning of Scripture or doctrine. Irenaeus writes that we must turn to the "most ancient Churches with which the apostles held constant intercourse, and learn from them what is certain and clear in response to the present question."[21]

Dale Allison, author of the commentary on Matthew in the International Critical Commentary series, agrees with the thrust of Irenaeus's statement: "For [the Fathers] were, in so many ways, closer to the first-century Christians than we are—for they, unlike most of us, lived and moved and had their being in the Scriptures." In many ways, the Scriptures—listened to for many years by patristic writers—were their popular music.

> They still read aloud. They still have a small literary canon. They still had, because of their educational methods, magnificent memorization skills. And they still heard Scripture chanted. They were accordingly attuned to *hear* things we no longer *hear*, things which we can only *see* after picking up concordances or doing word searches on our computers. I have come to believe that if we find in Matthew or another NT book an allusion to the OT that the Fathers did not find, the burden of proof is on us; and if they detected an allusion which we—here I am thinking of modern commentaries—have not detected, investigation is in order.[22]

To argue for the richness and sensitivity of patristic exegesis, however, is not to posit its infallibility. The Fathers are occasionally quirky in their

---

[21]Irenaeus *Against Heresies* 3.4.1, Ante-Nicene Fathers, 1:417.

[22]This quotation is from a lecture given by Dale C. Allison Jr., delivered at the Billy Graham Center, Wheaton College, for the first annual meeting of the Society for the Study of Eastern Orthodoxy and Evangelicalism, September 28, 1991.

reading of a text and sometimes outrageous. An example from Jerome will have to suffice. In what J. N. D. Kelly describes as "one of Jerome's most audacious feats of exegesis," Jerome dismisses the possibility that Abishag the Shunamite, the woman who slept with King David in his latter years to keep the aged king warm, could have been a literal, historical figure. To consider her to be such would be "crudely literalistic. . . . What she stands for in the story is the wisdom which glows in an old man."[23] Here Jerome's ascetic sensibilities appear to have blurred his interpretive vision.

The tradition of the church is not entirely reliable. If not, in what sense does tradition function as authoritative? How can we effectively distinguish between authentic developments in the church's tradition and mutations? And who possesses the authority to identify mutations when they occur?

The crucial criterion for evaluating the authenticity of a development, it seems to me, is whether the development faithfully, wisely and coherently expresses the truth found in Scripture. The apostolic teaching contained in the canonical Scriptures is the norm by which all developments must be tested. Picture this apostolic teaching as the genetic code or DNA that governs the development of the biblical message as the church reflects on the gospel across the years. This DNA must be faithfully replicated throughout church history to govern the ongoing proposal and development of theological models. But as the DNA replicates faithfully under the guidance of the Holy Spirit, faithful and creative theological reflection provides a new window into the original structure of the DNA. This is precisely the reason that our interpretation of the Bible today can be vastly aided by the church's great tradition, while the tradition itself does not rule out the possibility of creative developments.

Every orthodox development adds to our understanding of the gospel's original DNA.[24] Thus, we can have a postbiblical theological model such

---

[23]J. N. D. Kelly, *Jerome* (Peabody, Mass.: Hendrickson, 1998), p. 191.

[24]In the next few pages I freely draw on material from Christopher A. Hall, "What Evangelicals and Liberals Can Learn from the Church Fathers," *Journal of the Evangelical Theological Society* 49, no. 1 (March 2006): 81-95, and "The Role of Tradition in Evangelical Theology," *The Word Made Fresh* session, American Academy of Religion Meetings, Atlanta, November 2003.

as the Trinity required by the church as an orthodox statement of faith to which all Christians are called to attest, though we never run across the word *Trinity* in the Bible. Why? The genetic code found in the Scripture has replicated in the rule of faith and the great tradition of the church under the guidance of the Holy Spirit. The DNA in the rule of faith in turn serves as a reliable guide to the original DNA of the Bible. The teaching and practices of the church, under the Spirit's empowerment and guidance, directed the church in recognizing the faithfulness of the trinitarian model to the original gospel message.

Arianism or any other heresy represents a theological model that the church has perceived, on the basis of the great tradition, to contain defective or mutant DNA. Orthodox theological models are like oak trees that have sprouted from acorns. The mature tree is a natural, healthy development of the biological blueprint contained within the acorn. Heretical models, by contrast, resemble weeds that have erupted in a field where one expected lush grass. The DNA, even in a faulty model, will often resemble the original enough to warrant careful testing by the church to determine the model's authenticity.

Now, note well: if a model is finally gauged to be heretical, it is because the church has communally determined that the proposal in question distorts the truth, that it contains mutated DNA rather than a faithful representation of the original. Apart from this communal determination, any Christian at any time could challenge any doctrine on the basis of an idiosyncratic interpretation of Scripture. And if we can autonomously correct the church on any point, then we can correct the church on every point.

Most evangelicals, I would think, are fearful of an infallible magisterium. Because we believe the church may err, though, do we go to the opposite extreme and make each believer his own magisterium? By what appeal could one ever show a person that his peculiar interpretation is misguided? He is his only authoritative guide! But he would argue that it is the Scripture that is guiding him. And on the basis of the Protestant principle alone, he appears to be correct.

Positively, the conservative evangelical is deeply committed to the Scripture. Unfortunately, the same evangelical's commitment to the Bible is often divorced from the trustworthy safeguards of an authoritative church tradition. Frequently, we judge ourselves competent to overturn as much historical precedent as necessary to maintain our own interpretation of Scripture. The unhappy result is the rising tendency within the evangelical community to view each other with increasing suspicion and hostility, often on the basis of a reading of the Bible that is itself deeply idiosyncratic.

Can this impasse be resolved? I have noted already the unique status of Scripture as the DNA of the gospel. I have also referred to the rule of faith that authoritatively guides our understanding of the DNA structure we receive in our canonical texts. I am now prepared to add the principle—to me an obvious one—that the further one moves from the original DNA source, the more likely mutations become. Therefore, we are always wise to pay particular attention to the gospel as it was understood in the world of the church fathers.

Yet I must acknowledge that my position is exposed to a number of criticisms. Is it truly more likely that the genuine DNA of the gospel will manifest itself in the earliest years of the church, the acorn so to speak of the church's ancient life, or in the fully developed tree? David Mills, a convert to Roman Catholicism from the Episcopal Church, is convinced that we identify the DNA of the gospel more clearly by looking at the fully developed tree rather than the newly sprouted sapling. "The Church did not stop developing in the early centuries, and it is only by knowing where she got to that we know which strand of the ancient thought on the matter was right and the orthodox and the Catholic one." Traditionalizing Protestants such as I, Mill believes, desire to be traditional "without being submitted to the tradition as a Catholic would wish," and yet they claim "more authority for the tradition as the interpreter of Scripture than the Evangelical would wish."[25]

The Roman Catholic perspective articulated by Mills strikes me as fair and coherent. Why, then, do I not accept it? I, like other evangelical theologians, distinguish myself from those in the Roman communion by my

---

[25]David Mills, "Standing with Christ," *Touchstone* 16, no. 6 (July-August 2003): 83.

belief that the magisterium of the church can err in its understanding of the gospel with the result that the DNA of the gospel can mutate. Of course, the same can be said of Protestant attempts to understand the gospel and interpret the Scripture. Thus, unlike Mills, I believe infection and disease may mar the "fully developed tree" so that it requires pruning, whether the "tree" in question be Mills's Roman Catholic tradition or Hall's Anglican perspective.

The issue of Marian devotion is a case in point. What are we to make of the Roman magisterium's teaching regarding the conception, person and role of Mary? Catholic theologians themselves often acknowledge that the biblical basis for the immaculate conception of Mary is quite slim. When Pope Pius IX in the nineteenth century made the decision to promulgate Mary's immaculate conception as church dogma, he was advancing the tradition in a way that earlier developments of the gospel's DNA did not clearly demand or warrant. So I have to ask whether this new development in Marian thinking represents a faithful replication of the gospel DNA. It appears to me that the DNA has mutated at this point.

My application of the Protestant principle in response to Marian dogma is not foolproof. The problem that I and all Protestant theologians face is that of trusting that our understanding of Scripture is more valid and trustworthy than that of the Roman theologians who met in the nineteenth century. I could reject Pope Pius's decision solely on the basis of my own reading of Scripture, without reference to communal authority of any kind. But here we see the danger of an autonomous, individualistic reading of the Bible. On the same grounds—my individual rejection of a church dogma based on my reading of Scripture—I could reject anything whatsoever from the church's traditional interpretation, from a sacramental understanding of the Eucharist to a trinitarian understanding of the divine nature. If my rejection of Marian dogma is made autonomously, I cut my own theological throat, for the Protestant principle then becomes a weapon that any isolated Christian, with no communal ties of any kind, can wield against any doctrine he happens to dislike or disagree with, all the while claiming the illumination of the Holy Spirit.

So here is our dilemma. We cannot allow tradition to grow without accountability to the Scripture on which it purports to be based. At the same time, we cannot allow private interpretation of Scripture to occur without accountability to the tradition that must authoritatively guide it. If tradition automatically trumps Scripture, we are doomed; if private interpretation of Scripture trumps tradition, we are equally doomed.

I want to expand on a threefold proposal for tradition's role in evangelical theology that I have offered in the past. As for the proposal itself, first, as evangelicals we affirm our faith and confidence in the Bible as the fundamental resource for theological reflection and for the confirmation, correction and rejection of theological proposals. The Scripture is inspired of God and possesses an utterly unique authority for the church's faith and practice.

Yet the meaning of the Bible is not transparent to those who read it. Interpretation of the biblical text is unavoidable. While our own interpretations seem patently clear to us as the plain meaning of the text, they are rarely so to those who disagree with us. Therefore, second, we recognize that our interpretation of Scripture is no more infallible than the church's traditional reading. Our reading needs to be corrected by tradition, and tradition needs to be corrected by our reading.

Third, we affirm the richness of the traditions of our own distinct evangelical communions. Clark Pinnock points us to authoritative traditions such as the Formula of Concord, the Belgic Confession and the Thirty-nine Articles. Even within seemingly autonomous bodies such as independent Bible churches, interpretive traditions such as dispensationalism have played a prominent role in how Christians interpret the Bible.[26] As Kevin Vanhoozer observes, we are more likely to perceive "the full, intrinsic meaning potential of authorial discourse through a process of reading texts in contexts other than the original. Reading Scripture with, for example, Lutherans, Methodists, and Episcopalians may bring to light certain aspects of the biblical text that one might not have seen by one's Presbyterian self."[27]

---

[26]Clark Pinnock, *Tracking the Maze* (San Francisco: Harper & Row, 1990), pp. 35-43.
[27]Kevin Vanhoozer, "Four Theological Faces of Biblical Interpretation," in A. K. M. Adam et al., *Reading Scripture with the Church: Toward a Hermeneutic for Theological Interpretation* (Grand Rapids, Mich.: Baker Academic, 2006), p. 142.

We must also acknowledge the possibility, indeed, probability, that our own traditions contain mutations from the original DNA of the gospel. These mutations will become more readily apparent to us as we draw nearer to the broader tradition of the church, the great tradition represented in conciliar documents such as the Nicene Creed, the ancient rule of faith and the formative patristic period. The rule of faith and the conciliar documents of the church are indispensable aids in helping Christians understand and, as Stephen Fowl observes, remember "the dramatic framework for appropriately ordering the diversity of Scripture" and for judging between proposed interpretations.[28] As we immerse ourselves in the "basic plot" line of the Bible, assisted by the Christians who have come before us, our ability to "relate the various scenes in the theodrama to what God has done climatically in Jesus Christ" will increase, as will our talent for "grasping how we can go on following Christ in new situations so that our speech and action correspond to the truth of the gospel."[29]

Of course, it will be natural to prioritize our own tradition. As we encounter interpretive traditions other than our own, we can expect to experience theological cognitive dissonance, especially if we treat others' perspectives fairly. We may be drawn to reconsider some of our dearest perspectives, a process that is painful, anxiety-producing and disorienting. We must be willing, though, to read across borders and to allow the natives of the land we are exploring to be our guides. If we are going to study the Roman Catholic tradition, we need to read Roman Catholic writers, not Protestants writing about Roman Catholics. The same would hold true for Roman Catholics wishing to investigate the varied traditions of the Protestant world. We will be tempted to listen only to familiar voices because the unfamiliar is disorientating, confusing, threatening and fearful. Sooner or later we may have to ask the question, What if I am wrong?

I have sometimes employed the metaphor of God's holy church as a field within which a variety of flowers have blossomed over the course of

---

[28]Stephen Fowl, "Further Thoughts on Theological Interpretation," in A. K. M. Adam et al., *Reading Scripture with the Church: Toward a Hermeneutic for Theological Interpretation* (Grand Rapids, Mich.: Baker Academic, 2006), p. 129.

[29]Vanhoozer, cited by Fowl, ibid.

the church's history. The evangelical flower—picture it as a lilac—possesses its unique shape, fragrance and color. We have long rejoiced in its beauty, and rightly so. However, as our vision expands, we see more of the field—and perceive that it is not a field at all but a skillfully cultivated garden, with more types of flowers than we had ever imagined. Each displays its own delicacy, with its own attendant vulnerability. Each flower, and each variety, is beautiful, but greater than any individual flower is the glory of the garden as a whole. Is a cross-pollenization between the flowers of God's garden possible?

As I have offered this extended metaphor in the past, a number of suggestions and critiques have been offered. Baptist and Anabaptist friends have felt that my metaphor of an ecclesial garden and the possibility of cross-pollenation between flowers is overly optimistic and underplays the negative effects of tradition in the church's history. The Anabaptist tradition was birthed in times of fiery persecution from ecclesial authorities convinced that believers baptism wreaked havoc upon foundational Christian beliefs. Thus, there remains deep suspicion within Anabaptist communities—also reflected in many independent Bible churches—of church authority and tradition. For these Christians, tradition is more likely to be harmful than helpful.

Roman Catholic and Orthodox friends have also questioned my approach. My unwillingness to submit to the church's magisterium on issues such as Marian dogma strikes many Catholics as the classic Protestant tendency to elevate the Holy Spirit's illumination of the individual above the Spirit's illumination of the church. To both Roman Catholic and Orthodox, I illustrate the Protestant willingness to submit to the church's authority only when it fits my exegetical and theological fancy. When the church's teaching violates my interpretation, I too readily set the tradition aside. Indeed, am I not advocating a smorgasbord or Whitman's Sampler approach to church tradition, choosing those chocolates that appeal to my taste and leaving those with soft centers in the box. I will take the divinity of the Son, the hypostatic union and the deity of the Spirit, please. As for apostolic succession, Marian devotion or baptismal regeneration, no thank you.

How can we move forward? One group feels that I call for too much magisterium and another group for not enough. In addition, must we not acknowledge the danger of a theological and devotional aestheticism in which individual preference and experience becomes the arbiter of which traditions are accepted or rejected? Andy Crouch, for instance, speaks of encountering "many self-proclaimed postmodern Christians whose church practices reflect, often unwittingly and with the best of intentions, the enshrinement of personal choice and preference in all its gilded postmodern, or ultramodern, glory."[30]

My Whitman's Sampler illustration again comes to mind. The appropriation of the church's tradition turns into a spiritual consumer's dream: I choose what I like and ignore what I do not like, based on my preferences, without giving much thought to the life experiences and habitual patterns of behavior out of which my preferences emerge.

If such is the case, it may well be on the level of my experiences, habits, preferences and choices where the work needs to be done. A prolonged apprenticeship to proven masters of the faith, sages who may well question certain presuppositions and preferences I hold dear, may be just what the doctor orders if I am to escape from theological, historical and devotional narcissism. If so, a significant leap forward might initially entail a number of steps backward. To return to Sweet's metaphor of the pole vaulter, I need to reverse my steps to gain a running start into the future.

Is it too much to ask our Catholic friends to dedicate six months to a year studying Luther, Calvin or other Protestant worthies? In turn, is it too much to ask Protestants and more particularly evangelicals to enter the world of Athanasius, Augustine, Jerome, Gregory of Nazianzus, Basil the Great, John Chrysostom, Ambrose and Gregory the Great? Cross-pollenization occurs only when the pollen of one flower is carried to another, often by an industrious and adventurous bee.

To sum up my emphases and suggestions for the future: First, understand that the church's tradition is more than a set of doctrinal propositions. Tradition "denotes," as D. H. Williams puts it,

---

[30]Andy Crouch, "Life After Postmodernity," in *The Church in Emerging Culture,* gen. ed. Leonard Sweet (Grand Rapids, Mich.: Zondervan, 2003), p. 99.

the acceptance and handing over of God's Word, Jesus Christ *(tradere Christum)*, and how this took concrete forms in the apostles' preaching *(kerygma)*, in the Christ-centered reading of the Old Testament, in the celebration of baptism and the Lord's Supper, and in the doxological, doctrinal, hymnological and creedal forms by which the declaration of the mystery of God Incarnate was revealed for our salvation.[31]

Cary speaks of tradition "as a way of being educated, trained and formed in the virtues necessary for good theologizing," an emphasis we have already encountered in Athanasius and Gregory of Nazianzus.

In turn, the virtues inculcated in us through exposure to and practice in the church's tradition aid us in the acquisition and development of "particular skills, patterns of experience, habits of perception and portions of knowledge" essential for understanding, embracing and communicating the gospel well.[32]

I return to the metaphor of the Christian as an apprentice musician. An apprentice must learn more than musical theory, though the theory is essential if she is ever to create or play beautiful music. The apprentice must learn to be a practitioner of her craft. Along with the development of her mind, her muscle memory must also grow so that mind and muscle can ever more efficiently work together. What at first is quite difficult, even foreign to her natural inclinations, with practice becomes second nature. Discipline leads to freedom. As she listens, reads, watches and practices under the guidance of a skilled musical master, her habits, skills, experiences, preferences and choices are transformed.

She perceives, comprehends and appreciates notes, themes and meanings in a fresh manner that may indeed lead to innovation, but only because she now has the skills, knowledge, perceptions and insights to improvise. Her perceptions, judgments and musical experiences are quite different from those of persons who are musically illiterate. A well-trained musician will hear sour notes in a symphony performance much more acutely than one who does not possess a trained ear. Likewise, someone

---

[31]D. H. Williams, *Retrieving the Tradition and Renewing Evangelicalism* (Grand Rapids, Mich.: Eerdmans, 1999), p. 36.
[32]Cary, private e-mail.

properly formed in the great tradition will perceive doctrinal and behavioral false notes better than someone who has not be trained or catechized well. "Like the musician, things will be obvious to her that are not obvious to someone who is lacking the appropriate formation."[33]

Though some evangelicals and evangelical theologians look askance at the great tradition, it has often been operating in their lives in an unperceived, undetected fashion. Cary comments, "That's as inevitable as the Western musical tradition being operative in the life of a violinist. But, unlike most symphony violinists, evangelical theologians often fail to recognize that they are formed by the tradition to which they belong."[34] We need to understand more deeply the sources of our own intellectual habits, insights and practices. Our theological, ecclesial and devotional self-awareness must expand.

Self-awareness increases as we are exposed to the great tradition. Again, this exposure is similar to the way a student of the violin is initiated into the classical repertoire and learns to cultivate an ear for Mozart and Bach. Some schools might choose to train their students in a nineteenth-century repertoire more than the Baroque, just as some branches of the Christian tradition will look to Wesley or Luther rather than Aquinas. All, however, belong to the larger tradition reaching back to the church fathers.[35]

When we fail to ground ourselves in the great tradition, when we are concerned for doctrinal correctness but fail to understand the traditions in which doctrinal clarity developed and matured, ecclesial and theological shallowness and self-deception easily cripple our understanding and incarnation of the gospel. We are walking with a limp, for instance, when our churches fall into a therapeutic and consumerist practice of the gospel. It is one thing to employ candles in worship because Jesus is the light of the world, "God from God, light from light." It is another thing to employ candles because they are aesthetically pleasing to my personal tastes.

As we enter into the world of the Fathers and begin to cross borders that have divided Christians since the time of the Reformation, if not earlier,

---

[33]Ibid.
[34]Ibid.
[35]I owe this illustration to Cary.

our quest for an ever-deepening holiness can be supported by certain key dialogical virtues. Without the cultivation of these virtues, we will respond defensively and fearfully to models of Christian faith and practice that surprise, confuse, intimidate or repel us. Jay Wood warns against a whole catalog of dialogical vices that characterize philosophical, theological and ecclesial defensiveness and distrust: the tendency to "feel the persuasive power of a colleague's criticism of our views and to pretend otherwise"; the willingness to falsify data or to ignore counterevidence; the readiness to ignore, inflate, discount or subtly shade "the meaning of information unfavorable to our cherished opinions; the propensity to deliberately suppress the truth."[36] Virtues such as steadfastness, courage, empathy, honesty, gentleness, integrity and humility can significantly aid us as we build bridges to the world of the fathers and to the ecclesial worlds of our brothers and sisters in Christ today.

I return to my title: "Tradition, Authority, Magisterium: Dead End or New Horizon?" It should be clear that I am convinced neither tradition nor ecclesial authority is a dead end. Because of the pneumatological arc of the Holy Spirit across the church's history, we can expect to find in the church's tradition divine guidance, strength, wisdom and insight into the meaning of the gospel as given to us in apostolic testimony. The tradition does not lead us away from the Scripture; in its best moments it leads us into the Scripture's depth and riches. As Williams makes clear, "there is an inviolable unity between [Scripture and tradition] such that to reject tradition is to reject Scripture and vice versa. One cannot use the Scriptures and refuse to submit to the teaching of the Tradition. Likewise, one cannot claim the Tradition in support of a teaching that is denied or not supported in Scripture."[37]

We have also addressed the question of authority. I have argued that the tradition possesses inherent authority as it replicates the DNA of the gospel under the guidance of the Holy Spirit, but that it is possible for the gospel's DNA to mutate within tradition. Mutation is less likely the earlier we

---

[36]W. Jay Wood, *Epistemology: Becoming Intellectually Virtuous* (Downers Grove, Ill.: InterVarsity Press, 1998), pp. 61-62.
[37]Williams, *Retrieving the Tradition*, p. 95.

move in the church's history. The different communions that now compose the church as a whole bear the continuing responsibility to recognize the tradition's authority, to preserve and pass on the tradition's riches and to identify mutations in the tradition when they occur.

The church's authority has been abused in the past; it is not beyond the realm of possibility that abuse may occur in the future. Abuse is much less likely if we remember, as Robert Wilken observes, that authority in the church is much less connected to issues of power or coercion, as it is to trust. Generally speaking, the Fathers viewed authority as related to "trustworthiness, with the confidence a teacher earns through teaching with truthfulness, if you will. To say we need authority is much the same as saying we need teachers."[38]

The question is, then, whom will we trust? To which masters will we trustfully apprentice ourselves as we seek to understand and live out the gospel? Will we continue to hire ourselves "out as apprentices to a body of literature that is drawn almost wholly from the nineteenth and twentieth centuries," or will we move further back, further into the tradition? We ask not for infallibility but trustworthiness, a trust based in the final analysis on the continuing guidance and protection of the Holy Spirit over Christ's body on earth, the church.

---

[38]Wilken, *Remembering the Christian Past,* p. 174.

2

Old Books and Contemporary Faith

The Bible, Tradition and the Renewal of Theology

Brian E. Daley, S.J.

In his preface to a modern English translation of Athanasius's great treatise *On the Incarnation,* from the early fourth century, C. S. Lewis muses on the paradoxical importance, in our age obsessed with trendiness, of "reading old books." As a teacher of English literature, Lewis urges his readers to keep in touch generally with the classics that feed the bloodstream of our culture by reading formative original texts rather than modern historical summaries: "It is a good rule," he observes with characteristic directness, "after reading a new book, never to allow yourself another new one till you have read an old one in between."[1] This rule is even more important, he insists, when one is reading books on Christian subjects. Just as someone coming late to a discussion risks missing the drift of what is being said because he has not been there for the conversation's early stages, so in thinking about faith "the only safety is to have a standard of plain, central Christianity ('mere Christianity' as Baxter called it) which puts the controversies of the moment in their proper perspective."[2] With a sense of the long theological

---

[1] C. S. Lewis, introduction to Athanasius, *On the Incarnation,* trans. Penelope Lawson (New York: Macmillan, 1981), p. xiii.
[2] Ibid., pp. xii–xiii.

tradition, the reader has a chance, at least, of seeing beyond the real and tragic present divisions and confusions within the Christian family to "something positive, self-consistent, and inexhaustible," running through every age, something that expresses for us a still more fundamental unity in faith and moral vision. This "standard of plain, central Christianity," Lewis suggests, "can be acquired only from the old books."[3]

Lewis's stress on the importance of Christian classics, especially of classics from the formative debates and constructive essays of the first six or seven centuries of the church, would probably have seemed obvious to our ancestors, at least until the mid-seventeenth century. For John of Damascus or Bede, the successful doctrinal treatise or scriptural commentary was a distillation of mainstream earlier tradition, not a quest for revolutionary insights. For Peter Lombard or Thomas Aquinas, John Calvin or Johann Gerhard, producing a comprehensive survey of Christian teaching meant not only digging deep into the text of the Bible but also integrating the position one was arguing for into the long theological tradition, especially as that had been formed by the church fathers. It was only with the Enlightenment's stress on the autonomy of the critical human intellect that this interest in anchoring biblical interpretation and theological argument in the "old books" gradually began to fade, eventually to be eclipsed in the Catholic world by the deductive, rationalistic thinking of the scholastic manuals and in the Protestant world by philosophical apologetics, by the Romantics' effort to reconceive classical doctrine in experiential terms or by the evangelical attempt to encounter God's word in Scripture directly, apart from the creedal and doctrinal tradition in which it has been received and interpreted through the Christian centuries.

One of the most formative movements in twentieth-century Roman Catholic thought has been the recovery of an awareness of the importance of pre-Reformation Christian literature—especially the writings of the first several centuries of Christianity—precisely as sources for a deeper understanding of the gospel in our own world and for the renewal of our liturgy and the sustaining of our spiritual life. This emphasis on the return to the

---

[3]Ibid.

sources (often known by the French term *ressourcement*), so evident in the documents of the Second Vatican Council (1962-1965), paralleled, in Catholic intellectual culture, the new emphasis on critical scriptural scholarship and on the central role of the biblical text in theological argument that suddenly began to bloom in the years following World War II. This movement followed decades of suspicion on the part of church authorities, in the wake of the early twentieth-century modernist crisis, toward any kind of theology that seemed to suggest doctrinal development in history or that deviated too far from nineteenth-century scholasticism in form or content.

Much of the energy for this movement of biblical and patristic renewal came from professors in the French seminaries of the Dominican and Jesuit orders, who began, in the 1920s and 1930s, to offer a vision of Catholic theology that differed subtly but radically from what was almost universally available in the textbooks of the time: a theology that was deliberately crafted to break out of the clerical, apologetic, largely anti-Protestant and antimodern forms of thinking that had bound it for a century and more and to find in the textual roots of the Christian tradition inspiration for a theology more open to ecumenical dialogue, more engaged with the social needs of the modern world and more nourishing for the spiritual hunger of lay people.[4] Marie-Dominique Chenu, a French Dominican, for instance, published an influential article in which he argued powerfully that theology is not simply reasoning about the church's official teachings, organized formally into the kind of deductive structure Aristotle called a science, but that it expresses the mind's serious engagement with its own conversion to God through Christ Jesus. As a result, he insisted, theology is always radically historical in its way of reasoning, simply because God has revealed himself to human beings in the contingent events and characters of history. Chenu writes:

> The theologian works with a history. His "data" are not the natures of things, or the timeless forms; they are events, corresponding to an economy,

---

[4]For a discussion of the development of this new approach to Catholic theology and the sharp resistance it encountered until just before the Second Vatican Council in the 1960s, see Brian E. Daley, S.J., "*La Nouvelle Théologie* and the Patristic Revival: Sources, Symbols and the Science of Theology," *International Journal of Systematic Theology* 7 (2005): 362-82.

whose realization is bound to time. . . . The believer, the believing theologian, enters by his faith into this plan of God; what he seeks to understand, *quaerens intellectum,* is a divine initiative, a series of absolute divine initiatives, who essential trait is to be without a reason—both the general initiatives of creation, the incarnation, redemption, grace, and the particular initiatives of the gracious predestination of individuals: the sweet and terrible contingency of a love which needs give no account of his benefits or his refusal to benefit.[5]

The historical character of God's revelation of himself as Creator and Savior means, in other words, that our attempts to speak of him are not only framed by the historical contingency of our own speech and thought but also are anchored in the realization that God's ways, inexplicable in themselves, are understandable only as part of a developing consciousness that continually takes account of its own place in human history.

One area of Roman Catholic theology in which this new return to the sources had rich implications was ecclesiology: reflection on the Christian community, from the perspective of faith in what God has done in Christ. Ecclesiology, as such, was not a "treatise" in the panoramic medieval summas or a subject dealt with in theoretical terms by the church fathers; it was essentially a child of the Reformation controversies. Yet by turning again to patristic and medieval texts and reading them firsthand, as theological sources in their own right, theologians of this new stamp began to conceive of the reality of the church in a different way: as defined not by its boundaries and its authority structures so much as by its root identity as a people of faith—imperfect, contingent; called to holiness yet struggling to remain true to its mission; always incomplete until the eschatological kingdom of God brings its identity to fulfillment; always wounded by the disunity, the real but damaged communion, among those who profess the same Lord and are baptized in the same threefold name.

In 1937, Henri de Lubac—a young professor at the Jesuit theological faculty of Fourvière in Lyons—published his first book, in a new, ecumen-

---

[5]Marie-Dominique Chenu, "Position de la Théologie," *Revue des Sciences Philosophiques et Théologiques* 25 (1935): 247 (this author's translation).

ically and spiritually oriented series of Catholic theological monographs on the church, founded by the Dominican Yves Congar the previous year and called, significantly, *Unam Sanctam*. Lubac's book, *Catholicisme*,[6] was not, as its name might suggest, a summary of the characteristic teachings or practices of the Catholic church but rather, as its original subtitle, "The Social Aspects of Dogma," makes clear, a plea for a more socially active, genuinely corporate understanding of the church as Christ's body, drawing on an overwhelmingly rich range of scriptural, patristic and prescholastic medieval sources as its support. Here and throughout his later works, Lubac recognized that the revival of a more inclusive, socially incarnated sense of the church's reality and the rescue of Catholic ecclesiology from what he called "the bitter fruits of individualism,"[7] as well as from its apologetic, institutionally clerical edge, depended to a large extent on retrieving a more lively understanding of the long intellectual and spiritual tradition in which the church lives. More specifically, Lubac based his argument for a new conception of the church on a recovery, or at least a renewed understanding, of the essentially figural thought patterns of patristic theological argument and biblical interpretation, which embodied for him the early church's foundational understanding of God's continuous action in history to form and save his people.

For Chenu, Congar, Lubac and most of the young Roman Catholic theologians captivated by their project—people like Hans Urs von Balthasar, Jean Daniélou, Henri Bouillard, Hugo and Karl Rahner, and others—the key to the liberation of theology and the renewal of the church was the realization that our Christian understanding of God, the world and ourselves, and our Christian awareness of God's call, come not from a cohesive system of theses and dogmas, deduced from passages in the Scriptures and from authoritative later statements of bishops and theologians, so much as from the text of Scripture, read in its integrity and interpreted—as divine revelation—within the context of a continuing stream of Christian preaching and application.

---

[6]Henri de Lubac, *Catholicisme* (Paris: Éditions du Cerf, 1937). The most recent English translation is *Catholicism*, trans. Lancelot C. Sheppard and Elizabeth Englund (San Francisco: Ignatius, 1988).
[7]Lubac, *Catholicism*, p. 319.

This was clearly not a new idea, though scholastic manuals and Roman teaching practice had come to overlook it in the nineteenth-century rush to resist modern rationalism by a brand of ecclesiastical rationalism peculiar to the post-Reformation churches. Thomas Aquinas, for instance, makes it clear in the first question of part 1 of the *Summa Theologiae* that the science of theology, *sacra doctrina*, draws its inner coherence from the fact that the canonical Scriptures were its ultimate norm and first principle. Thomas emphasizes that theology, like any coherent branch of human knowledge, is properly open to debate; but while the arguments used in this debate may certainly include those from natural reason, "since grace does not destroy nature, but perfects it," the basis of all sacred doctrine is divine revelation; and this, Thomas insists, is normatively communicated to us in the Bible and uses human authorities and human reasoning merely for "extrinsic and probable arguments."[8]

For the theologians of the Catholic *ressourcement* movement of the mid-twentieth century, what was new was not the conviction that God's revelation is contained in a unique and unsurpassable way in the texts of Scripture but that the church's approach to hearing and understanding Scripture needs to be more direct, more focused on the text itself; if it is mediated through interpreters, as in some way our reading of the Bible always is, then it should be mediated not primarily through the secondary syntheses of post-Reformation manuals—what Lewis would label "new books"—but through the fathers of the church, who were the first to recognize and receive the Christian biblical canon. The Second Vatican Council's decree on divine revelation, *Dei Verbum*, published in 1965, sums up the spirit of the *ressourcement* by stipulating—in terms reminiscent of the sixteenth-century Reformers—that a new dedication to studying and preaching Scripture in its context must be the main source of Catholic renewal:

> The church has kept and keeps the scriptures, together with tradition, as the supreme rule of its faith, since the Bible, being inspired by God and committed to writing once and for all, communicates the word of God in an unalterable form. . . . Accordingly all the church's preaching, no less than the

---

[8]See Thomas Aquinas *Summa Theologiae* 1, q. 1, a. 8, resp. ad 2.

Christian religious life itself, ought to be nourished and ruled by Holy Scripture.[9]

What is characteristically Catholic here is the text's repeated insistence that the Scriptures serve as "the supreme rule of faith" "*together with* sacred tradition" *(una cum sacra traditione);* yet Scripture and tradition are explicitly presented in this document not in the earlier language of two sources of revelation but as "a single sacred deposit of the word of God,"[10] bringing to verbal form the truth of Jesus Christ, "who is in himself both the mediator and the fullness of all revelation."[11] And it is as witnesses to the tradition that surrounds and interprets the texts of Scripture, underlying the reception of the biblical canon and lighting up the framework in which the Bible was understood in the apostolic age, that the document also emphasizes the importance of studying the early church fathers and the history of Christian liturgy: "in this way the God who spoke of old still maintains an uninterrupted conversation with the bride of his beloved Son."[12]

For the twentieth-century renewal of Catholic theology and church life, then, a rediscovery of patristic thought, liturgy and exegesis has been inseparable from the retrieval of the biblical center of ecclesial faith and worship: in the patristic world, more clearly than in any later contexts, the tensions modern Christians often feel between Bible and theology, text and preaching, worship and ideas, had not yet entered the church's consciousness. All of these formed part of a single *traditio apostolica*, communicated to the community as a whole and preserved, in the midst of considerable diversity, in all the churches that recognized in each other branches of the same sacramental and spiritual body, sharers in the same communion.

A striking example of this understanding is the vision of church tradition in Irenaeus's *Against the Sects (Adversus Haereses)*, written in Gaul in the 180s to refute the revisionist theologies of communities claiming the secret, alternative views of redemption in Christ that came to be known as

---

[9]*Dei Verbum* 21, in G. Alberigo, *Decrees of the Ecumenical Councils* 2, ed. Norman Tanner, trans. Robert Murray (London: Sheed and Ward; Washington, D.C.: Georgetown University Press, 1990), p. 979 (altered).

[10]Ibid., 10 (Alberigo, p. 975).

[11]Ibid., 2, 4 (Alberigo, pp. 972-73).

[12]Ibid., 8 (Alberigo, p. 974); cf. 23 (Alberigo, p. 979).

Gnostic Christianity. Against the claims of the Valentinians and other Gnostic sects that their understanding of God, the world and human salvation represent revelation committed by the risen Christ to a favored few, higher in spiritual value and more liberating than the rather pedestrian faith of the wider Christian community, Irenaeus launches what is, in effect, an elaborate defense of ordinary Christian experience, as the place where God's redemptive grace is at work: this material and spiritual world, created by the one, transcendent, provident and loving God; this human body, destined for resurrection; this one publicly recognized, publicly persecuted community of Christian disciples; this one set of canonical Scriptures generally accepted by Christians—a Jewish canon, with additional writings about Jesus by the apostles; this one Christ of the four Gospels, giving his faithful ones life through the baptism and Eucharist the churches practice at his command. Irenaeus insists that a right understanding of all these things is communicated to us in a single rule of faith, accepted as normative by all the Christian communities throughout the known world.

> Having accepted this proclamation and this creed, as we have sketched it out, the Church—although scattered over the whole world—carefully preserves it, as if it dwelt in a single house. So also she believes these doctrines, as if she had one soul and the same heart, and she proclaims them in unison, and teaches them and hands them on, as if she had a single mouth.[13]

The last three books of Irenaeus's ample treatise are essentially an argument for the truth and cohesion of what is taught by the whole collection of sacred writings used as normative by the Christian churches—the Old Testament and the New. In the face of the Gnostic argument, however, that most of these texts no longer have validity as saving revelation, in view of the secret teachings the Savior had entrusted to chosen insiders, Irenaeus concedes, at the beginning of book 3, the priority of oral apostolic teaching over even the written Scriptures, but insists that this teaching has been communicated publicly to all who seek it and is "preserved by the suc-

---

[13]Irenaeus *Adversus Haereses* 1.10.2, ed. W. W. Harvey, 2 vols. (Cambridge: Cambridge University Press, 1857), 1:92-94.

cession of elders in the Churches."[14] Using the image of money deposited in a bank and available for all who need it to borrow, Irenaeus argues that even those incapable of reading the Christian texts we call the New Testament can draw on the same "water of life" through the universal teaching of the apostolic churches.

> For what would happen if the apostles had indeed not left writings behind for us? Would it not be necessary to follow the order of tradition, which they handed on to those to whom they entrusted the Churches? Many peoples among those foreigners [literally: barbarians] who believe in Christ assent to this arrangement, having salvation written in their hearts by the Spirit, without paper or ink, and preserving the ancient tradition carefully, believing in one God, the Creator of heaven and earth and all that is in them, and Christ Jesus the Son of God. . . . Those who believe this creed without written text are foreigners as far as our language goes, but as for thought and practice and manner of life they are, through their faith, extremely wise and pleasing to God.[15]

Irenaeus walks a fine line, then, between acknowledging that it is possible to profess an authentic Christian faith without direct access to the biblical text and still rejecting esoteric, originally oral traditions that thrive by contrasting themselves with the "crude" teaching of the Bible. The difference lies in the character and origins of the oral tradition and in its accessibility through a structured, open community.

Almost fifty years after Irenaeus composed his treatise, Origen of Alexandria dealt with the same fundamental issues of Scripture and creed in his own stunningly comprehensive work *On First Principles*. Here too the opponents are obviously Gnostic teachers—Alexandrian Valentinians, in all probability, like Heracleon, the first commentator on John's Gospel—who draw selectively on writings shared with mainstream Christians, as well as on their own texts, to develop a distinctive picture of God, the world and human salvation. Origen begins the preface to his treatise with a general reflection on Christian teaching. All those who believe that "grace and

---

[14]Ibid., 3.2.2; see also 3.1, 2; 2.1; 3.1.
[15]Ibid., 3.4.1-2.

truth came through Jesus Christ" (Jn 1:17), he says, and who believe that Jesus is himself the truth, seek a detailed knowledge of how to live in the words of Christ—which for Origen include not only the words of the Gospels but also those of the whole Bible, since all the sacred writers, Moses and the prophets as well as the Gospel writers and Paul, were filled with the Spirit of Christ.[16]

The problem, however, is that the text of Scripture, already in the second and third centuries, could be used to support a dazzling variety of positions, "not only on small and negligible matters, but also on great and even on the greatest things: on God, that is, or on our Lord Jesus Christ himself or on the Holy Spirit; and not only on these but on other creatures."[17] Origen continues:

> For this reason, it seems necessary first of all to lay down a clear line, or an obvious rule *(regulam)*, concerning each of these subjects, and then also to ask about other matters. For just as many Greeks and foreigners promised us the truth, but we gave up seeking it among all who attributed it to their false opinions after we came to believe that Christ is the Son of God, and were persuaded that we must learn the truth from him; so now—since there are many who think they share the mind of Christ, and not a few of them have different positions from their forbears, but the preaching of the Church, handed on from the apostles, is preserved by orderly succession and remains in the Churches until the present time—only that position is to be believed as truth that in no way varies from the tradition of the Church and the apostles.[18]

Origen immediately goes on to qualify what might seem to be shaping up as an excessively authoritarian notion of revelation. The apostles knew, he argues, that some points of their preaching were so fundamental that all believers, even the simplest of folk, needed to grasp them clearly, while other things could be simply asserted without full explanation; and even for the most fundamental issues, the underlying reasons for why things are so they left to the investigations of "those who were blessed with outstanding gifts of the Spirit."[19]

---

[16]Origen *On First Principles* pref. 1.
[17]Ibid., 2.
[18]Ibid.
[19]Ibid., 3.

Origen then lists what he considers the basic assumptions all Christians must keep in mind as a guide for interpreting the word of Scripture according to the mind of the apostles: that God is one, the sole creator, the God of the patriarchs and prophets and the Father of Jesus; that Jesus Christ, the firstborn Son of God, took on flesh like our own, died our death and was raised; that the Holy Spirit, however one understands his origin, "is united in honor and dignity with the Father and the Son"[20] and has inspired the prophets; that the soul will survive to be rewarded or punished for its deeds and that its body will rise in some form to share that retribution; that each of us has free will and is responsible for his or her own actions; that demons and angels exist and influence human actions; that the world is not eternal; and that the Scriptures "were composed through the Spirit of God" and have not only their obvious meaning but also hidden spiritual meanings that must be searched for by the help of the Spirit.[21] This list of basic Christian tenets—strikingly parallel to the formulations of the rule of faith that appear in Irenaeus, Tertullian and other early Christian writers—is in fact an outline of what Origen will set out systematically in his treatise, not once but twice, always developing his exposition of the faith with a primary emphasis on the scriptural basis for every point in his exposition.

In the final book (bk. 4) of the treatise, Origen turns to Scripture itself, as inspired by the Holy Spirit to nourish the faithful and lead them, through a right understanding of the text, to share in the life of God. The implication of his argument seems clearly to be that it is only those who already grasp the central drift and outline of Scripture's teaching, from Genesis to the book of Revelation, who are in the position to interpret particular texts correctly and to judge their place in the whole structure.[22] Like Irenaeus, Origen takes it for granted that the Scriptures of Israel and the Christian Gospels and letters (which seem to form for him a generally ac-

---

[20]Ibid., 4.
[21]Ibid., 8.
[22]For a fuller argument for this understanding of *On First Principles,* see Brian E. Daley, S.J., "Origen's *De Principiis:* A Guide to the Principles of Christian Scriptural Interpretation," in *Nova et Vetera,* ed. John Petruccione (Washington, D.C.: Catholic University of America Press, 1998), pp. 3-21. See also Brian E. Daley, S.J., "Incorporeality and 'Divine Sensibility': The Importance of *De Principiis* 4.4 for Origen's Theology," *Studia Patristica* 41 (2006): 139-44.

cepted, if not yet an officially designated, canon) are an organic whole, telling a single story and proclaiming a unified message of salvation, and that even the smallest details of Scripture carry a life-giving meaning for the believer if understood within that whole. Just as the priest in ancient Israel was appointed to cut apart the animal offered in sacrifice and lay it open on the altar, so the biblical interpreter—who is, for Origen, the true priest of the new law—has the task of "cutting up the flesh of the Word of God," exposing the inner joints and veins of the texts in which the Word has, since the time of Moses, concealed his divinity under "the veil of the letter."[23] Armed with a clear sense of the basic apostolic message conveyed by the rule of faith, the exegete and preacher, in Origen's view, carries out the central liturgical role in the Christian community: leading the people formed by the Word, "in whom the divine fire always is burning, always consumes the flesh,"[24] to offer themselves as a sacrifice of praise to God.

A century and three-quarters after Origen wrote *On First Principles,* Augustine engaged many of the same problems of Christian scriptural interpretation in his treatise *De Doctrina Christiana (On Christian Learning),* begun in 397 and finished thirty years later. Probably intended as a manual for training preachers, this work makes a sustained plea for the liberal arts, with all their appended subspecies of erudition, as a useful and appropriate way to form minds capable of seeking out the doubtful or hidden meanings of scriptural texts and of conveying those meanings powerfully in persuasive speech. But the most fundamental knowledge the scriptural interpreter needs, if he is to understand and proclaim the text correctly, is to grasp the message conveyed by the whole of what was now recognized as the biblical canon. When one encounters difficulties in a particular passage—difficulties of punctuation and construal, such as plagued ancient grammarians, or the more theoretical difficulties of distinguishing metaphors from literal assertions—Augustine, like Irenaeus and Origen before him, reaches to tradition: "You should refer it to the rule of faith, which you have received from the plainer passages of Scripture and from the au-

---

[23]Origen *Homilies on Leviticus* 1.4, Sources Chrétiennes (Paris: Éditions du Cerf, 1943-), 286:78-80; cf. 1.1 (66).
[24]Ibid., 4 (80).

thority of the Church."[25] And if our real purpose in reading Scripture is to find the will of God, to learn what we must do in order to reach our goal of life with him, then the practical heart of the rule of faith, as Augustine insists in book 1 of the work, is the double commandment of love, enunciated in the Torah and reaffirmed by Jesus: to love the Lord our God above all things—since he alone is the "thing," the reality, the *res* worth clinging to and "enjoying" as our ultimate good—and to love our neighbor as ourselves. Augustine puts his position with characteristic clarity:

> So if it seems to you that you have understood the divine scriptures, or any part of them, in such a way that by this understanding you do not build up this twin love of God and neighbor, then you have not yet understood them. If on the other hand you have made judgments about them that are helpful for building up this love, but for all that have not said what the author you have been reading actually meant in that place, then your mistake is not pernicious, and you certainly cannot be accused of lying.[26]

In Augustine's mode of thinking, such a love-centered hermeneutic is, at the same time, a church-centered hermeneutic: for him, the church of Christ, which is his body on earth, is held together by the love that the Holy Spirit pours forth in the hearts of the faithful—a tough, enduring love, international and transethnic in scope, which turns the eyes of the believer beyond his or her local community and tradition, and joins him to the whole company of disciples, journeying toward the heavenly Jerusalem. Learning how to read the Bible as an invitation to love is both the fruit and the foundation of life in a believing, human church.[27]

We may seem to have traveled a long way from musing, with Lewis, on the value of reading "old books," or even from the Catholic church's experience—unique perhaps, within its own twentieth-century struggles—of the transforming effects of *ressourcement*, of learning to read our common ancient sources again not for proof texts in argument but for the

---

[25] Augustine *On Christian Learning* 3.2.2, trans. Edmund Hill, *Teaching Christianity* (Hyde Park, N.Y.: New City, 1996), p. 169.

[26] Ibid., 1.36.40. On this hermeneutic of charity, see also 3.15.28.

[27] For Augustine's vision of the church as a body knit together by Christ's gift of love, see *Homilies on 1 John* 10.3.

renewal of our Christian life. The three examples I have briefly laid out here—well-known texts by familiar authors—are meant primarily to remind us of the early church's common conviction, which runs through all the variety of the Fathers' language and style: that our faith as Christians is wholly rooted in Scripture—in what we call the Old Testament, as our instrument for understanding Jesus, and in what we call the New Testament, as our lens for reading the Old through and in Jesus. Yet, that Scripture cannot be understood or interpreted authentically—cannot be read as expressing the divine revelation that culminates in the person of the incarnate Word—apart from the community's rule of faith, which is distilled from Scripture and leads us through the obscure thickets of its meaning to the way of Christ. Both preaching and liturgical worship, then, in this classical view, are focused on Scripture, live from Scripture; yet Scripture is only received, tested, recognized as canonical and internalized by individuals in the context of liturgy and in the light of preaching. Theology, as a rather dull subspecies of preaching, itself finds its home in the life of the worshiping community as the way (to use Gregory of Nazianzus's famous phrase) in which "faith brings reasoning to its perfection." And the figural exegesis of scriptural passages, which can seem so bizarre and arbitrary to our more prosaic modern minds, suddenly reveals its logic when we recognize that it expresses the constant awareness that we who now read the Bible as our book have been grafted by Christ, through the gift of his Spirit, into the living organism of his people through the ages: that the Bible is about us because the church, along with Israel, is part of his holy, pilgrim people.

All of these interpretive activities, the Fathers remind us, define and nourish the church, which is located within the human history where God reveals himself and which is a central actor in that history's final age. So it is only within a worshiping, discerning, interpreting, preaching church that Scripture becomes Scripture—is received as a canon and generates the rule of faith—and carries out its life-giving function as the Word of God. If our reading of Scripture is to be freed from the "slavery to the letter" Origen and Augustine feared, as well as from the privatizing, world-escaping tendencies of gnosis, it must be embedded in an implied ecclesiology that takes the world and its history seriously and be guided by an ecclesial sense of living tradition.

As Catholics and evangelical Christians, all of us need *ressourcement:* need to be able to stay close to the springs of our Christian faith. I am not in a position to say what this might mean for evangelicals today, but I am convinced—as a member of a Catholic order that has always seen itself as both "reformed" and "evangelical," in a broad Christian sense—that Catholics, at least, do this best by learning again what Scripture and its interpretation required, in the minds of the church fathers, and by accepting the fact that any whole-hearted return to our sources will have lasting, life-changing implications for the way we live and understand ourselves as a church. For the Roman Catholic community in the twentieth century, *ressourcement* has meant reclaiming a sense of the church as a worshiping, social body, formed by the gospel, with a history that matters. It has meant getting away from the literalism and polemical rationalism of nineteenth-century scholastic theology; recognizing that the Spirit of God continues to guide the church more deeply "into all the truth" (Jn 16:13), in ways that we cannot predict but that centrally involve both consistency and development; abandoning an individualistic sense of salvation and Christian duty, in order to recognize that our mission in the world, and our promised future at the world's end, belong to the whole body of Christ.

Lubac, whose great book *Catholicism* I mentioned earlier, emphasizes there the connection of the rediscovery of patristic biblical interpretation and the continuing life of the church in powerful terms:

> What we call nowadays the Old and New Testaments is not primarily a book. It is a twofold event, a twofold "covenant," a twofold dispensation which unfolds its development through the ages, and which is fixed, one might suppose, by no written account. When the Fathers said that God was its author—the one and only author of the Old and New Testaments—they did not liken him merely, nor indeed primarily, to a writer, but saw in him the founder, the lawgiver, the institutor of these two "instruments" of salvation, these two economies, two dispensations which are described in the Scriptures and which divide between them the history of the world. . . . Convinced that all therein was full of deep and mysterious meaning, the Fa-

thers bent over the inspired pages in which they could trace through its successive stages the covenant of God with the human race; they felt that, rather than giving a commentary on a text or solving a verbal puzzle, they were interpreting a history. History, just like nature, or to an even greater degree, was a language to them. It was the word of God. Now throughout this history they encountered a mystery, which was to be fulfilled, to be accomplished historically and socially, though always in a spiritual manner: the mystery of Christ and his Church.[28]

The reason Christians should read "old books," ultimately, is because they can form us all, with unparalleled freshness and power, into sharers in that mystery.

---

[28]Lubac, *Catholicism*, pp. 169-70.

3

Similis et Dissimilis

Gauging Our Expectations of the Early Fathers

D. H. Williams

When I left Chicago for central Texas five years ago, I decided to "go country," as the song says. I purchased cowboy boots and a few acres of land, put in a fence and a small barn and eventually bought two horses. One of the horses was a colt that I planned to break in and make a good riding horse. I had read some books, watched some videos and observed horse trainers. Why could I not do the same? After all, the horse is a domesticated animal that should respond to human instruction. Once I had done all the fieldwork and rope training, I figured it was time to climb on his back. I asked my wife to come out and take some pictures of my first ride with this horse. The instant I got into the saddle, the horse took off, wildly jumping and kicking until I fell off. I discovered, now sprawled on the ground, that it was I who would have to be trained with the horse. A year and a half later, after a broken leg, a fractured hip and scores of bruises, I was fully broken in and the horse was ready to ride.

Who would have thought a decade ago that one of the most vibrant and serious fields of Christian study at the beginning of the twenty-first century would be the ancient church fathers? There has been an opening of new avenues, especially among Free Church Protestants, by the almost overnight popularity of bishops and monks, martyrs and apologists, philosophers and historians who first fashioned a Christian culture fifteen hundred years ago.[1] We are seeing numbers of books, articles and large-scale projects of Scripture commentary produced by Protestant evangelical publishers, all which demonstrate that the study of the intellectual and spiritual life of postapostolic Christianity is moving into current reflections of evangelical theology, exegesis and piety.

As a long-time student of patristics, I welcome how Free Church traditions are seeking how to incorporate the early church into their perspectives.[2] When I entered the academic study of patristics in 1985, I could count on one hand the number of those who were doing serious study in this field and were not either Episcopalian or Roman Catholic. Much has changed. But I am also cautious about this newfound enthusiasm in the early fathers for the reason that evangelicals might be tempted to tame the early fathers by making them speak to our current situation in ways alien to the ancients themselves. There is much to be gained by introducing a new *ressourcement* of patristic Christianity to the contemporary challenges that Christian face. But as the twentieth-century *ressourcement* movement argued, we must be willing to be taught and "broken in" before we start adopting and adapting this doctrine or that practice for our own purposes in the twenty-first century. In order for the appropriation of the early fathers to become more than another trend among others within the history of evangelicalism, we must beware not to create the early fathers in our own image. In this essay I will make some comments on the ways in which the ancient fathers are dissimilar from and similar to Protestant evangelicalism with a view to establishing some fruitful ways of listening to the Fathers.

Make no mistake; there are high ideological and historiographical walls that have separated evangelical forms of faith from the faith of the early church. Barriers of ahistoricalism, anti-Catholicism and anticreedalism have stood and still stand in the way. Underlying these barriers has been the prevailing perception that Christianity after the apostles soon became distorted to the point of betraying the gospel. The rise of the episcopacy,

---

[1]As noted by R. R. Reno, "The Return of the Fathers," *First Things* (November 2006): 16.
[2]See D. H. Williams, ed., *The Free Church and the Early Church* (Grand Rapids, Mich.: Eerdmans, 2002).

the alleged dependency on tradition rather than the Bible, Christian emperors, veneration of martyrs, infant baptism and so on, all bespoke of a faith that had become misaligned and detached from the pristine spirituality of the New Testament. In practice this meant that most of the ecclesiastical and theological history from the death of the apostles to the time of the Reformers needed to be purged, not embraced, from the believing church.[3]

For many evangelical or Free churches the notion that Protestant Christianity has a heritage seated within the patristic tradition, much less a heritage to which one should make appeal, is still a foreign and even suspect one. Such longstanding suspicion is the result of marginalizing the postapostolic period as ephemeral to Christian faithfulness, leaving an enormous gap in the historical consciousness of evangelical spirituality, worship and biblical understanding. Despite the fact that the fifteenth- and sixteenth-century Reformers perceived their reforming efforts in continuity with the historic teaching of the catholic faith on most matters and relied extensively on the ancient sources for expounding theological orthodoxy, their later Protestant successors have tended to eschew these same sources as superfluous to the Christian identity, or even contrary to biblical authority, as the conflict against Roman Catholicism was waged. Much has been written about these problems, and I do not need to rehearse them here.

At the same time, evangelicalism's recent and growing fascination with the age of the early fathers may not be so surprising after all. For all their suspicion of the patristic era, many Protestants are still characterized by a general primitivist impulse when it comes to religious beginnings, that is, how the mark of authentic faith demands a return to Christian origins as the primary and normative age of the Spirit. Back to the faith of the New Testament church is the ideal for today's church. The mentality behind "back to the Bible" seems to have the same connotations. This does not mean that there is an invested interest in actual historical or traditional connections. The point, rather, is that the time of the primordial Christian church is al-

---

[3]For details alleging the Constantinian "fall," see D. H. Williams, *Retrieving the Tradition and Renewing Evangelicalism* (Grand Rapids, Mich.: Eerdmans, 1999), chap. 4.

ways repeatable. Whether it dates back to the sixteenth century with Mennonites or the Reformed movement or to nineteenth-century America via the Disciples of Christ, Pentecostalist movements or the Churches of Christ, Protestant Christianity has perceived its central task as reclaiming the apostolic faith as witnessed in the New Testament. Indeed, it has been observed that the restorationist idea may be the most vital single assumption underlying the development of American Protestantism.[4]

Once the theological and ideological wall that separates the New Testament from what follows it is lowered, the search for restoring the church is opened to the way in which the apostolic deposit unfolded in subsequent centuries. We discover immediately that that which is apostolic, or apostolicity, was a concept developed after the apostles, mainly pertaining to the conservation and continuation of what the apostles taught.[5] The familiar lines that have been drawn between the New Testament and postapostolic Christianity are artificial and often polemically motivated. The important concept of canon is itself a patristic construct.[6] With good reason, therefore, did George Florovsky declare, "The Church is apostolic indeed, but the Church is also patristic."[7]

Another reason for the rise of interest in early fathers is that they may help ameliorate the problematic issues of identity that have beset evangelicals since the mid-twentieth century. To ask what precisely defines an evangelical still generates a variety of answers to the point that only a few core propositions can be made. The wide array of influences from evangelicalism's historical heritage and religious cultural development,[8] as rich as

---

[4]Richard Hughes, ed., *The American Quest for the Primitive Church* (Chicago: University of Illinois Press, 1988), p. 7.

[5]The word *apostolic* is first used in Ignatius of Antioch's preface to his letter to the Trallians (c. 117) in reference to the imitation of a personal model, but Irenaeus provides us with what would become the standard understanding: "The church . . . has received from the Apostles and their disciples the faith." He then proceeds to give a summary of that faith in *Against Heresies* 1.10. See Irenaeus *Against Heresies* 1.10.2, Ante-Nicene Fathers (Peabody, Mass.: Hendrickson, 1994), 1:331.

[6]D. H. Williams, "The Patristic Tradition as Canon," *Perspectives in Religious Studies* 32 (2005): 357-79.

[7]George Florovsky, *Bible, Church, Tradition* (Belmont, Mass.: Nordland, 1972), p. 107.

[8]See J. A. Carpenter, "The Fellowship of Kindred Minds: Evangelical Identity and the Quest for Christian Unity," in *Pilgrims on the Sawdust Trail,* ed. T. George (Grand Rapids, Mich.: Baker Academic, 2004); D. W. Dayton and R. K. Johnston, eds., *The Variety of American Evangelicalism* (Downers Grove, Ill.: InterVarsity Press, 1991).

it is, have prevented the creation of a unifying platform, with exception of institutional associations (i.e., National Association of Evangelicals).[9] Thus, the search for a common ground that transcends the battles of the sixteenth and seventeenth centuries has gained traction over the last two decades. The slow demise of the usual denominational categories has added to the evasiveness of evangelicalism, which also means its quest for locating some unifying principles or a shared earlier history has become more urgent. It is not implausible, then, to argue that the appropriation of formative Christianity might assist in creating a rootedness or an identifying center to which evangelicals could point.

Dissimilis

In turning to the early fathers, let me say that the patristic faces that evangelicals meet will not all be familiar or even comfortable ones. Clearly the ancient Christians had ways of expressing themselves and their times that are *dissimilis,* or unlike, our notion of religion. Despite a fascination with the early fathers, evangelicals will find some wholly unique features about the patristic age that will not easily be squared with their religious worldviews.

First, let me mention a few issues that are a cause for stumbling for contemporary translators or theologians. One is the anti-Judaism—sometimes quite strongly worded—that is found in many ancient Christian writers. By the end of the second century, the acceptable currents of Jewish Christianity were fading out and were being replaced by a more polarizing conception. Hostilities between the two overwhelmed the deeper truth of their shared legacy. Already by the first decade of the second century, we hear Ignatius of Antioch declare in an open letter that "it is utterly absurd to profess Jesus Christ and to practice Judaism."[10] Even in the very saintly account of Polycarp's martyrdom, we are told that Jews incited his death and convinced Ro-

---

[9]Evangelicals are very generally marked by four characteristics: commitment to the authority of Scripture, the atoning work of Christ, the necessity of personal conversion and the imperative to evangelize others. A problem, of course, is that a quarter to a third of Roman Catholics, Eastern Orthodox and mainline Protestants in America also answer to those characteristics.

[10]Ignatius of Antioch *To the Magnesians* 10.3, in *The Apostolic Fathers in English,* ed. Michael Holmes (Grand Rapids, Mich.: Baker Academic, 2006), p. 107; cf. *To the Philadelphians* 6.1.

man authorities to destroy his body.[11] By the third century, whole works by Christian authors will be devoted, as the title implies, *Adversus Iudaeos*.[12] We likewise see in the sermons of John Chrysostom little sympathy for the Jews and no hope of their salvation.[13] It is an unfortunate side of the patristic mentality and remains problematic for the modern Christian reader.

Another issue, like that of the New Testament, is the patristic accep-tance of institutional slavery. After Constantine, bishops were given au-thority to manumit slaves, but the practice was an exceptional one and not the result of social change. Christian masters were committed to practice the Christian virtues with their slaves, and slaves (with their owner's per-mission) could be baptized. The practice of slavery was completely indig-enous; slaves comprised almost two-thirds of the Roman population. In-deed, it was rumored that Callistus, the bishop of Rome (A.D. 217-222) had once been a slave.[14] Without laboring the point, we may observe that the same architects who contributed toward our doctrines of Christology and trinitarianism simply assumed the acceptability of slave holding.

Yet another matter we have to acknowledge in early Christianity was the way it gradually elevated the pursuit of asceticism to a position of spiritual su-periority over that of faithful Christians married and living in communities. By the 370s the *Life of Antony* was a bestseller across the Mediterranean as well as other stirring accounts of holy men successfully contending with the devil and human weaknesses, which freely flowed from Syria, Egypt and eastern Asia Minor. Given the extent and depth to which the ascetic life had taken hold of the Christian conception of living a holy life in the world, anything less was subjugated to second place. Jerome spoke for this general trend when he pronounced that marriage was good and given by God, but the completely

---

[11]*Martydom of Polycarp* 17.2 in *The Apostolic Fathers in English*, ed. Michael Holmes (Grand Rapids, Mich.: Baker Academic, 2006), p. 146.

[12]E.g., Tertullian *Against the Jews;* Cyprian *Three Books of Testimonies Against the Jews;* Novatian *On Jewish Foods.*

[13]See Lee M. McDonald, "Anti-Judaism in the Early Church Fathers," in *Anti-Semitism and Early Christianity,* ed. Craig A. Evans and Donald A. Hagner (Minneapolis: Fortress, 1993), pp. 215-52. Ambrose of Milan threatened to cut the emperor Theodosius from communion if he persisted in making the bishop of Callinicum pay for the rebuilding of the synagogue that a group of Christians burned down; Ambrose *Epistle* 74 [40].7-8.

[14]Hippolytus *Refutation of All Heresies* 9.7 (*ANF* 5:129).

virginal life was better because it continued the martyr's life of complete self-sacrifice. How ironic it is to read a monk, Helvidius, vigorously argue for the equal value of virginity and the married state against Jerome's position which set celibacy and ascetic life as the preferred and more acceptable state of Christian living before God.[15] By the later fourth century, fewer bishops were marrying, soon leading to the merger of the bishop and the ascetic and eventually to the priesthood and celibacy in the West. As far as Ambrose was concerned, the relation of celibacy to marriage was comparing good with good, "so that what is superior may be that much more apparent."[16] Christian churches were now becoming two-tiered in the way in which they defined spirituality.

One further difference, though not the last, between the early and the evangelical churches has to do with the practice of evangelism. Most assuredly, the intention of the early church was not to be user-friendly, much less seeker-sensitive. In fact, it was the reverse: there were many occupations that would prevent one from becoming a Christian even when a person sought to convert. A Roman list from around A.D. 215 shows that not only pagan priests, sorcerers or the immoral were prohibited, but so were sculptors, painters, some kinds of athletes, soldiers and actors. In effect, any lifestyle or occupation that was counter to the culture of the church would not be admitted to baptism. But wasn't the early church committed "to make disciples of all nations"? Once in the church, however, believers were told to preserve the *arcana disciplina* ("secret practices") that the faith confessed, and that church teaching was not for general consumption or public knowledge. One manual on church practice from Rome says,

> If there is anything else, which needs to be told [about the faith], the bishop shall tell it privately to those who receive baptism. None but the faithful may know, and even them only after receiving baptism. This is the white stone about which John said, "A new name is written on it, which no one knows except the one who received the stone."[17]

---

[15]Jerome *Against Helvidius* 24, Nicene and Post-Nicene Fathers, Series 2 (Peabody, Mass.: Hendrickson, 1994), 6:346.

[16]Ambrose *On Virgins* 1.7.35; cf. 1.3.10: "For virginity is not praiseworthy because it is found in martyrs but because it itself makes martyrs" (*NPNF* 2, 10:365).

[17]*Apostolic Tradition* 21.40. The reference is to Revelation 2:17.

It may be that persecution of Christians and fear of informers originally lay behind these secretive practices, but these were not the primary reasons. It seems that the church's greater worry was the pollution of the mysteries of faith. This was one interpretation of Matthew 7:6: "Do not give dogs what is holy; and do not throw your pearls before swine." Moreover, baptism was an initiation into the church's mysteries that the believer was to retain in the heart, not on paper. The saving gospel was to be permanently etched on one's mind and soul. So Augustine tells baptismal candidates that once they have received the church's central teachings via the North African creed ("Symbolum"), "in no way are you to write it down, in order to retain the same words; but you are to learn it thoroughly by hearing, it, and by heart, keep and go over it in your memory."[18]

In sum, the actual mechanics of evangelistic activities is almost unknown to us after the apostolic times, as is any emphasis on missions to foreign peoples.[19] An exception is Ulfilas, an Arian missionary to the Goths in the later fourth century who translated the Bible into their language.[20] The story of Patricius or Patrick and Ireland in the fifth century is well known.[21] Like Ufilas, Patrick had been captured as a youth in a raid by those to whom he would later return to begin a church. But these are noteworthy exceptions during the first five centuries. If there was a norm in the method of spreading the faith, it seems not to have been on mass conversions or missionary exploits but on the one-to-one communication within already established networks of communities.[22] By their lives of high moral standards, self-sacrifice to the point of martyrdom and liberal charity in times of plague or poverty to Christian and non-Christian alike,[23] the churches attracted converts— and in large numbers.

---

[18]Augustine Sermon 212.2.

[19]The single reference that Eusebius of Caesarea makes about missionary endeavors (Ecclesiastical History 3.37.3) is spoken of in the past: it occurred with the disciples of the apostles.

[20]Socrates Ecclesiastical History 4.33.

[21]Among many choices, see E. A. Thompson, Who Was St. Patrick? (Rochester, N.Y.: Boydell, 1985).

[22]Rodney Stark makes a compelling case for this in The Rise of Christianity (Princeton, N.J.: Princeton University Press, 1996), pp. 73-94.

[23]The extent of social compassion displayed by Christians was begrudgingly admitted by a number of pagan critics. There is the well-known remark by the pagan emperor Julian, "These godless Galileans [his word for Christians] feed not only their own poor, but others, while we neglect our own" (Epistle 84a).

How Not to Use the Ancients

In their newfound zeal for appropriating the early fathers as a means of opposing theological modernity, evangelical writers are inclined toward romantic presentations of the Fathers and their value for us. It is easy to idealize the Fathers so that most everything they said provides good guidance for today's church. One can resort to the patristic legacy as a golden age or in a nostalgic sense in which the years of formative Christianity are recalled from the past, as if invoking them ushers into the present a sort of historical magic. This would not be the first time that ancient texts were used in this way. An exceptional find in the Egyptian desert some years ago was a small papyrus fragment that contained a portion of the text of the Nicene-Constantinopolitan creed (381). The fragmentary portion dates from the later fifth century, and scholars think it may have been used as a kind of amulet.[24] Evidently, the wearer of this creedal formula thought that the creed possessed power such that it could invite God's blessing or ward off evil spirits and misfortune!

In our reclamation of the early church's faith, the patristic legacy must not be treated as if it were an ecclesiastical charm bracelet, nor should it be interpreted to mean that reclamation of all or any one aspect of the ancient tradition will solve ecclesiastical discipline and doctrinal muddles that beset contemporary Christianity. The notion of *ressourcement* is not about quixotically reappropriating the early fathers as if they hold the answers for contemporary Christians and churches. Even the staunchest defender of the relevance of patristic resources will admit that not everything the patristic fathers taught is true or even valuable.

While we may agree that the ancients were less fragmented than is the Christianity of the present age, the church's historic witnesses must always be heard within the rough-and-tumble world of interchurch polemics, doctrinal uncertainty and no one agreed-on method of biblical exegesis. It is more accurate to say that the early church was truly engaged in a search—sometimes haphazardly—for a Christian doctrine of God, rather

---

[24]"Fragment of the Niceno-Constantinopolitan Creed," in *New Documents Illustrating Early Christianity*, ed. G. H. R. Horsley (New South Wales, Macquarie University, The Ancient History Documentary Research Centre, 1981), pp. 103-4.

than slowly unveiling what it knew implicitly all along (as one finds in the late-nineteenth-century editorial opinion in the Ante- or Post-Nicene Fathers series). There was both development and changes in early centuries, which lay behind the construction of those categories "orthodoxy" and "heresy." When it comes to acknowledging the foundational creeds, therefore, we are faced with viewing them not merely as doctrinal touchstones but as diachronic statements of faith whose theological and polemical contexts are just as important as the words of the creeds.

Related to this issue is the way contemporary appeals are made to the writers of the early church as if the church possessed a monolithic stance on its opinions and practices. There were indeed some common threads that manifested themselves through the rules of faith, catechetical addresses and major confessions of faith, but as we obtain a more detailed understanding of the early church we discover it was not uniform historically or theologically. In his definition of the catholic faith, Origen admitted that certain Christians disagreed with other Christians. These differences, he pointed out, were not just on "small and trivial things" but about "most important matters" (*On First Principles* praef.). Both Athanasius and Arius vehemently declared that their respective views represented the Christian tradition. It may be that Arius was ultimately wrong, but it was nevertheless true that both of them were drawing on selected portions of a body of tradition that existed and yet was not formulated to answer the new questions of their time that were being raised.

On the whole, it was not always a matter of orthodox versus heretic but of the faithful conflicting with the views of other faithful. The controversy that exploded in the fifth century over christological issues is a good case in point.[25] All parties were seeking to guard the complete divinity of Christ while militantly opposed to one another over the proper logic and terminology of expressing his divinity in the light of his true incarnation. Cyril of Alexandria condemned Nestorius, Flavian condemned Eutyches, and Leo of Rome's position regarding the two natures at Chalcedon used

---

[25]For a good accounting, see Susan Wessel, *Cyril of Alexandria and the Nestorian Controversy*, Oxford Early Christian Studies (Oxford: Oxford University Press, 2004).

Nestorian language to defend the original intention of Cyril. The council of Chalcedon only partially solved the problems.

The danger of using the patristic era as a wondrously united age is that early Christianity becomes too easily subject to our own agendas for using it. It is difficult to disprove general claims that make appeal to a church age that never existed—the ancient church becomes another Lake Wobegon, "where all the women were strong, the men good-looking and the children above average." Such a patristic age may serve our needs for creating a model that we may better beat back the postmodernists or theological liberals, but we do this at the cost of misconstruing ancient historical and theological realities. Before we are tempted to remake the patristic church in our own image, let us first encounter it with its own problems and solutions.

I would submit that this is a potentially serious problem now facing evangelicals who are discovering and utilizing the ancient fathers. Frankly, this problem is not much helped by presenting to evangelical readers bite-size passages of the early fathers—small clips of patristic writings in anthologies or biblical commentaries that are devoid of context and the flow of argument. I say this with some uneasiness since I am the volume editor for Matthew in the The Church's Bible series! In this series, paragraph-size extracts are chosen from select early fathers on most verses in a format that reminds one of Thomas Aquinas's *Catena Aurea (The Golden Chain)*, where patristic comments were lined up one after the other as they pertained to a biblical passage. The comments had no extrinsic relation to one another except that each was addressing the same biblical section. It was impossible to know the mind of the early church from these small links, even if there was presented some valuable insights on the Bible.

Although I admit this is not the best way to acquire the depth of meaning or thought processes of the early fathers, the *catena* format is a start for the beginner. Widely used in the Middle Ages, the catenae were meant to act as mnemonic aids for the reader. And like all such collections, they were supposed to spur the believer on to further investigation of an ancient author or follow a train of thought that exegetical sound bites could not do. If evangelicals continue to follow after the ancient voices, they will need to confront this issue.

A third mishandling of the early church is looking for proto-Protestant doctrines or practices in the ancients that support the evangelical point of view. There have been recent attempts to find a "patristic principle of *sola scriptura*" in Irenaeus[26] or in Athanasius, from which the conclusion is reached, "*Sola scriptura* has long been the rule of believing Christian people, even before it became necessary to use the specific terminology against later innovators who would usurp the Scriptures' supremacy in the church."[27] The concern is a polemical one: reading the ancient fathers through the lens of post-Reformation Protestantism and looking for criteria, such as *sola Scriptura,* embedded within the religious consciousness of the patristic church. The point, presumably, is that an ancient vindication of such religious ideas would further the Protestant claim as the upholders of true faith contra Roman Catholicism, which also claims the authority of the early fathers and councils.

Not only do such approaches misconstrue the dynamic of the ancient sources, but more ominously, they are continuations of the old Protestant versus Roman Catholic contest of the sixteenth and seventeenth centuries. With great polemical fervor, scholars in this period from both sides rushed off to find patristic sources and citations that would demonstrate that their side could truly claim to be in continuity with earliest Christianity. This sort of accessing the ancient Christians was tantamount to approaching their writings as a theological grab bag, hoping to find some foundational principle that reinforced the claims of one church against another. Those days of using the early fathers like authoritative bricks to throw at Roman Catholics should now be over and should stay that way.[28]

---

[26]E.g., *Roman Catholicism,* gen. ed. John H. Armstrong (Chicago: Moody Press, 1994). It should be noted that the views of the editor have changed since this book was published.

[27]*Sola Scriptura!* gen. ed. Don Kistler (Morgan, Penn.: Soli Deo Gloria Publications, 1997), p. 53. See especially James White's essay titled "Sola Scriptura and the Early Church."

[28]Imposing doctrines like *sola Scriptura* on the early church is not merely failing to recognize the great anachronism but also that there was no category in believers' minds that the authority of Scripture or point of faith could rightly function in the church apart from the church's tradition. Were it to do so, there was scarce assurance that an orthodox Christian faith would be the result. See D. H. Williams, "The Search for *Sola Scriptura* in the Early Church," *Interpretation* 52 (1998): 338-50.

Similis

There are a number of likenesses in Christian antiquity from which today's church might profit: the development of theological norms, the di-
alectic of apologetic treatises or a rigorous catechetical system, and so on.
It is arguable that we are witnessing a Protestant version of *ressourcement*
of the twenty-first century, which is not the mere elevation of the writings of the early church in an idealized sense but a critical utilization of
the Fathers as the church's primary witnesses and architects for the
present task of faithfully undertaking scriptural and theological interpretation. The very idea of *ressourcement*, as among twentieth-century
French Roman Catholics, began with immersion in the thought world
and hermeneutics of the early church. It was learning Latin, Greek, Syr-
iac and Coptic so that one may enter into this world. Undertaking *ressourcement* was de facto a renewal movement, a rediscovery of the
church's resources by returning to the fountainhead of its doctrinal and
ecclesial beginnings.[29] It was an orientation aimed at constructing a new
reunification between the aims of theology and the task of the church.[30]
Theology had to speak relevantly and pastorally to the church's present
situation, and the key to modern theology's relevance lay in the creative
recovery of its past.

What Can We Gain from the Ancient Fathers with Patience

Evangelicals need to discover how to better instill within believers a
sense of the Christian corporate memory when it comes to preaching
and worship.[31] Generally speaking, anamnesis (the process of remembering) was the primary way of worship for the ancient Christians. This
makes sense for a culture that had a functionally literate population of

---

[29]This movement led to the 1942 beginning of the series *Sources Chrétiennes* (Paris: Editions du Cerf),
perhaps the finest patristic text editions and French translations in the world. It now numbers 511
volumes with 8 more in preparation.

[30]Hence the name "la nouvelle théologie," which was given to the movement. Henri de Lubac disliked
the term because it created the false impression that a uniform set of ideas existed among its proponents and especially because the name contradicted the impetus of the movement, which was to renew modern theology by a return to its biblical and patristic sources.

[31]I leave the matter of biblical exegesis to other writers.

10 percent or less. But there was more to it than these limitations. The memory of Christ centered on his death and resurrection, and the brief narrative of birth, suffering, death, burial and resurrection formed the core of early Christian tradition. As we find in catechetical addresses of Cyril of Jerusalem or Gregory of Nyssa or Ambrose of Milan, the faith was developed from this core, which was the heart of the church's teaching. A new believer was made to understand that Christ's body was a horizontal entity, past, present and future, in which the believer could participate and share. There was no personal ownership, as it were, of this faith in a privatized sense. Note, for example, that the tradition of the Christian faith, usually in the form of a creedal confession, was handed over to the baptismal candidate, who after learning and reflecting on it would "return" it by rendering it orally, before the congregation. The faith was not his to keep but to partake. Thus, one was brought into the Christian tradition as one who was joining himself or herself to that corporate memory.

A significant part of the church's memory was that of persecution and suffering for the faith (before and after Constantine). This called forth a consciousness in Christian communities on retelling and reliving the martyrdom accounts, affecting the identity of the church. Indeed, it has been suggested that there is a critical link between the memory of suffering and the making of a Christian culture,[32] a kind of formation that is presently occurring in the churches of mainland China.

But even without an ongoing consciousness of suffering, Christian believers' entry and growth within the church should be built on the formative touchstones of the church's memory. For in this memory is found the constituents of what Christians believe and hope for, manifested in expressions of worship, music, catechesis and service. And thus the mind of the church's past becomes the primary means of forming our present mind as opposed to our present infatuation with technique. For it is the tradition as memory, not the latest technique in church growth, that will enable believers to discern the truth of God when they are presented with

---

[32]Elizabeth A. Castelli, *Martyrdom and Memory* (New York: Columbia University Press, 2004), p. 173.

The Da Vinci Code or the Gospel of Judas.[33]

There is an indissoluble connection in many early Christian thinkers between theological and exegetical insight and moral goodness and purity of heart. Among Latins and Greeks, the pursuit of wisdom and contemplation *(theoria)* could not be found without self-purification, since without them, the mind is not able to comprehend or see the truth. A true philosopher is one who has denied himself worldly pleasures, lived what we would call an ascetic life, in order to obtain intellectual fullness and experience the Good or the Absolute. In the Christian mind and for different reasons, Jesus' words "Blessed are the pure in heart, for they shall see God" (Mt 5:8) were interpreted as demonstrative of this same interconnection. Of all the Beatitudes, this one most grabbed the spiritual imagination of the early church and set a course for the way a believer may achieve divine understanding. Palladius, author of the *Lausiac History,* taught that the soul of the one who loves God should desire to hear his Word. The proper approach to reading Scripture was to purge the body first of all uncleanness, feelings of pride and boastfulness.[34] Holy Scripture must be read by those who are holy. Without the pursuit of purity in mind and heart, one can gain only the most superficial understanding of the Bible. Anyone is capable of grasping only the surface (i.e., literal) meaning of the text, which breeds shallowness in the work of interpretation. But intellectual or spiritual purification is necessary in order that the eyes of the heart may see God, that is, perceive the divine meaning. This is a frequent refrain of Origen, who appeals to the Beatitude of Matthew 5:8:

> For what else is "to see God in the heart" but to understand and know Him with the mind. . . . By this divine sense, therefore, not of the eyes but of a pure heart, that is, the mind, God can be seen by those who are worthy.[35]

No amount of historical-textual methodologies can replace this prereq-

---

[33]Not unexpectedly, two books have been released questioning the veracity of the Gospel accounts: Bart D. Ehrman, *The Lost Gospel of Judas Iscariot* (New York: Oxford University Press, 2006); Elaine Pagels and Karen L. King, *Reading Judas* (New York: Viking Adult [Penguin], 2007). For a written a response, see N. T. Wright, *Judas and the Gospel of Jesus* (Grand Rapids, Mich.: Baker, 2007).

[34]Palladius *Lausiac History* prologue 14.

[35]Origen *On First Principles* 1.1, 9.

uisite for acquiring this kind of vision. It is for this reason that Gregory of Nazianzus declared in his opening theological oration,

> I tell you, [theology] is not for everyone—it is no such inexpensive or effort-less pursuit.... It is for those who have been tested, and found a sure footing in contemplation. More importantly, it is for those who have undergone, or at the very least are undergoing, purification of body and soul. For the one who is not pure to lay hold of pure things is dangerous, just as it is for weak eyes to look at the sun's brightness.[36]

Just as God's own being far exceeds human rationality, philosophical inquiry or historical-critical approaches cannot in themselves illuminate the meaning of the revelation of God, certainly not its more profound meanings. Augustine took this one step further. Because our spiritual ability to perceive is so weak, we cannot endure the truth when it confronts us: "The mind of man . . . is too weak to hold on to that changeless light and enjoy it; it is too weak even to endure that Light."[37] He advocates, therefore, that our minds must be healed and purified by faith: "Our manner of life cannot behold that pure, genuine and unchangeable Truth . . . the soul must be purified before it can understand."[38]

I submit that there are many instructive elements here for how the future task of theology and that of pastoral expectation should and must complement one another such that intellectual learning is not a threat to faith but an important means of producing Christian *paideia*.

A third area of patristic contribution may have to do with evangelicals who have diligently sought to articulate the means and assurance of salvation. Once a new convert has accepted Christ, what precisely are we expecting him or her to become? The patristic notion of *theosis* or divinization is all about how the life of God is imparted to the believer so that he or she may participate or share in the triune life. Athanasius puts it most succinctly: "The Son of God became man so we might become God."[39] Since humanity is made in the image of God and intended to be "partakers

---

[36]Gregory of Nazianzus *Oration* 27.3.
[37]Augustine *City of God* 11.2.
[38]Augustine *On Christian Combat* 14.
[39]Athanasius *On the Incarnation of the Word* 54.

of the divine nature" (2 Pet 1:4), the work of salvation is the restoration of that likeness that was originally within this image. While we cannot directly know or experience the very essence of God, we are made in the image of God, and as such, receive all that is in the divine life, which was lost in the Fall.

Among other things, this means the believer's growth is not a personalized matter of claiming God's gift of salvation as if it were a gift meant for the consumption of each Christian. The Holy Spirit brings us into the divine stream from which we are given to drink and be transformed. But let us be clear here, the concept behind "God became man so that man could become God" does not mean there is an ontological change of the believer into the divine. Rather, we may think of *theosis*, in one sense, as the restoration of the lost likeness to those redeemed in Christ,[40] a process of Christification. However we word it, the idea is that salvation is a reintegration into the divine life. Given the growing *rapprochment* between evangelicals and Eastern Orthodoxy, it behooves us to learn more about this teaching that is so central to Orthodox ideas of salvation.

The roots of both its expression and application are found among select early fathers—and not all of them Greek. Irenaeus seems to be first to suggest that a proper view of the incarnation insures the divine co-inhering with fallen humanity.[41] A christological emphasis is also found in the Latin writer Hilary of Poitiers, who writes that Christ sought to raise humanity to divinity.[42]

John Paul II had a strong interest in the importance of deification as the consummation of God's promises to the human being by becoming through grace what Christ eternally is by nature. Not untypical of his the-

---

[40]Robert Rakestraw, "Becoming Like God: An Evangelical Doctrine of Theosis," *Journal of the Evangelical Theological Society* 40 (2006): 258.

[41]Irenaeus *Proof of the Apostolic Gospel* 31: "So He united man with God and brought about a communion of God and man."

[42]Hilary of Poitiers *On Matthew* 5.15: "A sin against the Spirit is to deny the fullness of power to God and to abrogate the eternal substance in Christ, by which God came into man, so man will become as God"; *On the Trinity* 9.38: "But the Incarnation is summed up in this, that the whole Son, that is, His manhood as well as His divinity, was permitted by the Father's gracious favor to continue in the unity of the Father's nature, and retained not only the powers of the divine nature but also that nature's self. For the object to be gained was that man might become God."

ology is his view that the human person is most human, only truly human, when partaking of divinity.[43] Made in God's image, the human person finds his completion solely in union with God.

While there are different nuances in the complexity of its meaning, divinization brings about transformation that is assuredly God-given. Grace is not only a divine pardon from sin, forgiveness from God's wrath and being made righteous despite ourselves, but it is no less the divine energy that comes from God's own nature, unites us to Christ and changes us so that "Christ is formed in [us]" (Gal 4:19).[44] This has the means of elevating the purpose and course of salvation in a positive light, so to speak.

One last and most obvious benefit from the early fathers could come in the form of putting the teaching of the Fathers in song and liturgies. Since the days of the apostles, the worship of the church was meant to serve as a critical vehicle for imparting *doctrina,* that is, ordered teaching about the Christian faith. Christian leaders found that worship was too good an opportunity to waste on anything but supplying the believer with the concrete foundations of how to think and live christianly. There was a reciprocal relation between worship and doctrine, between the act of praise and the task of theology. Like homilies, early hymns and theological poetry were constructive exercises in conveying scriptural truths and the tradition.

If we would be instructed by the early fathers, let us put some of their wisdom and reflection to music or alternate readings in worship so that singing may not be mere exercises in creating emotional enthusiasm or a preparatory activity for the sermon.

It was in the fourth century when the practice of using hymns for conveying sound doctrine becomes widespread. A famous orator in the city of Rome, Marius Victorinus, converted late in life to Christianity, a conversion that is described by Augustine in *Confessions.* Sometime after his baptism, Victorinus wrote several technical philosophical works defending the

---

[43]D. V. Meconi, "Deification in the Thought of John Paul II," *Irish Theological Quarterly* 71 (2006): 133.

[44]Rakestraw, "Becoming Like God," p. 269.

Nicene form of faith that contemporaries said could be understood only by the very learned.[45] About the same time, he composed a set of three hymns. Victorinus was the first Latin intellectual to make a defense for the Nicene faith, and his hymns provided another avenue for his efforts. And it may be that his hymns, on account of their profundity in simpler terms, did greater good than his treatises for extending sound trinitarian teaching in the church.

One of his hymns opens with the words:

True Light, assist us,
  O God the Father all powerful!
Light of Light, assist us,
  mystery and power of God!
Holy Spirit, assist us,
  the bond between Father and Son!
In repose you are Father,
  in your procession, the Son,
And binding all in One, you are the Holy Spirit.[46]

Taking this hymn, Kurt Kaiser has put it to music so that we can sing it, as it was intended.[47]

I have only scratched the surface in this essay. Evangelicalism's encounter with the early fathers is the necessary next step for contemporary evangelicalism that it might grow with theological integrity and ecumenical prudence in a cultureless culture and Christless spirituality. There are ominous characteristics of the current ecclesial changes that include the gradual loss of the church's militant character and the ready acceptance of hyper-individualism. In too many instances, the message and ethic that guides evangelical churches differs only minimally from that of the surrounding culture. The maxim that "we need to be like them, in order to win them" (to Christ) has backfired.

---

[45]Jerome *On Illustrious Men* 101.

[46]*First Hymn* 1-7, in *Marius Victorinus,* trans. Mary T. Clark (Washington, D.C.: Catholic University of America Press, 1981), p. 315.

[47]My deepest thanks to Dr. Tony Payne of Wheaton College Conservatory for playing this music with chorale singers at the conference.

True Light, Assist Us
(SATB)

Text: M. Victorinus - 4th Century
Translation/Adaptation: D.H. Williams

Music: Kurt Kaiser

© 2006 Kurt Kaiser Music

If the church is a culture in its own right,[48] it is called to transform cultures, not merely accommodate itself to them. A Christianity whose moral and social behavior is hardly more than a sanctified version of even the best of secular society is clearly in trouble. This is especially true "when the culture patently lacks any consensus about an agreed (much less objective)

---

[48]Cf. Robert Wilken, "The Church as Culture," *First Things* 142 (April 2004): 31-37: "The Church is a culture in its own right. Christ does not simply infiltrate a culture; Christ creates culture by forming another city, another sovereignty with its own social and political life."

code of morality, and in which the fundamental moral good is the market 'virtue' of choice."[49] If, indeed, the church must create its own culture in order to preserve a distinctive existence in the midst of the decay of Western culture, then it must provide resources drawn from the wealth and memory of its formative past for believers so they may discover their roots and establish a future Christian identity.

[49]Eamon Duffy, "Tradition and Reaction: Historical Resources for a Contemporary Renewal," in *Unfinished Journey*, ed. A. Ivereigh (New York: Continuum, 2003), p. 58.

PART TWO

Reading Scripture

The Setting and Promise of
Patristic Exegesis

4

The "Pagan" Background of Patristic Exegetical Methods

Michael Graves

In discussions among Christians about how to interpret the Bible correctly, the charge has sometimes been made that a certain method for doing scriptural exegesis is not valid because it was borrowed from a non-Christian source. Thus, many modern scholars have criticized patristic allegory on the grounds that it represents little more than pagan Hellenistic allegory applied to the Bible. Conversely, some recent Christian writers have expressed interest in patristic allegory specifically as a means of discovering a distinctively Christian way to read Scripture. In this essay, I will briefly consider the dependence of patristic exegetical methods on pagan learning. My goal will be to show that, in reality, both sides of one of the key hermeneutical conversations in the early church drew heavily on pagan learning and through this borrowing (not just in spite of it) each made a positive contribution to the Christian understanding of the Bible.

We will begin by looking at Origen's allegorical interpretation of the Bible and its connections with non-Christian Greek allegory. Origen (c. 186-255) practiced a mode of interpretation that distinguished multiple senses in the biblical text and gave prime importance to the spiritual sense.[1] For Origen, the realities of biblical history conceal mysteries, such that beneath each biblical event or detail there lies a hidden sense or senses to be discovered.[2] Among other terms, "to allegorize" is one way that Origen talked about discovering the spiritual sense,[3] and by the fourth century the word *allegoria* came to be particularly associated with his approach. Origen exerted great influence on the development of Christian thought, especially in the area of biblical interpretation. Around 358, Basil the Great and Gregory of Nazianzus compiled an anthology of texts from Origen's writings (the *Philocalia*), mostly dealing with the interpretation of Scripture.[4] Jerome's affirmation that Origen was "the second teacher of the churches after the apostle" captures well the sense of authority attached to Origen's exegesis in the fourth century.[5] In the seventeenth century, Richard Simon summed up Origen's influence by saying, "Most of the fathers who lived after Origen merely copied his commentaries and other treatises upon the scriptures; those who held opinions contrary to him could not help reading them and thereby profiting from them."[6] Henri de Lubac demonstrates Origen's centrality to the Christian exegetical tradition in the first volume of his *Medieval Exegesis*, in which he has a nine-page discussion of Origen, a ten-page discussion of "Origen's Descendants" and a sixty-four-page chapter titled "The Latin Origen."[7] Origen's methods were extremely influential on the development of patristic exegesis.

Already in antiquity, it was perceived that Origen's use of the Bible had some close relationship with non-Christian Greek intellectual traditions.

---

[1]Perhaps less well-appreciated are Origen's significant contributions to the technical study of the language and form of the biblical text, as seen most clearly in his multicolumn Old Testament known as the *Hexapla*.

[2]Henri de Lubac, *Histoire et Esprit* (Paris: Éditions du Cerf, 2002), pp. 139-40.

[3]E.g., Origen *Philocalia* 1.29.

[4]See Gregory of Nazianzus *Epistle* 115; see John A. McGuckin, *St. Gregory of Nazianzus* (Crestwood, N.Y.: St. Vladimir's Seminary Press, 2001), pp. 102-4.

[5]Preface to Origen's *Homilies on Ezekiel*. Although Jerome later renounced Origen on doctrinal grounds, he never ceased to make use of Origen's writings, especially in the area of scriptural interpretation; for example, see Jerome *Epistle* 61.2.1-2.

[6]Richard Simon, *A Critical History of the Old Testament*, "translated into English by a person of quality" (London, 1682), bk. 3, chap. 10, p. 62 (translation slightly updated).

[7]Henri de Lubac, *Medieval Exegesis*, trans. Mark Sebanc, 2 vols. (Grand Rapids, Mich.: Eerdmans, 1998), 1:142-50, 150-59, 161-224.

The first source that clearly associates Origen's biblical interpretation with pagan learning is a quotation from Porphyry, the well-known critic of Christianity, preserved in Eusebius of Caesarea's *Ecclesiastical History*. Eusebius quotes the passage in order to show that Origen's great learning was acknowledged even by a hostile source. Porphyry says:

> Some, in their eagerness to find an explanation of the wickedness of the Jewish writings [i.e., the Old Testament], rather than give them up, had recourse to interpretations that are incompatible and do not harmonize with what has been written, offering not so much a defense of what was outlandish as commendation and praise of their own work. For they boast that the things said plainly by Moses are riddles, treating them as divine oracles full of mysteries, and bewitching the mental judgment by their own pretentious obscurity; and so they put forward their interpretations. . . . But this kind of absurdity must be traced to a man whom I met when I was still quite young, who had a great reputation, and still holds it, because of the writings he has left behind him, I mean Origen, whose fame has been widespread among the teachers of this learning.[8]

Later, after conceding that Origen was well educated in Greek learning, Porphyry criticizes Origen for running headlong toward the barbarian recklessness of Christianity. Porphyry concludes:

> while his manner of life was Christian and contrary to the law, in his opinions about material things and the Deity he played the Greek, and introduced Greek ideas into foreign fables [i.e., the Old Testament]. For he was always consorting with Plato, and was conversant with the writings of Numenius and Cronius, Apollophanes and Longinus and Moderatus, Nicomachus and the distinguished men among the Pythagoreans; and he used also the books of Chaeremon the Stoic and Cornutus, from whom he learnt the figurative interpretation, as employed in the Greek mysteries, and applied it to the Jewish writings.[9]

By the time of the fourth century, a period of many intellectual and political conflicts within the church, we find that there was a reaction against

---

[8]Porphyry, in Eusebius *Ecclesiastical History* 6.19.4-5, ed. J. E. L. Oulton, Loeb Classical Library 265 (Cambridge, Mass.: Harvard University Press, 1932).
[9]Ibid., 6.19.6-8.

Origen's approach to allegory.[10] Two of the most prominent critics of Origen in the fourth century were Diodore of Tarsus and Theodore of Mopsuestia, who are generally associated with an Antiochene movement that stressed the importance of the "literal" sense *(kata lexin)* and the reality of the subject matter of the text *(historia)* as the basis for the spiritual sense, which they called *theoria*.[11] Both Diodore and Theodore wrote works against allegory: Diodore's *On the Difference Between Theoria and Allegoria*, and Theodore's *Against the Allegorists*. Unfortunately, neither work is preserved,[12] but we can get a sense of their arguments against allegory from comments that are preserved in other works, and both of them criticized allegory for being pagan in origin.

The main points of Theodore's argument may be summarized as follows: the allegorical method of interpretation came from pagans, who invented this approach in order to explain away their myths. Christian allegorists likewise use this method to explain away the real facts in the divine Scriptures.[13] In reality, it was Philo who first applied pagan allegory to the Old Testament, making biblical texts appear false and fraudulent like the pagan myths.[14] For example, Philo introduced into the teaching of Moses, regarding the creation of the world, the "arithmetic

---

[10]See Frances Young, "The Fourth-Century Reaction Against Allegory," *Studia Patristica* 30 (1997): 120-25; W. Telfer, "The Fourth-Century Greek Fathers as Exegetes," *Harvard Theological Review* 50 (1957): 94-96; H. N. Bate, "Some Technical Terms of Greek Exegesis," *Journal of Theological Studies* 24 (1923): 60-61. Not only were reservations expressed about allegory by figures like Diodore, Theodore and John Chrysostom, but even Basil, who was an admirer of Origen, criticized allegorists "who do not admit the common meaning of the Scriptures" and "who consider themselves wiser than the revelation of the Spirit" (*Homilies on the Hexameron* 9.1, trans. Agnes Clare Way, Fathers of the Church (Washington, D.C.: Catholic University of America, 1963). A pro-allegory and pro-Origen response to these criticisms was offered by Gregory of Nyssa; see Ronald E. Heine, "Gregory of Nyssa's Apology for Allegory," *Vigiliae Christianae* 38 (1984): 360-70.

[11]On *historia* in the Antiochenes, see Christoph Schäublin, *Untersuchungen zu Methode und Herkunft der Antiochenischen Exegese* (Köln-Bonn: Peter Hanstein Verlag, 1974), pp. 156-58. For a discussion of Antiochene *theoria*, see Bradley Nassif, " 'Spiritual Exegesis' in the School of Antioch," in *New Perspectives on Historical Theology*, ed. Bradley Nassif (Grand Rapids, Mich.: Eerdmans, 1996), pp. 343-77.

[12]Our knowledge of Diodore's work comes from the *Suda* (*D* 1149); see also *Preface to the Commentary on Psalms* 118. Regarding Theodore's anti-alligorical treatise, Facundus (*In Defense of the Three Chapters* 3.6.13) indicates that it was directed against Origen.

[13]Lucas van Rompay, *Théodore de Mopsueste: Fragments syriaques du Commentaire des Psaumes*, Corpus Scriptorum Christianorum Orientalium 436 (Louvain: Peeters, 1982), pp. 11, 13.

[14]Ibid., p. 15.

of human contemplation," claiming that the world was created according to the principles of this "arithmetic," so that Philo rejected some of the historical context of what Moses said and accepted only part of it. Origen followed this lead.[15] In contrast to pagan allegory, Theodore claims to follow the interpretive method traced out by the Lord, Paul and the Evangelists.[16]

Porphyry, Diodore and Theodore all thought that Origen's exegesis was derived in some way from non-Christian Greek allegory. But were they correct? Was there a substantive connection between Origen and Hellenistic allegory? The answer appears to be yes.

Let us first review a few basic details about the history of Greek allegory and then consider some specific points of similarity between Origenian and non-Christian Greek allegory. What was later called *allegoria* was in earlier times referred to as *hyponoia*, the "under sense," that is, the sense concealed beneath the surface meaning. The names and activities of deities were most often interpreted in terms of physical phenomena; another common type of allegory was found in ethical teachings; in some cases, a real occurrence was thought to be the original basis of a myth. Although we have no evidence from the earliest period, Porphyry ascribes the beginnings of allegorical interpretation to Theagenes of Rhegium, who lived in the sixth century B.C. and who is said to have made use of allegory to explain the battle between the gods in *Iliad* 20, which otherwise presented an "unsuitable" view of the gods.[17] This "defensive" motive for allegory is often thought to have arisen in the sixth century in response to criticisms of the Homeric myths, as when Xenophanes said, "Homer and Hesiod have attributed to the gods all sorts of things which are matters of reproach

---

[15]Ibid., pp. 15-16.

[16]Ibid., p. 14.

[17]Hermann Diels and Walther Kranz, *Die Fragmente der Vorsokratiker*, 3 vols. (Berlin: Weidmann, 1961), 1:8.A.2. On the origins of allegorical interpretation, see Luc Brisson, *How Philosophers Saved Myths*, trans. C. Tihanyi (Chicago: University of Chicago Press, 2004), pp. 5-40; Andrew Ford, *The Origins of Criticism* (Princeton, N.J.: Princeton University Press, 2002), pp. 67-89. J. Tate argues that the practice of allegorical interpretation can be traced back to another figure, Pherecydes of Syros (sixth century B.C.), based on Origen's testimony in *Against Celsus* 6.42; see J. Tate, "The Beginnings of Greek Allegory," *Classical Review* 41 (1927): 214-15. For Tate, this evidence supports his view that the origins of allegory were more positive than negative.

and censure among men: theft, adultery, and mutual deceit."[18] However, it has recently become clear that there were also positive motives for the introduction of allegory. Philosophers sought to expound their teachings through the authoritative myths and were not simply trying to defend the poets' reputations.[19] Both of these trends continued throughout antiquity: some later authorities, including Plato, continued to attack the poets (giving rise to allegorical defenses), while others, including the Stoics, continued to look for their doctrines in the poets. We will consider Origen's place within Greek allegory with respect to both of these motives, "defensive" and "positive."

Heraclitus (late first or early second century A.D.) wrote an allegorical treatise on Homer titled *Homeric Problems,* which he begins by saying, "It is a weighty and damaging charge that heaven brings against Homer for his disrespect for the divine. If he meant nothing allegorically, he was impious through and through, and sacrilegious fables *(mythoi),* loaded with blasphemous folly, run riot through both epics."[20] Heraclitus goes on in this work to expound philosophical teachings through Homeric texts, thereby reconciling the surface presentation of the deity in Homer with the more lofty philosophical conception of the divine.[21] Origen, in *On First Principles,* makes a similar comment while describing the need to move beyond the literal sense in scriptural interpretation:

> Moreover, even the simpler of those who claim to belong to the Church, while believing indeed that there is none greater than the Creator, in which they are right, yet believe such things about him as would not be believed of the most savage and unjust men. Now the reason why all those we have mentioned hold false opinions and make impious or ignorant assertions

---

[18]Xenophanes, quoted in J. H. Lesher, *Xenophanes of Colophon* (Toronto: University of Toronto Press, 1992), fr. 11.

[19]On this subject, see especially J. Tate, "Plato and Allegorical Interpretation," *Classical Quarterly* 24 (1930): 1-10, and "On the History of Allegorism," *Classical Quarterly* 28 (1934): 105-14.

[20]Heraclitus *Homeric Problems* 1.1-2; see *Heraclitus: Homeric Problems,* ed. and trans. D. A. Russell and D. Konstan (Atlanta: Society for Biblical Literature, 2005).

[21]For an example, see Heraclitus *Homeric Problems* 21-22 on the attempted binding of Zeus: "There is only one remedy for this impiety: to show that the myth is an allegory."

about God appears to be nothing else but this, that scripture is not under-stood in its spiritual sense, but is interpreted according to the bare letter.[22]

As Origen later explains, problematic or seemingly useless passages in the biblical text often serve a special purpose, namely, to point the reader to a higher meaning:

> But if the usefulness of the law and the sequence and ease of the narra-tive were at first sight clearly discernible throughout, we should be un-aware that there was anything beyond the obvious meaning for us to understand in the scriptures. Consequently the Word of God has ar-ranged for certain stumbling-blocks, as it were, and hindrances and im-possibilities to be inserted in the midst of the law and the history, in order that we may not be completely drawn away by the sheer attractive-ness of the language, and so either reject the true doctrines absolutely, on the ground that we learn from the scriptures nothing worthy of God, or else by never moving away from the letter fail to learn anything of the more divine element.[23]

Passages that, according to Origen, require spiritual interpretation in-clude the statements in Exodus saying that God hardened Pharaoh's heart, since if they are taken at face value, they are unworthy of a just God;[24] the statement about the destruction of Ai in Joshua 8:22, "and Israel smote them, until there was left none that survived or escaped," which refers to the slaying of demons within, since the literal sense would encourage peo-ple to become cruel and thirst after human blood;[25] and John's account of Jesus' cleansing of the temple, because it is unlikely that a carpenter's son could have gotten away with such an act,[26] and because the picture of Jesus

---

[22]Origen *On First Principles* 4.2.1-2; see *Origen: On First Principles*, trans. G. W. Butterworth (Lon-don: SPCK, 1936).

[23]Origen *On First Principles* 4.2.9; cf. *Philocalia* 1.28: "But if in reading the Scripture you should some-times stumble at a meaning which is 'a stone of stumbling and a rock of offense,' blame yourself. Do not despair of finding meanings in the stone of stumbling and rock of offense, so that the saying may be fulfilled, 'He that believes shall not be ashamed.' First believe, and you will find beneath what is counted a stumbling-block much gain in godliness." See *The Philocalia of Origen*, trans. G. Lewis (Edinburgh: T & T Clark, 1911); translation slightly updated.

[24]*Philocalia* 27.1-2.

[25]Origen *Homilies on Joshua* 8.7.

[26]Origen *Commentary on the Gospel According to John* 10.145-46.

whipping people makes the Son of God look self-willed, rash and undisciplined.[27] In sum, it appears that Origen does reflect something of the defensive motive of pagan Greek allegory, that is, the desire to use allegory to rescue the authoritative text from charges of error or blasphemy.[28]

As for Origin's relationship to positive Greek allegory, a general assessment of Origen's practice of reading foreign subject matter into the Old Testament would be exceedingly complex. I will therefore restrict myself to a few examples where Origen clearly uses the Old Testament as a basis to expound some particularly Greek idea. Our first example is Origen's discussion of the three parts of philosophy and the three senses of Scripture in his *Commentary on the Gospel According to Matthew* 17.7 (on Mt 21:33-43).[29] Origen describes the Lord's vineyard as the teachings of divine Scripture related to "physics," that is, the highest teaching on the world and God; the fruit of the vineyard is life according to virtue, that is, "ethics"; and the fence around the vineyard is "logic," identified as the literal meaning of Scripture, since it protects the hidden sense of Scripture and guards it from outsiders. This tripartite division of "physics," "ethics" and "logic" reflects a widespread Greek system, which the Stoics expounded by likening philosophy to a fruit garden, where physics corresponds to the height of the plants, ethics is the richness of the fruit, and logic is the strength of the walls.[30] Philo also reports that the threefold division of philosophy was likened to a field, with physics ("that part which deals with nature") compared with trees and plants, morality compared with fruits and crops and logic with the fence that encloses the field, since logic protects the other two parts of philosophy like the fence protects the fruits and

---

[27]Ibid., 10.147; cf. 10.181-84.

[28]Other cases of what appear to be defensive allegory in Origen include *Homilies on Numbers* 25.3, where the five kings of Midian killed by Israel (Num 31:8) become five vices against which the Christian must fight; *Homilies on Ezekiel* 4.7, where the bears that kill the children in 2 Kings 2:23 are demonic bears; and *Commentary on the Gospel According to John* 1.229, concerning the statement in Matthew 10:34, "I came not to send peace, but a sword," where Origen says that this relates to severing the injurious union between body and soul.

[29]On this passage, see Marguerite Harl, "Introduction," in *Origène: Philocalie, 1-20,* Sources Chrétiennes 302 (Paris: Éditions du Cerf, 1983), pp. 110-18.

[30]Sextus Empiricus *Against the Logicians* 1.16-19. Philosophy is also likened to an egg (ethics = yolk, physics = white, logic = shell) and to an animal (physics = blood and flesh, logic = bones and sinews, ethics = soul).

plants.[31] The flow of thought from the stoics to Philo and to Origen is clear.

As another example, we may cite Origen's exegesis of Numbers 33, which recounts the stages of Israel's journey out of Egypt, as an account of the journey of the soul toward perfection.[32] Heraclitus represented the wanderings of Odysseus as a story of overcoming ills through philosophy and virtue.[33] According to Numenius, as preserved in Porphyry's allegorical treatise *On the Cave of the Nymphs,* Odysseus was to Homer "the symbol of man passing through the successive stages of *generation* and so being restored to his place among those beyond all wavecrash," which, following Plato, is said to refer to moving beyond the material universe.[34] Odysseus's goal is to conquer the passions, and the plausibility of this interpretation is defended by Porphyry on the basis of Homer's "perfection in every virtue."[35] The whole concept of the soul's journey or return to something higher is an important element that Origen shares with the Platonic tradition.[36]

The same may be said of Origen's doctrine of the preexistence of the soul,[37] which he used to explain why Jacob was loved and Esau hated before they were even born: this does not reflect injustice on God's part but rather reflects the judgments given to Jacob and Esau based on their own behavior before they entered their bodies.[38] Origen's rationale for the soul's preexistence is different from that of Plato,[39] but the doctrine itself clearly reflects Origen's Platonism.

---

[31]Philo *On Husbandry* 14-16.

[32]Origen *Homilies on Numbers* 27.

[33]Heraclitus *Homeric Problems* 70.

[34]See Robert Lamberton, *Porphyry: On the Cave of the Nymphs* (Barrytown, N.Y.: Station Hill Press, 1983), p. 39.

[35]Ibid., p. 40.

[36]See Karen Jo Torjesen, *Hermeneutical Procedure and Theological Method in Origen's Exegesis,* Patristische Texte und Studien 28 (Berlin: Walter de Gruyter, 1986), p. 121; Jean Daniélou, *Origen,* trans. W. Mitchell (New York: Sheed and Ward, 1955), pp. 92-93.

[37]See Joseph W. Trigg, *The Bible and Philosophy in the Third-Century Church* (London: SCM, 1985), pp. 103-15; Hal Koch, *Pronoia und Paideusis* (Berlin: Walter de Gruyter, 1932), p. 33.

[38]Origen *On First Principles* 3.1.22; *Commentary on the Gospel According to John* 2.191-92.

[39]Henri Crouzel, *Origen,* trans. A. S. Worrall (Edinburgh: T & T Clark, 1989), pp. 207-9. For Plato, the concept of the soul's preexistence is part of his theory of knowledge: the soul knew the Forms in its pre-bodily existence and is reminded of those Forms by perceiving things in the physical world that participate in them. By way of contrast, for Origen the preexistence of the soul gave him a way to answer both the Valentinian doctrine that there are fundamentally different kinds of souls and the Marcionite charge against the goodness of God on the grounds that people are not all born into equally desirable conditions of life.

It may justifiably be said that Origen's approach to allegory does resemble Greek pagan (and Philonic) allegory. But Origen's Greek outlook should not be taken simply as an impediment to his understanding the biblical text. For one, Origen's willingness to address some of the hard passages of the Bible is noteworthy; these questions have not ceased even to the present day. In addition, there are ways in which Origen's Hellenistic framework helped him to make sense of the Christian Bible as a whole within the context of the church.

As one example, we may observe that a good deal of what Origen says about the figural reading of the Old Testament, even when said in a Platonic way, follows a path already set out by the New Testament,[40] and his Platonism sometimes helps him to understand the New Testament expression of the ideas. Thus, when Origen connects Jesus with the Passover Lamb, he does so under the authority of Paul (1 Cor 5:7) and the first chapter of the Gospel of John (Jn 1:29).[41] The fact that he makes this connection in his comments on the "Bread from heaven" discourse in John 6, with regard to eating Jesus' flesh, is theologically very suggestive. It is statements like John 6:63, "the words that I have spoken to you are spirit and life," that probably led Origen to say, "We must not suppose that historical things are types of historical things, and corporeal of corporeal. Quite the contrary: corporeal things are types of spiritual things, and historical of intellectual."[42] In fact, as Henri Crouzel has pointed out, there are times when Origen talks about the higher world where he is simply following the lead of the Gospel of John, and not just Platonism.[43] Many of Origen's comments in book 19 of his *Commentary on the Gospel According to John* sound very Platonic, and they are no doubt said in a Platonic way; but when we realize that he is commenting on John 8:23, "You are from below, I am from above; you are of this world, I am not of this world," and he is connecting it with

---

[40]See Daniélou, *Origen*, pp. 139-73.
[41]Origen *Commentary on the Gospel According to John* 10.110.
[42]Ibid.
[43]Crouzel, *Origen*, p. 81. On the ways that Origen distanced himself from Platonic thinking, see Mark Edwards, *Origen Against Plato* (Aldershot: Ashgate, 2002).

similar passages elsewhere in the Gospel of John, then we can begin to see that Origen's exposition of John's thought may have something real to offer.[44] On a similar note, it is significant that Eugène de Faye, who situated Origen along with Philo in the tradition of Hellenistic allegory, also situated the book of Hebrews in that tradition, acknowledging the connection between Origen and Hebrews.[45] Even if one cannot justify every exegetical move that Origen makes from within the tradition of the New Testament, it is also true that Origen does frequently follow leads found in the New Testament when interpreting the Old and that his Hellenistic framework may sometimes help him to unpack the New Testament's reading of the Old.[46]

As another example, Origen used Stoic physics to conceptualize the theological unity of the Bible, thereby giving to the church one of its first systematic theologies of Scripture. In brief, the Stoics believed that all things, including God, are corporeal.[47] What is known as God is an artistic fire *(pyr technikon),* a pneumatic power *(dynamis pneumatike),* a rationality *(logos)* that penetrates and extends throughout all of existence, giving order and purpose to all things.[48] This logos-rationality is not a personal God but a universal nature or Providence *(pronoia)* that insures the best ordering and outcome of all events.[49] Even if something appears at first sight to be evil or without reason, one may assume that, from the perspective of the whole, it accords with the good purpose of

---

[44]Origen *Commentary on the Gospel According to John* 19.127-50.

[45]Eugène de Faye, *Origène,* 3 vols. (Paris: Éditions Ernest Leroux, 1923), 1:94 ; see also Lubac, *Medieval Exegesis,* 1:150.

[46]As for Origen's view, he appealed to 1 Corinthians 9:9-10 and Galatians 4:21-24, among other texts, as evidence that the apostle Paul practiced allegorical interpretation (*On First Principles* 4.2.6; cf. *Against Celsus* 4.44.). Origen also believed that it was a teaching of apostolic tradition that "the contents of scripture are the outward forms of certain mysteries" (*On First Principles* prol. 8); see Albert C. Outler, "Origen and the *Regulae Fidei*," *The Second Century* 4 (1984): 139.

[47]On Stoic physics, see Giovanni Reale, *The Systems of the Hellenistic Age,* ed. and trans. J. R. Catan (Albany: State University of New York Press, 1985), pp. 237-59; A. A. Long, *Hellenistic Philosophy* (Berkeley: University of California Press, 1986), pp. 147-60.

[48]A. A. Long and D. N. Sedley, *Hellenistic Philosophers,* vol. 1 (Cambridge: Cambridge University Press, 1987), 46 A, B, G, H; 47 G, L; 49 J; 55 M. See also Diogenes Laertius 7.156; Cicero *The Nature of the Gods* 2.57.

[49]Long and Sedley, *Hellenistic Philosophers,* 54 A, P; 55 M, N. See also Cicero *The Nature of the Gods* 2.58.

the universal *logos*.[50] Origen applies this concept, with all its attendant ideas, to the logos in Scripture,[51] although Origen, like other middle Platonists before him such as Philo and Clement, understood the permeating *logos* as something incorporeal.[52] According to Origen, just as providence governs the whole world, so also the divine character—the *logos*—extends throughout Scripture, even to the smallest detail, ensuring that every part is good when seen from the perspective of the whole, even if the goodness or usefulness of some parts is not immediately clear.[53]

As Karen Jo Torjesen has shown, Origen's doctrine of the presence of the *logos* in Scripture was central to his exegetical method.[54] For Origen, the universal coming of the *logos* in the incarnation was a paradigm for the coming of the *logos* to the individual soul through Scripture.[55] Scripture is applied to the individual through "the mediating activity of the *Logos*," which both reveals the *logos* to the individual (so that it is self-revealing) and leads the soul through progressive stages to moral and mystical perfection (cf. Origen's Platonism).[56] The task of exegesis for Origen is to allow the hearers of Scripture to receive this instruction from the *logos*. Thus, Origen's expositions often follow a basic trajectory moving from the literal sense, as defined by the nature of the book being studied,[57] to the spiritual sense, which is presented in such a way as to lead the soul to progress toward perfection. Thus, in his homily on Jeremiah 1:1-10, Origen leads the

---

[50]Long and Sedley, *The Hellenistic Philosophers*, 54 O, Q, R, T. See also Plutarch *Against the Stoics on Common Conceptions* 1065.a-c; cf. Long, *Hellenistic Philosophy*, pp. 169-70.

[51]Harl, "Introduction," pp. 60-74. On Origen's conception of the *logos* and Stoic thought, see also de Faye, *Origène*, 3:123-25.

[52]David Dawson, *Allegorical Readers and Cultural Revision in Ancient Alexandria* (Berkeley: University of California Press, 1992), p. 191. There were, of course, significant differences between Origen and the Stoics on the divine *logos*. For the Stoics, God is materialistic and immanent in the physical world, which is the only world thought to exist; in addition, the operation of the divine rationality in the universe leads to a strong conception of fate that excludes human freedom. For Origen, God is immaterial and transcendent, there is an eternal world different and more real than the material world (Platonic), and human freedom is given a place within the governance of providence; see Koch, *Pronoia und Paideusis*, p. 207.

[53]Origen *On First Principles* 4.1.7; *Philocalia* 2.4-5.

[54]See Torjesen, *Hermeneutical Procedure*, pp. 108-47.

[55]Ibid., pp. 114-18.

[56]Ibid., p. 119.

[57]Ibid., pp. 68-69.

reader from the recognition of sin, to the turning away from sin through good works, suffering and Christ's power, to the purification of the soul like the temple.[58] Origen's theology of the *logos* in Scripture, although Hellenistic in mode of thought, is in fact built up into a scriptural system by Origen, and it may offer some suggestive ways for Christians today to expound the biblical text with the edification of the hearers in view.

Having considered Origen's debt to non-Christian Greek thought, we may now turn to look at one of Origen's critics in the patristic period, Theodore of Mopsuestia. In spite of Theodore's insistence that he was simply maintaining the apostolic mode of interpretation, recent research, especially that of Christoph Schäublin on the origin and methods of Antiochene exegesis, has shown that the Antiochenes also owed a heavy debt to pagan learning.[59] Whereas Origen's allegory was influenced by a stream of pagan thought that flowed from the philosophical schools and found its expression in philosophically oriented commentaries on ancient myths, the Antiochenes reflected the intellectual world of the rhetorical schools, as part of the fourth-century revival of sophistry that followed the so-called Second Sophistic of the first and second centuries.[60] Thus, John Chrysostom and Theodore of Mopsuestia studied with the greatest rhetorician of their day, Libanius, who was a fervent supporter of paganism, and even gave the funeral oration for the emperor Julian ("the Apostate").[61] The rhetorical schools of antiquity had their own ways of teaching and using literature. We will cite here just two examples of how the pagan rhetorical/literary environment influenced Theodore.

The first example is Theodore's use of the term *hypothesis* in his commentaries. Each biblical book, according to Theodore, should be interpreted against the backdrop of the specific historical situation addressed by the writer. For Old Testament books, this situation should be located

---

[58]Ibid., pp. 100-105.

[59]See n. 11. See also Frances Young, "The Rhetorical Schools and Their Influence on Patristic Exegesis," in *The Making of Orthodoxy*, ed. Rowan Williams (Cambridge: Cambridge University Press, 1989), pp. 182-99.

[60]Telfer, "The Fourth-Century Greek Fathers as Exegetes," p. 93.

[61]J. N. D. Kelly, *Golden Mouth* (Ithaca, N.Y.: Cornell University Press, 1995), pp. 6-8. See Libanius *Orations* 17.

within Old Testament history. The subject matter of the book, based on the particular historical situation being addressed, was called the *hypothesis*.[62] Theodore's use of the word *hypothesis* in this sense is strikingly similar to its usage in the *hypothesis* literature known from ancient literary and rhetorical studies, where the term *hypothesis* referred to an introductory preface that provided a summary of the work in question, along with some brief analysis.[63] Insight into the nature of Theodore's indebtedness to this tradition can be gleaned from the *hypotheseis* written for Demosthenes by Theodore's teacher, Libanius. For each speech of Demosthenes, Libanius gave an introduction *(hypothesis)*, indicating the historical situation addressed in the speech and the main purpose of the speech.[64] In addition, these *hypotheseis* would often survey the general contents of the speech and even note critical problems where necessary.[65] In the case of Theodore, such a *hypothesis* can be found at the beginning of each Psalm in his commentary on that book, and we also find a similar introduction for each of the Minor Prophets.[66] The similarities between Libanius and Theodore in the details of these introductions are a clear indication of Theodore's debt to the pagan rhetorical tradition.[67]

Although pagan in origin, this procedure had a positive influence on Theodore's *Commentary on the Twelve Prophets*. A prophetic book, much like a speech given by Demosthenes, addresses a specific situation in the history of a specific people. Although within the work itself such informa-

---

[62]Schäublin, *Untersuchungen zu Methode und Herkunft*, p. 84.

[63]Ibid., p. 92.

[64]Richard Foerster and Carl Münscher, "Libanios," *Realenzyklopädie der klassischen Altertumswissenschaft* (Stuttgart: Druckenmüller, 1927), 12:2522; see R. Foerster, *Libanii Opera*, 12 vols. (Leipzig: Teubner, 1915; reprint ed., 1963), 8:600-681.

[65]Schäublin, *Untersuchungen zu Methode und Herkunft*, pp. 93-94.

[66]Theodore uses both biblical materials, including the books of Maccabees, and extrabiblical sources such as Josephus and Herodotus in order to describe the historical contexts of biblical books (ibid., 88-92). This practice may also be compared with that of Libanius, who made use of various biographical materials besides the speeches of Demosthenes in his *hypotheseis* on Demosthenes (Foerster and Münscher, "Libanios," p. 2522).

[67]Schäublin, *Untersuchungen zu Methode und Herkunft*, p. 94. Cyril of Alexandria, coming after the time of Diodore and Theodore and either influenced by them or influenced by the same tradition, discusses in connection with the *skopos* of Scripture many of the same issues dealt with by the Antiochenes under the category of *hypothesis*; see Alexander Kerrigan, *St. Cyril of Alexandria: Interpreter of the Old Testament* (Rome: Pontifical Biblical Institute, 1952), pp. 95-110.

tion could be taken for granted, later readers might be totally unaware of the events giving rise to the original presentation. It would be like trying to understand a contemporary state-of-the-union address without knowing anything about the historical context. For this reason, it was natural and beneficial for Theodore to appropriate the *hypothesis* format for his comments on the minor prophets, although this approach did not always produce the best results when applied to the Psalms, which often lack specific historical contexts.

As our second example, we may mention what may be called Theodore's critical spirit. For instance, Theodore is reported to have made the following comment on the book of Job:

> The name of the blessed Job . . . was famous among all the people, and his virtuous acts as well as his ordeals were related orally among all the people and all the nations from century to century and in all the languages. Now, after the return of the Israelites from Babylon, a learned Hebrew who was especially well versed in the science of the Greeks committed in writing the history of the just, and in order to make it larger he mingled the story with exquisite utterances borrowed from the poets, because he composed his book with the purpose of making it more pleasant to the readers.[68]

Theodore later calls the behemoth of Job "a dragon of pure fiction created by the author according to his thoroughly poetic manner; it is thus that he has also composed many speeches in the name of Job and his friends, and in the name of God, which neither agree with nor correspond to reality."[69] One can see in this comment the kind of literary criticism indicative of Hellenistic scholars like Aristophanes of Byzantium and Aristarchus of Samothrace and their Roman-age descendants.[70] Theodore's understanding of the behemoth as a beast of "pure fiction" created according to the author's "poetic manner" may be likened to Aristarchus's judgment at *Iliad* 5.385, regarding the story of Ares being bound and kept

---

[68]See Dimitri Z. Zaharopoulos, *Theodore of Mopsuestia on the Bible* (New York: Paulist, 1989), pp. 46-47. The source for this quote is the ninth-century writer Isho'dad of Merv.

[69]Ibid.

[70]See Rudolf Pfeiffer, *History of Classical Scholarship* (Oxford: Clarendon, 1968), pp. 171-279; John Edwin Sandys, *A History of Classical Scholarship*, vol. 1: *From the Sixth Century B.C. to the End of the Middle Ages*, 3rd ed. (Cambridge: Cambridge University Press, 1921), pp. 169-250.

in a jar for thirteen months, that one should understand the text simply as a myth composed according to poetic license, and that one should not go beyond what was said by the poet.[71] In the scholion preserving this statement, Aristarchus's comment is followed by historical, physical and ethical allegories of the passage; it was probably against allegories like these that Aristarchus first gave his interpretation.[72] In other words, according to Aristarchus, one should view the story through a mythic/poetic lens rather than through a didactic/allegorical one. Theodore's understanding of the Behemoth in Job follows along the same lines. One should simply accept the poetic fiction for what it is and not seek to find a hidden meaning.[73] Theodore's appropriation of Greek pagan thinking is not without value as a model for today. One may see in Theodore the combination of a biblical critic who paid attention to the origins and particular literary forms of biblical books and a bishop who believed in the divine inspiration of the Bible and was concerned for the spiritual well-being of his readers.

Looking back on the patristic period, we can see that both Origen and Theodore made use of pagan Greek learning in the development of their exegetical approaches. One may perhaps see in this conflict a Christian manifestation of the classical Greek dispute between rhetoric and philosophy, as it played out in the school environments of late antiquity. Yet, we should not be dismayed that early Christians borrowed ideas and methods from pagan scholarship. The period of the New Testament bequeathed to the church the proclamation of Christ and a theological understanding of history, both of which have transforming implications for how one reads Scripture. But in the strictest sense, the earliest church did not create its

---

[71]C. G. Heyne, *Homeri Ilias*, 2 vols. (Oxford: Clarendon, 1821), 1:258.

[72]Ibid., pp. 258-59.

[73]Although Theodore objects to Philo's allegory on the grounds that Philo is treating Scripture like a pagan myth, he nevertheless accepts the idea of poetic fiction in Scripture, provided that it is seen as a literary device and not as a method for uncovering hidden meaning. On the critical spirit shared by Aristarchus and Theodore, see also Schäublin, *Untersuchungen zu Methode und Herkunft*, pp. 37-38. Theodore was something of an inspiration for Rudolf Bultmann, who disparaged Theodore's excessive interest in formal linguistic matters along the lines of ancient rhetoric but praised Theodore for his sensitivity to the peculiarities of biblical language and for his historical sense and appreciation for historical phenomena as such; see Rudolf Bultmann, *Die Exegese des Theodor von Mopsuestia*, posthumously published by H. Feld and K. H. Schelkle (Stuttgart: Verlag W. Kohlhammer, 1984), p. 67.

own literary scholarship. This simply was not the concern of the apostolic period. But as time went on, biblical texts needed to be copied, translated, understood on their own terms and explained in new times and contexts; and in the church, as in the philosophical schools, the explanation had to show the contemporary relevance of the text. In the early church, especially starting with Origen, Christians began to take the tools of scholarship available to them and apply those tools to the Bible. We can be grateful for the services that these early Christians performed, even if we do not accept everything that they did and even if we disagree about what were the best and worst features of their exegesis.

Christians borrowed methods of textual interpretation from the pagan intellectual world and combined these methods with their own theological views of Scripture to create a Christian biblical scholarship.[74] It is therefore of limited value to condemn any literary method applied to the Bible as un-Christian solely on the grounds that it was borrowed from outside the church, since this was how literary scholarship came into the church in the first place. Other arguments should be used to evaluate the validity of methods applied to Scripture: for example, how well does the method allow the interpreter to achieve the goals of understanding the biblical text and explaining its significance? How well does the method accord with the Christian belief that the gospel is to be proclaimed through the interpretation of Scripture? Questions like these, rather than questions of origins, should guide our discussions about method in biblical exegesis.

---

[74]For example, one of the most successful and widely accepted appropriations that Christians made from classical scholarship was the commentary genre, especially as applied to Scripture.

5

The Quadriga or Something Like It

A Biblical and Pastoral Defense

Peter J. Leithart

Caesarius, a fifth-century bishop of Arles in Gaul, said in a sermon on 1 Samuel 17 that the story of David and Goliath reveals the Trinity, and particularly Christ, whom David "typified." David's arrival at the battlefield is a type of the incarnation: "Jesse sent David to search for his brothers, and God sent his only-begotten Son," who came to "seek his brothers." David bears an ephah of flour, and since an ephah is "a quantity of three measures," the ephah points to "the mystery of the Trinity." David's ten cheeses are "the Decalogue of the Old Testament," and together with the ephah the cheeses reveal that "Christ was to come with the Decalogue of the law and the mystery of the Trinity to free the human race from the power of the devil." The battle takes place in a valley, a sign that Christ would come "in order to lift up the human race from the valley of sin and tears," and the armies of Israel hesitate in the presence of Goliath because they are not "able to fight against the devil before Christ our Lord freed the human race from his power." David's brother Eliab "maliciously chiding David who typified our Lord, signified the Jewish people who jealously slandered

Christ the Lord even though he had come for the salvation of the race."[1]

John Calvin had little patience for this sort of thing. He rejected detailed allegorizations as "puerile" and "childish" and insisted that edification of the church, not interpretive ingenuity, was the goal of biblical interpretation.[2] Protestants, and evangelicals in particular, have sided with Calvin over Caesarius; Protestants are more at home with edifying literal interpretation than with supposed allegorical fancy. In his recent fine commentary on 1 Samuel, Dale Ralph Davis deals with the story of David and Goliath within this Calvinistic framework. Unlike Caesarius, who finds Jesus in every nook and cranny, Davis does not mention Jesus. He examines the chapter's literary style and structure, noting David's faith but emphasizing the theocentric theme of Yahweh's honor and David's zeal to defend it. He notes the sixfold repetition of the verb *harap* ("reproach, defy," vv. 10, 25, 26 [2x], 36, 45) and concludes by asking if we are as concerned with God's reputation as David was, or as we are with our own.

Of course, Protestant interpretation has always been more complex than this simple contrast suggests. Not all Protestants have been equally hostile to allegory. In his early writings, Martin Luther followed a modified version of the medieval fourfold method, and through applying this method to the Psalter Luther inched his way toward justification by faith.[3] Though he attacked allegory, Calvin was favorable to typology, claiming in various commentaries that David, Zedekiah, Joseph, Aaron, Samson, Zerubbabel and Cyrus were all types of Christ. At times, the lines between allegory and typology blur, as Calvin permits himself to speculate on the symbolic import of the priestly robes or furnishings in the tabernacle.[4] Later Calvinists also

---

[1]John R. Franke, ed., *Joshua, Judges, Ruth, 1-2 Samuel*, Ancient Christian Commentary on Scripture, Old Testament 4; gen. ed. Thomas C. Oden (Downers Grove, Ill.: InterVarsity Press, 2005), pp. 268-70. The quotations are taken from Caesarius *Sermon* 121, found in its entirety in *Saint Jerome*, trans. John N. Hritzu, Fathers of the Church 53 (Washington, D.C.: Catholic University of American Press, 1947-).

[2]See David L. Puckett, *John Calvin's Exegesis of the Old Testament*, Columbia Series in Reformed Theology (Louisville, Ky.: Westminster/John Knox, 1995), pp. 106-13.

[3]Alister E. McGrath, *The Intellectual Origins of the European Reformation*, 2nd ed. (Oxford: Blackwell, 2004), chap. 5; David P. Scaer, "God the Son and Hermeneutics: A Brief Study in the Reformation," *Concordia Theological Quarterly* 59, nos. 1-2 (1995): 49-66; Gerhard Ebeling, *Luther* (Philadelphia: Fortress, 1964), pp. 93-109.

[4]Puckett, *John's Calvin's Exegesis*, pp. 115-17.

used typological and allegorical methods,[5] and contemporary evangelicalism has become more favorable to patristic and medieval interpretation.[6]

Calvin had a point. I do not think that patristic and medieval commentators always did a good job on particular texts. I seriously doubt that David's ten cheeses represent the Decalogue, nor do I see a trinitarian allusion in the fact that an ephah contains three measures of flour. More seriously, the traditional distinction of literal and spiritual senses has sometimes been infected with a Platonizing dualism that ends up conceding far too much to Marcion. In his treatise "On the Spirit and the Letter," Augustine explains that Old Testament promises "are earthly and temporal, good things of this corruptible flesh," and as such they were "figures" of "eternal and heavenly goods belonging to the New Covenant," which promises "a good of the heart itself, a good of the mind, a spiritual good which is an intelligible good."[7] While Augustine's construction has some basis in the New Testament, it suppresses passages where the New Testament fulfillment is just as earthy as, though more expansive than, the Old Testament promise. According to Paul, after all, Yahweh promised that Abraham would be heir not of a spiritual realm but of the world (Rom 4:13).

I admire Calvin's biblical work as much as his theology. But as I have worked on Old Testament texts as a theologian, commentator and preacher, I have increasingly felt that something like the medieval fourfold method of interpretation, or quadriga, presents the best way of integrating the various demands of preaching and teaching Scripture. In fact, I believe the quadriga

---

[5]Typological interpretation, sometimes verging toward allegory, was popular among later generations of Reformed commentators. See Stephen J. Stein, "The Quest for the Spiritual Sense: The Biblical Hermeneutics of Jonathan Edwards," *Harvard Theological Review* 70 (1977): 99-113; Thomas H. Luxon, "'Not I, But Christ': Allegory and the Puritan Self," *English Literary History* 60 (1993): 899-937.

[6]In addition to Oden's Ancient Christian Commentary on Scripture series, see Christopher A. Hall, *Reading Scripture with the Church Fathers* (Downers Grove, Ill.: InterVarsity Press, 1998); Eugene H. Peterson, *Eat This Book* (Grand Rapids, Mich.: Eerdmans, 2006); R. R. Reno and John O'Keefe, *Sanctified Vision* (Baltimore: Johns Hopkins University Press, 2005); Moises Silva, *Has the Church Misread the Bible?* Foundations of Contemporary Interpretation 1 (Grand Rapids, Mich.: Zondervan, 1987).

[7]*On the Spirit and the Letter* 36 (Corpus Scriptorum Ecclesiasticorum Latinorum 60:189): *quia in eo . . . promissa terrene et temporalia recitantur, quae bona sunt huius corruptibilis carnis, quamvis eis sempiternna atque caelestia ad novum scilicet testamentum pertinentia figurentur, nunc ipsius cordis bonum promittitur, mentis bonum, spiritus bonum, hox est intelligibile bonum.*

is almost unavoidable, and that trying to avoid the quadriga can only lead and has led to hermeneutical and theological confusion. In this essay, I offer biblical and pastoral arguments in support of those claims. After a brief description of the quadriga, I examine what appears to be a minor question about the order of the four senses as an opening to a biblical and pastoral defense of the "method."[8] For clarity, I limit myself to discussing the interpretation of the Old Testament, specifically Old Testament narrative.

The Four Senses of Scripture

The *Catechism of the Catholic Church* gives a concise definition of the quadriga:[9] "one can distinguish between two senses of Scripture: the literal and the spiritual, the latter being subdivided into the allegorical, moral, and anagogical senses."[10] The fully developed "fourfold" did not appear in the earliest patristic writers. Augustine generally worked with a dual hermeneutic, distinguishing "literal" and "spiritual" senses,[11] while other church fathers, inspired by a trichotomist anthropology, trinitarian theology or the Vulgate's use of "tripliciter" in Proverbs 22:20, sought out a triple sense. As a developed scheme, the quadriga first appeared in the *Conlationes* of John Cassian in the fifth century,[12] from whom it was transmitted to medieval students of Scripture through the *glossa ordinaria* that came from the

---

[8]Though he does not set out to defend the quadriga, Adventist scholar Richard M. Davidson elicits something very close to the quadriga from a study of *typos*-structures in the New Testament, *Typology in Scripture*, Andrews University Seminary Doctoral Dissertation Series (Berrien Springs, Mich.: Andrews University Press, 1981), p. 393.

[9]The most detailed treatment of this development is found in Henri de Lubac, *Medieval Exegesis*, trans. Mark Sebanc, 2 vols. (Grand Rapids, Mich.: Eerdmans, 1998, 2000), esp. vol. 1. See also James Samuel Preus, *From Shadow to Promise* (Cambridge, Mass.: Harvard University Press, 1969), pp. 9-149. The Latin word means "four-horse chariot," and though it had various allegorical meanings in the Middle Ages, Luther seems to be the first to use the word to refer to the fourfold method of interpretation. See Kenneth Hagen, "Biblical Interpretation in the Middle Ages and Reformation," available at <www.wls essays.net/authors/H/HagenMiddle/HagenMiddle.rtf>.

[10]U.S. Catholic Church, *Catechism of the Catholic Church* (Mahwah, N.J.: Paulist, 1994), p. 33.

[11]Augustine occasionally employs a fourfold model, though his four senses—*historia, allegoria, analogia* and *aetiologia*—do not match the senses of the later system. See Preus, *From Shadow to Promise*, p. 21 n. 26.

[12]John Cassian *Conlationes* 14.8 (Corpus Scriptorum Ecclesiasticorum Latinorum 13/2:404): "For there are three kinds of spiritual knowledge, tropology, allegory, anagogy, concerning which in Proverbs it is said, 'But you, write those things for your self triply over the breadth of your heart'" *(Spiritalis autem scientiae genera sunt tria, tropologia, allegoria, anagoge, de quibus in Proverbiis its dicitur: 'tu autem describe tibi ea tripliciter super latitudinem cordis tui').*

school of Anselm of Laon.[13] After Cassian, the four-senses model became standard throughout the medieval period, though never universal.[14]

A Latin lyric cited in 1330 by Nicholas of Lyra summarizes the meaning of each sense:

> The letter teaches events, allegory what you should believe, Morality teaches what you are to do, anagogy what mark you should be aiming for.[15]

Each passage records events, communicates doctrine, exhorts us to obedience and nurtures Christian hope. Some medieval commentators associated the threefold spiritual sense with the theological virtues of faith (allegory), love (tropology) and hope (anagogy).[16] Cassian's example of Jerusalem was used widely. Literally, Jerusalem is the city of David, the capital city of ancient Israel; allegorically it is the church; tropologically, each of us is a city in which God dwells, and what applies to the whole city applies to each citizen; anagogically, it is the future Jerusalem, the eternal dwelling place of the saints.[17]

Thomas Aquinas's fourfold explanation of the opening fiat of Genesis 1, "Let there be light," provides another illustration of the fourfold in operation:

---

[13]The *glossa ordinaria* defines the senses differently from John Cassian: "history, which speaks of things done; allegory, in which one thing is understood from another; tropology, that is, moral speech, which deals with the ordination of morals; anagogy . . . through which we are led to higher things to be drawn to the superior things" (*historia, quae res gestas loquitur; allegoria, in qua aliud ex alio intelligitur; trpologia, id est moralis locutio, in qua de moribus ordinandis trantatur; anagoge . . .per quem de summis et coelestibus tractaturi, ad superiora ducimur*). As Preus points out (*Shadow to Promise*, p. 26), *allegoria* here is identical to what Augustine called the figurative sense, and the anagogical sense is more mystical and heavenly than eschatological.

[14]In the twelfth century, Hugh of St. Victor claimed that Scripture had a "triplex inteligentia" and eliminated anagogy from the scheme. In other writings, however, Hugh distinguishes between "simple allegory" and an allegorical sense that stretched toward anagogy (Preus, *From Shadow to Promise*, p. 27 n. 7).

[15]Lubac, *Medieval Exegesis*, 1:1. The Latin is more musical: *Littera gesta docet, quid credas allegoria, moralis quid agas, quo tendas anagogia*.

[16]Gerhard Ebeling, "The New Hermeneutics and the Early Luther," *Theology Today* 21, no. 1 (1964): 38-39.

[17]John Cassian *Conlationes* 14.8 (Corpus Scriptorum Ecclesiasticorum Latinorum 13/2:404): "Four figures proclaimed in one thus . . . flow together, that one and the same Jerusalem can be understood in four ways: according to history the city of the Jews, according to allegory the church of Christ, according to anagogy the heavenly city of God . . . according to tropology the soul of man, which frequently by this name either is rebuked or praised by the Lord" (*praedictae quattuor figurae in unum ita, si volumus, oconfluunt, u tuna atque eadem Hierusalem quadrifarie posit intellegi: secundum historiam civbitas Iudaeorum, secundum allegorian ecclesia Christi, secundum anagogen civitas dei illa caelestis . . . secundum tropologiam anima hominis, quae frequenter hoc nominee ut increpatur aut laudatur a domino*).

When I say, "Let there be light," while referring literally to corporeal light, it is to the literal sense. [If "Let there be light"] be taken to mean "Let Christ be born in the Church," it pertains to the allegorical sense. But if one says, "Let there be light," i.e., as meaning "Let us be conducted to glory through Christ," it pertains to the anagogical sense. Finally, if it is said, "Let there be light," i.e., "Let us be illumined in mind and inflamed in heart through Christ," it pertains to the moral sense.[18]

Though later derided as justification for a hermeneutical free-for-all, the quadriga was proposed as a speed bump to slow fantastic traffic on the interpretive highway.[19] It tied interpretation to the dogmatic tradition of the church, partly by anchoring allegory in the literal sense. While the relation of literal and spiritual senses was formulated in different ways, medieval Bible teachers all believed the literal sense was the foundation for all the other senses.[20] Thomas offered a classic formulation of this point in the opening question of the *Summa Theologiae*. According to Thomas, the quadriga works not because the words of Scripture have multiple senses or referents, which could only introduce confusion. Rather, words have a single sense, the historical or literal sense, and refer to actual events and persons. The other senses do not proliferate from the words of Scripture but from the significant events, institutions and persons to which those words refer. Thus "David" refers to the boy-shepherd who defeated Goliath, but God writes history with things and not merely with words and thus employed the actual boy, David, to foreshadow his greater Son, Jesus. Scripture's words signify things, but, in the providence of God, the things signified by the words of Scripture signify future things.[21] In this way, the literal blossoms into a series of spiritual senses.

---

[18]Thomas Aquinas *Commentary on Saint Paul's Epistle to the Galatians,* trans. F. R. Larcher (Albany, N.Y.: Magi Books, 1966), p. 138, as quoted in Scott Hahn, *Scripture Matters* (Steubenville, Ohio: Emmaus Road, 2003), p. 53.

[19]Ebeling, "New Hermeneutic and the Early Luther," pp. 38-39.

[20]For variations on this question, see Beryl Smalley, *The Study of the Bible in the Middle Ages* (Notre Dame, Ind.: University of Notre Dame Press, 1964).

[21]Thomas Aquinas *Summa Theologiae* 1.1. 10. Ebeling helpfully notes that, following Augustine, Thomas describes a double form of signification: In addition to word-thing signification, God is able to signify things with other things. In this, Hugh anticipated Thomas's way of rooting the spiritual in the literal; see Preus, *From Shadow to Promise,* pp. 28-31.

Order of Redemption, Order of Interpretation

One of the advantages of the quadriga lies in the way it resists and subverts trends of modern scholarship. Modern interpretation fragments the Scriptures as it scratches about for evidence of sources and symptoms of editorial tampering and institutionalizes the separation of Old and New Testaments by confining them to separate hallways and assigning them different departmental letterhead. By contrast, the quadriga assumes the unity of the Bible and enacts that unity in its readings. Modern biblical scholarship, moreover, pries apart theological inquiry from religious devotion in an effort to conform biblical study to the standards of objective scientific pursuit.[22] This is achieved, in part, through the application of method, which, in modern theology, has often pretended to be a theologically neutral foundation for theology: Before we begin to think theologically, we construct a framework using nontheological materials. In hermeneutics, we establish methods of textual and historical analysis that do not depend on theological commitments and then interpret the Bible within the bounds of those rules and principles. The whole process is a ruse. No method is theologically neutral, and method often functions as a way of determining ahead of time what the text can and cannot be allowed to say. Though sometimes described as the fourfold method of interpretation, the quadriga makes no pretense to being a neutral science but is self-consciously theological and spiritual.

The theological basis of the quadriga becomes clearer when we explore what initially appears to be a tediously inconsequential difference in the order of the four senses. Some early writers, such as Jerome and Cassian, as well as later writers, such as Isidore of Seville and Peter Lombard, move from the literal sense to tropology or moral application and then to allegory. Jerome states that the Scriptures have a threefold sense: "In the first place, we are meant to understand them historically, in the second place, tropologically, and in the third place, according to a spiritual understanding."[23] Origen's order varies. At times, he follows the same triple order as

---

[22]Ebeling blames Johann Semler for establishing the distinction of theology and religion in modern theology; see *Luther*, pp. 93-94.
[23]Jerome, quoted in Lubac, *Medieval Exegesis*, 1:139.

Jerome does. Scripture, he claims, must be interpreted for the simple in a "bodily way," which he also describes as "the common and historical understanding." Some Christians have advanced further and can be edified by the "soul" of Scripture, while the "perfect" are "edified by the spiritual law itself." Origen's method reflects an anthropological scheme: "just as man is said to consist of body, soul, and spirit, so also does Holy Scripture, which has been given by the bounty of God for the salvation of men."[24] At other times, Origen moves from history to allegory to morality,[25] and in this many medieval commentators follow him. The Venerable Bede, better known in medieval times as a biblical commentator than as a historian, employs this second order: "In Sacred Scripture there is a threefold meaning . . . namely historical, allegorical, and anagogical," he says in his *Hexameron,* and he reiterates the point using different terms in his commentary on Leviticus: "truly an understanding of Scriptures is threefold: historical, mystical, and moral."[26]

Examining this fine hermeneutical distinction, your head may well be filling with visions of pinheads and dancing angels, but Henri de Lubac makes a convincing case that the question of how to order the quadriga goes to the theological heart of biblical interpretation. He points out that using the first model, in which moral applications are drawn directly from the literal sense, an interpreter can derive moral applications from Scripture that "have nothing specifically Christian" about them.[27] Jerome's method implies that virtue and ethics are prior to faith and thus represents a hermeneutical moralism. In the second arrangement, which places allegory before tropology, the order of interpretation follows the order of redemption, putting into hermeneutical practice the principle enunciated by Gregory the Great: "One is not brought into contact with the faith by means of the virtues, but with the virtues by means of faith."[28] The Old Testament records actual events, but these events, by God's providential

---

[24]Origen, quoted in ibid., 1:143. The quotation is from Rufinus's Latin translation of Origen's *Periarchon.*

[25]Lubac, *Medieval Exegesis,* 1:145.

[26]Bede, quoted in de Lubac, *Medieval Exegesis,* 1:92.

[27]Lubac, *Medieval Exegesis,* 1:147.

[28]Gregory the Great, quoted in ibid., 2:31.

design, foreshadow the redemptive work of Christ (allegory). The Spirit incorporates us into him by faith so that his life of love may be lived out in us (tropology) as we look in hope for the consummation (anagogy).[29]

I am not suggesting that an interpreter must rigorously and consciously follow this order for every passage or that a preacher must cover each of these senses in every sermon. To employ the quadriga in that fashion would be to turn it into a method in the modern scientific sense. Rather, this order exposes the theo-logic of the quadriga.

In following the order of redemption, the second order—literal, allegorical, tropological, anagogical—reflects the theological hermeneutics of the New Testament. This is true, first, because it offers a christocentric reading of the Old Testament, which is precisely the New Testament's reading of the Old. Jesus explicitly teaches that the entire Old Testament reveals the suffering and glory of the Christ (Lk 24:26-27, 44-48), and the New Testament is packed with christological readings of Old Testament institutions and practices (temple and sacrifice), persons (Moses, David, Elisha and Jeremiah), offices (priest, king and prophet) and events (exodus, conquest and return from Babylon).

In the New Testament, this christological/allegorical sense is simultaneously an ecclesiological sense, because the church is the body of Christ, the community united to the incarnate Son.[30] Ecclesial allegory assumes an identification of Christ with his church that is confirmed not only by the pervasive New Testament teaching concerning union with Christ but also by some of Paul's explicit statements concerning the church: "As the body is one and yet has many members, and all the members of the body, though they are many, are one body, so also is

---

[29]It is striking that Davis, and many Reformed and evangelical commentators with him, tends to follow the first model. Instead of interpreting David and Goliath as a narrative foreshadowing of Christ, they draw moral exhortations from the narrative without any explicit reference to Christ. It seems far more Protestant to put grace (allegory) before works (tropology). It seems far more evangelical to say that the chief message of the Old Testament, as of the New, is the evangel, and that the Old Testament applies to *our* lives because Jesus first fulfilled it. I suspect that the moralism that dogs evangelical Protestantism arises in some measure from this triumph of tropology and the eclipse of allegory.

[30]I differ here with Richard B. Hays, who claims that Paul's hermeneutic is ecclesiocentric rather than Christocentric; see his *Echoes of Scripture in the Letters of Paul* (New Haven, Conn.: Yale University Press, 1993). I submit that for Paul, and Augustine, this distinction would make no sense.

Christ" (1 Cor 12:12).[31] Furthermore, by taking the church as his bride, Paul says, Jesus becomes "one flesh" with her, which implies that the church is the "flesh" of the Christ (Eph 5:31-32). As body and as bride, the church is one with her head and husband.

Before the development of an explicit fourfold sense, Augustine had laid out the *totus Christus* as a hermeneutical principle. Following the rules of Tychonius the Donatist, he notes that "the head and the body—that is, Christ and his Church—are sometimes indicated to us under one person."[32] As he works his way through the Psalms, Augustine interprets the voice of the psalmist sometimes as the voice of Christ, sometimes the voice of the body, sometimes the polyphonic voice of both together. So close is the union of Christ with his body that the Psalter speaks with a single harmonious voice: "So let Christ speak," Augustine says, "since the Church speaks in Christ, and Christ speaks in the Church; and the body in the head, and the head in the body."[33] The New Testament supports this hermeneutical application of *totus Christus* ecclesiology. Israel's forty-year temptation in the wilderness, for instance, finds fulfillment in Jesus' forty days of trial (Mt 4:1-11; Lk 4:1-12), but, as Paul says, Israel's temptations were also examples for the Corinthians (1 Cor 10:1-4).

Tropology follows from allegory, not only "methodologically" but theologically. In fact, when allegory extends beyond allegories of Jesus to allegories of the *totus Christus*, tropology is already implicit within allegory. That is, precisely because an Old Testament event is about Jesus, it is also about us in him. The relation of allegory and tropology has been understood in two ways. On the one hand, the quadriga anticipates what contemporary New Testament scholars describe as the "indicative-imperative" pattern of New Testament, and particularly Pauline, ethics. Paul's exhortations often take a "be what you already are" form: "You have died with Christ, therefore put the sinful nature to death; you are a new creation in Christ, so walk in newness of life; you are filled with the Spirit, so keep in

---

[31]Scripture quotations in this essay are from the New American Standard Bible, updated edition.

[32]Augustine *On Christian Doctrine* 3.31.44, in Nicene and Post-Nicene Fathers, first series, ed. Philip Schaff, trans. J. F. Shaw (Peabody, Mass.: Hendrickson, 1995).

[33]Augustine, quoted in Lubac, *Medieval Exegesis*, 2:92.

step with the Spirit." On the other hand, as Richard B. Hays points out, the ethical demands of the gospel are "logical entailments" of God's redemptive work, not the product of an independent act of will on the part of the believer. Newness of life is not something the believer strives to achieve; it is how the work of Christ and the Spirit manifests itself in an individual life.[34] To transpose Hays's ethical-theological point into a hermeneutical principle, the quadriga needs only a slight nudge in a Lutheran direction. In Luther's early work on the Psalms, the tropological sense is not about moral demands but about the work of Christ in the believer. Tropology is just as much about God's acts as allegory is, though the field of action is different: Allegory speaks of God's acts in the history of Jesus, tropology of God's acts in the history of an individual person.[35] Whether we understand tropology as "moral demand" or as "God's work in the individual," the quadriga places faith in Christ and his work (and, consequently, union with Christ) before works and treats works of love as a fruit of faith.

Fittingly, the last sense is the anagogical, the eschatological sense. To the last, the order of interpretation follows the order of salvation. Here again, the quadriga reflects the deepest strains of New Testament theology. Over the past century, scholars have rediscovered the pervasiveness of eschatology in the New Testament, and despite many differences in formulation, there is widespread agreement that New Testament eschatology is structured by an "already-not yet" pattern.[36] The last things, Paul an-

---

[34]Richard B. Hays, *The Moral Vision of the New Testament* (San Francisco: Harper, 1996), p. 39.

[35]McGrath, *Intellectual Origins*, pp. 161-62: "an important difference between Luther on the one hand, and Erasmus and Bucer on the other, must be noted. For Erasmus, the tropological sense of scripture is concerned with the moral demands, which are made of the believer. Thus his discussion of the faith of Abraham ends with an exhortation to children to emulate the virtues of their parents. Luther, however, adopts a quite different understanding of this sense of Scripture: for him the tropological sense refers to the gracious work of Jesus Christ in the individual believer, so that the *bonum tropologicum* is to be defined as faith. As Ebeling points out, Luther treats the concept as pertaining to God's *acta* rather than man's *facta*. *Via dei est, qua nos ambulare facit*. Thus Luther interprets *iudicium Dei, institia Dei* and similar terms tropologically in terms of what God does for man, rather than in terms of what God expects of man.... [I]t is evident that Luther regards the central message of scripture—both Old and New Testaments—to concern the *acta Dei*. Three particular arenas of this work of God are identified: the *acta Dei* in Christ, in the Church, and in the individual believer."

[36]For an early and valuable contribution to this development from a Reformed theologian, see Geerhardus Vos, *The Pauline Eschatology* (Phillipsburg, N.J.: Presbyterian & Reformed, 1930).

nounces, have already come: Resurrection life has erupted into the dead world, the Spirit has been poured out from on high, whoever is in Christ—behold, a new creation! At the same time, Paul looks ahead to a future resurrection of the dead, a final triumph over death and a judgment that sorts out every disorder and injustice and brings in everlasting righteousness. The believer lives by faith in the accomplished salvation in Christ and the Spirit, and waits in hope for the consummation. The quadriga incarnates the New Testament's already-not yet eschatology in hermeneutical practice. Allegory establishes the already—what Jesus accomplished in his first advent—while anagogy reminds us that, at every point, an eschatological surplus is yet to come.

The New Testament's use of temple imagery provides a specific illustration of the integration of *totus-Christus* allegory with tropology and anagogy. Solomon built a literal temple in Jerusalem, but Solomon's temple is an allegory of the *totus Christus* foreshadowing both Christ (Jn 2:13-22) and his church (Eph 2:11-22; 1 Pet 2:5). The New Testament implicitly develops some of its atonement theology from this allegory. Because the temple was a place of sacrifice, Jesus as the temple offers himself in sacrifice; because the temple was ruined and rebuilt, Jesus as the temple dies and rises; in Ezekiel 47, water flows from the temple to renew the land, and water pours from Jesus' side to transform the desert into a garden (Jn 19:32-34). In union with Christ, the church as the temple likewise offers sacrifice in worship ("sacrifice of praise") and in life ("living sacrifices"), and it is also the house from which flow living waters. From this Christo-ecclesiological allegory, Paul draws individual tropologies: Each believer is a temple and must guard the sacred space of his body, scour out all that is unclean and preserve himself undefiled (1 Cor 3:16-17; 6:19-20).[37] Finally, though the church is already the temple of God, it looks in hope for the temple-city that will descend from heaven (Rev 21:1-8); though each of us is already a tent, an earthly outpost of the Spirit, we groan in hope for the house from heaven that awaits us (2 Cor 5:1-5).

---

[37]We may note in passing here that the quadriga neatly integrates individual and corporate applications of Scripture, because it assumes a mutual symbolic relation between the church and the individual member of it.

The quadriga does not offer a neutral method but a theological interpretation of the Old Testament shaped by the theology of the New and by the New Testament's interpretive example. Nor does the quadriga depend on a linguistic theory. As noted above, it is a thoroughly theological hermeneutical scheme. From the viewpoint of the quadriga, moreover, we can test hermeneutical alternatives. Strictly literal interpretation of the Old Testament places us in the unwelcome company of Marcion, with a Christless and perhaps a Godless Hebrew Bible. Pure allegory leaves us with an imperative-less indicative of antinomianism, while pure tropology produces the indicative-less imperative of moralism. Allegory and tropology without anagogy yields an overrealized eschatology, while anagogy without allegory and tropology is eschatologically underrealized. In short, alternatives to the quadriga, which have developed from fragments of the quadriga, embed distortions of biblical theology into hermeneutical theory and perpetuate those distortions in interpretive practice.

David and Goliath

Let us return to where we began, to young David in the valley between Socoh and Azekah. What ought we do with David? Let us try to quadrigize him. According to the *sensus literalis,* David fought and defeated a Philistine giant in single combat, which sparked a major Israelite victory over the Philistines. Even at the literal level, the story is already theologically charged, because the armies of Israel are Yahweh's armies, because Goliath is insulting Yahweh of hosts and because David, like Joshua before him, is conquering the land by defeating giants. Above all, the narrative records a crucial moment in the fulfillment of God's promise to give David the kingdom. At the beginning of the following chapter, Jonathan, with astonishing humility, hands over the insignia of the crown prince to his rival David (1 Sam 18:1-5).

According to the *sensus allegoricus,* David's defeat of Goliath foreshadows the greater David's conquest over the serpent. In addition to the surface similarity of the stories (a despised hero overcomes unequal odds to defeat an apparently stronger enemy), details of 1 Samuel 17, examined in a larger biblical context, support this christological interpretation. Among other things, Goliath is the Bible's first metallic man, dressed in bronze armor from head to toe (1 Sam 17:4-6), and thus anticipates Nebuchadnezzar's vision of a multimetallic statue in Daniel 2. By the time of the exile, armored Goliath has grown into a giant imperial figure, which will be reduced to powder at the coming of the kingdom of God.[38] That statue, like Goliath, is felled by a small stone (Dan 2:44-45), this time flung without hands. Suffering in exile, Israel is assured that Gentile empires will give way to the fifth monarchy, the empire of Yahweh, who can throw down Alexander and Caesar as easily as David beats Goliath. Together, David's triumph over Goliath and the Lord's triumph over Gentile empires typify Jesus, Jesus the Rock, Jesus the rejected stone, Jesus the choice cornerstone.

Goliath is a metal man; Goliath is also a beast. David convinces Saul to let him fight Goliath by regaling him with shepherd war stories: "Your servant has killed both the lion and the bear; and this uncircumcised Philistine will be like one of them" (1 Sam 17:34-36). David is a new Adam, the beast tamer, who is confident that he can take on a giant because he has successfully wrestled wild animals. In this way too he anticipates another vision of Daniel, in which "one like the Son of Man" receives the kingdom that has been held by a series of increasingly ferocious beasts, including a lion and a bear (Dan 7:1-8). It is no accident that Goliath dies of massive head trauma—first a stone in the forehead, followed by decapitation: He is a type of the dragon (and, by the way, dressed in scales, 1 Sam 17:5), and one defeats serpents by crushing their heads (Gen 3:15).

David is in all these ways a type of his greater descendent, Jesus; and Jesus' pattern of life works, by the Spirit, to mold the life of his church and each member of it. The allegory of conquest leads into a tropology, and at this point all the homiletical flourishes on this passage come to the foreground. With all the odds against him, David trusted Yahweh to deliver

---

[38]I agree with James Jordan that this imperial structure was initially set up as a protective nest for Israel. As Jeremiah said, Judah was to submit to Nebuchadnezzar, whom Yahweh had established as a new Adam (Jer 29). Yet, these imperial powers were still destroyed by the coming of God's kingdom, and in that respect there is a connection with the story of Goliath. Before the new Israel could recover the land/world, the Goliath of imperial power had to be felled with the Rock of Israel. For further discussion, see Jordan's commentary on Daniel (Atlanta: American Vision Press, 2007).

him; so should you. David defended Yahweh's honor; so should you. The story is about crisis management and teaches that we should confront the Goliaths that surround us with the faith of David.[39] The God who defeated Goliath through David is the God who raised Jesus from the dead, and he can raise you from your personal Sheol. Notice that, operating by the quadriga, these exhortations to confidence, faith and courage are not generalized moral encouragements but, because they grow out of an allegorical reading of the story, are specific forms of imitation of Christ, the greater David.

Finally, the story also implies an anagogy, for the church of giant killers lives between allegorical fulfillment and anagogical consummation. Allegorically, 1 Samuel 17 is fulfilled in the cross, through which, as Jesus announced, "the prince of this world is cast out." Satan, the lion who stalks us, is defeated now. Yet, we still hope for the day when the dragon and all his hosts will be dumped into the lake of fire forever. Between the times, we are called to act in hopeful expectation of that final victory. In the end, all the gigantic enemies of Jesus, every last Goliath—death finally included—will lie decapitated at his feet. Using the quadriga, we are not only refreshed in faith (God has defeated Satan in Christ) and love (out of faith, we live in courageous obedience to Christ) but also in hope (God will finally defeat every enemy).

Here my pastoral defense of the quadriga rests. As with all pastoral theology, the proof is in the pudding, and I trust that the foregoing has demonstrated that the quadriga turns 1 Samuel 17, in a way that even Calvin might approve, to the purposes of edification.

Conclusion

In closing, I want to stress that I am not offering the quadriga as a toy for texts. On the contrary, I believe something like the quadriga is necessary if we are going to preach and teach the Old Testament faithfully, fully and effectively.

Believing the Bible is true and that ours is a historical faith, we affirm

---

[39]This is the theme of a sermon on the text by Steve May, found at <www.preachingtoday.com/32769>.

the historical reality of the events the text records. We interpret *secundum historiam*. No Christian preacher, however, will be content to recount the past. To the letter, therefore, we must add a spiritual sense. This "must" is not only the "must" of obligation but the "must" of hermeneutical necessity. As soon as we do more than tell what happened, we have stepped, whether we know it or not, into the realm of the quadriga. We might want to limit ourselves, as many Protestants do, to tropology. Quite apart from the danger that this may produce a Christless moralism, it is simply impossible. As soon as we move from history to tropology, we have already made a series of implicit allegorical equations: David = the believer; Goliath = whatever threatens us; Israel = the church; David's faith is the model of ours. Preaching *secundum tropologiam* is already implicitly *secundum allegoriam*. Once we have swallowed that implicit allegory, there is every reason to take the next step and read the text as an allegory or typology of Jesus. After all, if we compare ourselves with David, how much more should we compare David with his greater Son? In fact, it is not clear how we can even begin to find ourselves in David's story unless we have already assumed we are in the story of Jesus. As soon as we move from text to tropology, we are implicitly agreeing with Augustine's *totus Christus*. And how can we stop there? Once we say that the Old Testament is about the Christ, we cannot help but remember that Christ has finished his work that is, at the same time, yet to be finished. Because the kingdom is now and not yet, preaching *secundum allegoriam* is also preaching *secundum anagogen*.

All preaching that aims to cultivate faith, love and hope will end up working with something very like the quadriga. If our preaching and teaching is to be a smooth stone flung against the giants of the land, we can hardly aim for less.

6

Irenaeus and Lyotard
Against Heresies,
Ancient and Modern

Nicholas Perrin

In his five-volume work *Against Heresies,* Irenaeus, the second-century bishop of Lyons, famously writes as follows:

> The Gospels could not possibly be either more or less in number than they are. Since there are four zones of the world in which we live, and four principal winds, while the Church is spread over all the earth, and the pillar and foundation of the Church is the gospel, and the Spirit of life, it fittingly has four pillars, everywhere breathing out incorruption and revivifying men. (*Against Heresies* 3.11.8)

Among contemporary students of the New Testament canon, the bishop's remarks have met with everything from skepticism to amusement. Hans von Campenhausen, for example, describes Irenaeus's reasoning as "somewhat violent."[1] More recently, Harry Y. Gamble sees the bishop's stance on the fourfold canon as "a tortured insistence on its legitimacy."[2] According to Lee MacDonald, the passage would not have been "the most

---

[1]Hans von Campenhausen, *The Formation of the Christian Bible,* trans. J. A. Baker (1972; reprint, Mifflintown, Penn.: Sigler Press, 1977), p. 199.

[2]Harry Y. Gamble, *The New Testament Canon* (1985; reprint, Eugene, Ore.: Wipf & Stock, 2002), p. 32.

convincing line of reasoning even in the ancient world!"[3] More recently still, Bart Ehrman, in his runaway bestseller, *Misquoting Jesus*, summarizes the same passage with an inimitable sarcasm: "In other words, four corners of the earth, four winds, four pillars—and necessarily, then four Gospels."[4]

For many scholars, then, Irenaeus's argument appears as little more than a desperate contrivance or an empty rhetorical flourish. As such it cannot be seen as having persuaded readers in his own time, much less as contributing grist for the mill of contemporary theological reflection. By most modern accounts, the bishop of Lyons has fallen flat. His argument for the fourfold Gospel canon, feeble as it is, must be relegated to the museum of historical theological oddities—and kept there safely under lock and key.

This essay proposes, in the first place, to challenge this particular understanding of Irenaeus as a misunderstanding. For by examining the bishop's argument closely, it becomes clear that his insistence on four Gospels, far from arbitrary, is rooted in a biblical theological logic that can be appreciated only by first appreciating the bishop on his own terms. From here, a proper appraisal of the dynamic tension between the four Gospels and the one gospel of Jesus Christ, made possible by this biblical theological reading, not only has important implications for our understanding of his doctrine of revelation but also yields instructive comparisons with Jean-François Lyotard's criticism of modern epistemology, as worked out in *The Postmodern Condition*. The striking parallels between Irenaeus's attack on the doctrine of the Gnostics and Lyotard's assault on the pretensions of scientific knowledge raises the question as to whether contemporary postmodern Christian thought, implicitly critical of Christian modernity, finds an ally in the bishop of Lyons.

Irenaeus's Case for the Fourfold Gospel

It would cut against the grain of all available evidence if we were to maintain, as Elaine Pagels does, that Irenaeus sets down his reasoning for four Gospels as a part of an abrupt bid to overpower Gnostic dissenters within

[3]Lee Martin MacDonald, *The Formation of the Christian Biblical Canon* (rev. 1988; reprint, Peabody, Mass.: Hendrickson, 1995), p. 96.
[4]Bart D. Ehrman, *Misquoting Jesus* (New York: HarperSanFrancisco, 2005), p. 35.

the church.[5] That Irenaeus is the first to adopt a position of "these four and no more" (to the exclusion of other Gospels) is viable only if we set aside the witness of Justin, the Muratorian Fragment and the material evidence of late-second-century Gospel manuscripts.[6] Moreover, the matter-of-fact quality of Irenaeus's argument suggests that the bishop is trying not to convince his audience of something new but to bolster a well-established practice theologically.

Even if modern readers may be initially suspicious of numerological arguments like the one we meet here, we need not imagine that the bishop of Lyons induced the appropriate number of Gospels by, say, turning to neo-Pythagoreanism or one of its arcane philosophico-mathematical principles. Nor do we need to believe that Irenaeus's argument is a posteriori. That is, it should not be assumed, as has been done, that had the bishop been obliged to vindicate three or five or some other number of Gospels, he would have somewhere found the numerological backing for those arguments too.[7] If this were the case, we might fairly write the bishop off as capricious and say that he is compensating for the opacity of his argument by throwing up whatever rhetorical window dressing is at hand. A better approach holds out the possibility that there is method to Irenaeus's madness.

For many readers it may come as a surprise that Irenaeus, in a fascinating discussion in book 2, chides the Gnostics because they "prosecute inquiries respecting God by means of numbers, syllables, and letters" (*Against Heresies* 2.25.1). He objects not because numbers have no meaning. On the contrary, because numerical realities (for example, the number of apostles) are ordered by Providence, we should expect these realities to bear meaning in the mind of God.[8] The problem with the Gnostics, ac-

---

[5]Elaine Pagels, *Beyond Belief* (London: Pan Books, 2005), pp. 110-15.

[6]See also Nicholas Perrin, *Lost in Transmission? What We Can Know About the Words of Jesus* (Nashville: Thomas Nelson, 2007), chap. 10.

[7]As argued, e.g., by Campenhausen (*Formation*, pp. 199-200) and E. Ferguson, "Factors Leading to the Selection and Closure of the New Testament Canon: A Survey of Some Recent Studies," in *The Canon Debate*, ed. Lee Martin McDonald and James A. Sanders (Peabody, Mass.: Hendrickson, 2002), p. 301.

[8]Irenaeus is committed to the notion that the created order is a reflection of the Creator (cf., e.g., *Against Heresies* 2.9.1).

cording to our heresiologist, is that their cosmogonies, stuffed with enumerations of supercelestial beings, can make any and every hypothesis plausible. Gnostic numerological arguments prove at once too much and too little. The better route, according to the bishop, is to begin with reality as empirically found in creation and work back from there. Numerological interpretation gains credence if it can

> adapt the numbers themselves, and those things, which have been formed, to the true theory lying before them. For storyline (*regula*) does not spring out of numbers, but numbers from a storyline; nor does God derive His being from things made, but things are made from God. For all things originate from one and the same God. (*Against Heresies* 2.25.1)

While wary of those spinning the cloth of mythography from the threads of abstract numbers (as many Gnostic patently did), he is open to inferring numerological significance from the story of creation. For Irenaeus, creation is the baseline and root of all theological ramification. But the creation of humanity is not just the once-for-all act of God's shaping Adam out of the dust; rather, it includes God's perfecting of Adam's race through redemptive history, which for all intents and purposes is an extension of creation. Thus, as the bishop sees it, because the four Gospels are part of redemptive history, they are no less a creational reality than the four corners of the world.

This is rather different from the way most modern readers of the Bible understand things. And perhaps it is precisely at this point of difference that our problems in understanding Irenaeus begin. If we mistakenly presume that he, like most of us, sees creational realities as being temporally and logically prior to and detached from salvation-historical realities, then we will also likely presume, again mistakenly, that he proceeds deductively: again as Ehrman puts it, "four corners of the earth, four winds, four pillars—and necessarily, then four Gospels." But if for Irenaeus creation and redemption are virtually synchronized and are correlated not horizontally, in relation to each other, but vertically, connecting in the mind of God, then this added dimension of theological perspectivalism will naturally inform his reasoning.

Given Irenaeus's stated ideal of "harmonizing" numbers with "what actually exists" (*Against Heresies* 2.25.1), I propose we are best off surmising that the bishop's argument proceeds not deductively (four corners, therefore four Gospels) but intuitively or (if we need to put this in logical terms) abductively. Observing a correlation between four Gospels and four world zones, he infers the significance of four in the mind of God. This inferred significance is so weighty that he turns it around again as the most excellent explanation as to why there are four Gospels; on account of its excellence, it is a necessary explanation: "the Gospels could not possibly be either more or less in number than they are."

This symmetry between the four authoritative portrayals of Christ and the four zones of the inhabited earth is only paralleled and reinforced by a more fundamental correspondence between Irenaeus's anthropology (his doctrine of the first Adam) and christology (his doctrine of the second Adam). Because Christ is the recapitulation of Adam, it is only fitting that Christ, the embodiment of new creation as contained in the four Gospels, should be analogous to Adam, the embodiment of creation as constituted by the four world zones.[9] We may only see the bishop drawing explicit attention to "four" in this sound-byte paragraph, but this is only the tip of the iceberg. That which is below the surface is the correlation of the first Adam and the second Adam, larger narratives, of which four corners and four Gospels are a part.

Why then are there four Gospels? The bishop's logic can be summarized with his own refrain: "it is fitting, it is possible, therefore it is" (*Against Heresies* 1.9.4; 1.22.1). As Irenaeus the biblical theologian sees it, the congruence of any two realities ("it is fitting"), if plausibly reinforced ("it is possible"), necessarily speaks to a real connection ("therefore it is"). He assumes that the burden of proof falls on the one wishing to deny this symmetry. At the end of the day, it is not, as so many modern commentators have suggested, Irenaeus who is doing violence to all reasoning, but it is the commentators who are doing violence to the reasoning of Irenaeus by abstracting it out of its biblical theological framework.

---

[9]See, classically, Gustaf Wingren, *Man and the Incarnation* (Philadelphia: Muhlenberg, 1959); J. T. Nielsen, *Adam and Christ in the Theology of Irenaeus of Lyons* (Assen: Van Gorcum, 1968).

Irenaeus and Lyotard

In reading Irenaeus, it is striking how so many of his themes anticipate certain strands in the writing of Jean-François Lyotard, including Lyotard's most well-known book, *The Postmodern Condition*.[10] This is particularly the case when it comes to issues of epistemology (the theory of knowledge): Lyotard's critique of knowledge, as conceived in modernity, is hauntingly similar to Irenaeus's criticism of *gnosis* ("knowledge"), as understood foremost by the Valentinian heretics. I begin with a survey of Lyotard himself.

Lyotard and the postmodern condition. The essence of postmodernity, Lyotard begins, is "an incredulity toward metanarratives."[11] Frustatingly, Lyotard fails to take up the question as to whether and to what extent the scriptural story may be considered a metanarrative; he focuses instead on the other great philosophies of history, not least the philosophy of Enlightenment and its handmaiden science.[12] Because the "scientific knowledge" or "instrumental knowledge" has had such a decisive effect on Western culture, and because that effect in recent decades has been all the more intensified through the "mercantilization of knowledge," our generation must admit to being witnesses of an epistemological transformation. Increasingly transmuted into a tranferable commodity, knowledge is becoming more and more objectivized, "exteriorized" and abstracted from the human context.[13] Primal or narrative knowledge, by contrast, sees knowing as inseparable from personal development *(Bildung)* and an array of social relations, which are fraught with political and ethical judgments. Because of modernity's technological advances, this narrative knowledge is becoming increasingly delegitimized.

Yet these two forms of knowledge, scientific knowledge, on the one hand, and the narrative knowledge of the peoples, on the other, remain co-

---

[10]Jean-François Lyotard, *The Postmodern Condition,* Theory and History of Literature 10 (Minneapolis: University of Minnesota Press, 1984).

[11]Ibid., p. xxiv.

[12]For a discussion on the application of Lytoard to Christianity, see James K. A. Smith, "A Little Story About Metanarratives: Lyotard, Religion and Postmodernism Revisited," *Faith and Philosophy* 18 (2001): 353-68; Merold Westphal, "Onto-theology, Metanarrative, Perspectivism and the Gospel," *Perspectives* (April 2000): 6-10; J. Thacker, "Lyotard and the Christian Metanarrative: A Rejoinder to Smith and Westphal," *Faith and Philosophy* 22 (2005): 301-15.

[13]Lyotard, *Postmodern Condition,* pp. 4-5.

existent. Drawing on Wittgenstein's concept of the "language game," whereby every utterance presupposes a social grammar and vice versa, Lyotard affirms that narrative knowledge is superior to scientific knowledge, because while narrative knowledge is self-legitimizing by virtue of its social and cultural embeddedness, the latter, having neither social grammar nor social grounding, lacks legitimation altogether. Again, the narrative of the people finds it final justification in cultural self-identity. Invoking Wittgenstein once more, Lyotard writes, "they are legitimated by the simple fact that they do what they do."[14]

Scientific understanding of knowledge eschews such ethnography in the name of objectivity, but in so doing it is forced to restrict knowledge to only that which can be verified.[15] When science advances claims, which implicitly presumes the answer to certain fundamental questions ("who decides what knowledge is, and who knows what needs to be decided"), it is necessarily dishonest about the fact that such claims are inevitably political, social and ethical in nature.[16] It must be dishonest, if it hopes to preserve the purported objectivity of its claims regarding its alleged transcendence over and superiority to tribal narratives. The breakdown of science's ability to legitimize itself has led to the balkanization of legitimizing structures. We are cast about in a world of epistemological islands. This is the heart of the postmodern condition.

Lyotard's critique and Gnosticism. When we turn to the finer details of Lyotard's restatement of scientific knowledge, we find certain interesting comparisons with the Gnosticism of Irenaeus's day. There are undoubtedly a number of avenues that could be profitably explored, but I will limit myself to several points.

First, as Lyotard points out, scientific knowledge establishes its own narrative by which it seeks to delegitimize other narratives, more precisely, competing local and particular expressions of knowledge. It aspires to a universal status as a "perfectly sealed circle of facts and interpretations"; its goal is in the "destroying the traditional knowledge of peoples, perceived

---

[14]Ibid., p. 23.
[15]Ibid., p. 25.
[16]Ibid., p. 9.

. . . as minorities or potential separatist movements destined only to spread obscurantism."[17] Indigenous knowledge is incommensurate with scientific knowledge; it is deemed illegitimate by modernist, Western culture because it cannot verify its own claims by the rules of science.

The role of science in Western society is, I submit, analogous to the role of the construct of *pleroma* ("fullness") in Gnostic thought. The *pleroma* is that which is imagined to be beyond the Creator God and that which contains God. For the Gnostics, knowledge of this *pleroma* constitutes the highest knowledge by which God may be understood and judged. By appealing to a ground of being apart from the Creator and creation, the Gnostics were able to maintain a superficial form of Christianity but avoid the philosophically awkward implications of the incarnation, namely, that universal truth could be revealed in history and in the particulars of creation. Like science, the Gnostic myth regularly involves incontestable pronouncements from a small circle of experts; they are pronouncements that claim a universal and totalizing validity. Moreover, both the modern expert and the ancient Gnostic mediator are perceived as having arrived at truth outside of the social bond without being answerable to it. The only ones authorized to interpret the experts are the experts themselves, not the community that receives scientific/Gnostic revelation.

In the scientific world, as in Gnosticism, the unicity of the referent (that which is under discussion) is necessarily assumed. Thus, truth must be strictly narrowed down to denotative statements, that which can be registered as true or false. After all, if science is to maintain its hegemony as final arbiter of truth, it must limit "truth" to that which can be verified. The scientific pronouncement, like the Gnostic myth, refuses to take up the social, political, aesthetic and ethical implications of its claims. Moreover, because scientific and Gnostic knowledge is inherently impersonal, it is binary. The consistent Gnostic believer—much like the modern product of the Enlightenment—is condemned to vacillate between the poles of absolute certainty (that which can be incontrovertibly demonstrated) and utter skepticism.

---

[17]Ibid., pp. 12, 30.

The degree of overlap between Gnostic knowledge and scientific knowledge prompts the question as to whether Irenaeus's criticism of Gnosticism may also be extended to modernity. Does Irenaeus, in other words, anticipate Lyotard and the line of postmodern thinking so suspicious of modernist epistemology? Toward focusing this question, I will return to the paradox of the one gospel with four Gospels.

The significance of the four Gospels and the one gospel of Jesus Christ. When we consider Irenaeus's understanding of the four Gospels and the one gospel of Jesus Christ, we find *in nuce* a statement of theology that rejects not simply the substance of Gnostic claims but their epistemological implications as well. Against the Gnostics, who sought to establish in place of Christian revelation a universal body of truth issuing from outside of creation, Irenaeus affirmed both the universality and particularity of revelation. In order to prepare for this claim, he insists that there is no *pleroma* beyond the Creator God. The Creator God is the highest God and the ultimate point of reference (*Against Heresies* 1.5). He is self-attesting through Scripture. Since this god is the God of the creation and all its particulars, which itself reflects the truth that is God, Gnostics have no right either to disparage positive revelation on account of its particularity or to rule out the possibility that God saw fit to reveal himself in the flesh of a socioculturally situated man.

For the bishop, Jesus Christ's being revealed simultaneously in the one gospel and in four is a very practical point. He wishes to show why the Gnostics are wrong in falling back on Gospels outside the fourfold canon and why they are equally wrong in neglecting to use all four. According to his report in *Against Heresies* 3.11.7, the Ebionites use Matthew "but are confuted out of the same"; Marcion retains Luke only, but is condemned by the same text; the Docetists use only Mark, but Mark is incompatible with their position; finally, the Valentinian sect employs John alone, but John alone is sufficient to make a compelling case against the same Valentinians. Whatever the sect and their Gospel of choice, there is enough material within each individual Gospel to refute the heresy in question. Each Gospel is self-contained and stands on its own two feet, lacking nothing as a faithful guide toward truth. The discrete Gospels are perspicacious;

their claims are universally binding.

All the same, there is another sense in which one Gospel is not enough. There must be four—no more, no less. According to Irenaeus, this is because "there are four zones in the world in which we live" and "four principal *(cathalokoi)* winds." Here it is possible that the bishop is recalling the well-known messianic text of Isaiah 11, which speaks of the "Spirit of the LORD" (Is 11:2) in connection with the gathering in of the Gentiles: "He will raise an ensign for the nations, and will assemble the outcasts of Israel, and gather the dispersed of Judah from the four corners of the earth" (Is 11:12). But if Irenaeus did not have this famous Isaianic passage in mind (we cannot be certain), he most assuredly was thinking of Ezekiel's fourfold cherubim, who (he understands to) reappear in the final book of the New Testament:

> After this I saw four angels standing at the four corners of the earth, holding back the four winds of the earth, that no wind might blow on earth or sea or against any tree. Then I saw another angel ascending from the rising of the sun, having the seal of the living God, and he called with a loud voice to the four angels who had been given power to harm earth and sea. (Rev 7:1-2)

In this context, the four angels are simultaneously those who superintend creation but also attend the throne (mercy seat) of God. They are mediators, entrusted with the task, which ultimately results in the worship of the nations. Like Isaiah 11, the bishop's most obvious subtext is decidedly missiological.

Irenaeus goes on to explain that the faces of the cherubim, as reported in Ezekiel 1, are the "activity of God." The first creature is a lion, symbolizing Christ's royalty. The second face is that of an ox, indicating Christ's priestly role. The third face is that of a man, showing Christ's "human guise." The fourth face is that of the flying eagle, which stands for the giving of the Spirit. He concludes, "Now the Gospels, in which Christ is enthroned, are like these" (*Against Heresies* 3.11.8). Four Gospels are necessary—no more, no less—because it was necessary to convey Christ's person from different angles: his royal and priestly status, as well as his human and divine nature.

But if a fourfold gospel is required to emphasize the various aspects of Christ's self-revelation, an event of universal implications, four Gospels are also necessary for a proper reception of the gospel among the indigenous nations. This is borne out by Irenaeus's comparison between the four Gospels and the four pillars *(styloi)* of the church (cf. 1 Tim 3:15). Given that the same term, "pillar" *(stylos)*, is used to signify the outer frames of the tabernacle (Septuagint, Ex 26:15-37), and given too that he goes on to describe Christ as the one seated among the cherubim, the bishop is clearly correlating Israel's tabernacle with the church.[18] This works well for his purposes. Both tabernacle and church represent a visible manifestation of God to humanity. The pillars are that on which the tabernacle quite literally depends; they mark off the holy space in which Yahweh's presence dwells. So too the Gospels, "held together by one Spirit," mark off the space in which Christ dwells. Neither outer walls of the tabernacle nor the Gospels provide exhaustive knowledge of the one God, but both tabernacle and Gospels are an adequate and faithful public display of God's presence. But this revelation is in accordance with created particularities: "For since God made all things in due proportion and adaptation, it was fitting also that the outward aspect of the Gospel should be well arranged and harmonized" (*Against Heresies* 3.11.9).

For Irenaeus, the dangers of Gnosticism were not simply doctrinal; there were dire ecclesiological consequences as well. In his view, the Marcionites, Encratites and Montanists share this one attribute: they "hold themselves aloof from the community of the brothers" (*Against Heresies* 3.11.8). This aloofness, the bishop hints, corresponds to a hermeneutical aloofness implied in giving one Gospel priority over the other three, or in the case of Valentinus, the privileging of a metagospel outside the four (the Gospel of Truth) over the four. To settle on one Gospel then is to reject the de facto canon. But more than that, it is to dissolve the interpretive community of the four Evangelists, who together are in turn an emblem and analogy of another interpretive community, the church. In Gnosticism,

---

[18]This is a common motif in the patristic writings; see Margaret Barker, *The Great High Priest* (London: T & T Clark, 2003), chaps. 7, 8.

with its radical commitment to one metanarrative, involving a single inter-pretation of a single Gospel yielding a single interpretation, the interpre-tive act ceases to be a social act. The authorized expert, the mediator of the Gnostic vision, acquires a totalizing force and community is rendered re-dundant, at least as far as interpretation goes. By contrast, in the church, partly because there are four Gospels, Christian reflection retains an in-trinsically communal or dialogical quality. If Irenaeus associates the meta-Gospel within the four or outside the four with pride and schism, the pluriformity of the gospel implies a certain degree of catholicity and lati-tude in interpretation, or to borrow Brian McLaren's borrowed phrase, "a generous orthodoxy."[19]

On the other hand, Irenaeus insists on the accessibility of "truth" and refuses to allow the knowledge of God to be severed from the objective moorings of Scriptures, the church and the church's beliefs. For him, these three elements form a tripod on which responsible scriptural inter-pretation is to take place. Of these three elements, it is first and foremost Scripture that is critical to the interpretive process. The church's tradi-tion and its rule of faith are corroborative; they are of second order for a proper interpretation of Scripture. So there are right readings of Scrip-ture; there are false readings of Scripture. Because there is one gospel and one Spirit, which binds the four together, individual perspectivalism is ruled out. For Irenaeus, the propounding of mutually contradictory doc-trines was the lot of Gentile philosophers, not Christians (*Against Here-sies* 2.27.1). Comprehensive understanding of reality was of course unat-tainable, but truth itself was. For the bishop of Lyons, the attainment of truth was one thing that distinguished Christians from the Gnostics, who had made a virtue out of skepticism: "Wherefore they also imagine many gods, and they always have the excuse of searching [after truth] (for they are blind), but never succeed in finding it" (*Against Heresies* 3.24.2). Irenaeus claims to have found the truth and does not betray the last embarrassment in saying so.

---

[19]The phrase serves as the title of his book: Brian D. McLaren, *A Generous Orthodoxy* (Grand Rapids, Mich.: Zondervan, 2004).

In sum, while Irenaeus's *Against Heresies* bears instructive parallel to the Lyotardian critique of modern epistemology, this does not necessarily make Irenaeus a postmodernist. The tension between the four Gospels and the one gospel of Jesus Christ is reflective of a dialectical tension in his epistemology: truth is certainly attainable but only in terms of adequation. If modern *ressourcement* wishes to follow the lead of the bishop of Lyons in terms of epistemology, we must somehow steer a clear course between the modernist Scylla of verificationism and the postmodernist Carybdis of individualist perspectivalism.

Conclusion: Implications for *Ressourcement*

In applying Irenaeus's criticism of Gnosticism to our day, we may find then that neither modernist nor postmodernist gets off so easily. Clearly, Irenaeus would be deeply suspicious of the modernist Christian tendency to equate intellectual assent to a certain set of theological propositions with the apprehension of truth. Certain strands of evangelical and fundamentalist Christianity, in which one's "personal decision for Christ" can overshadow the call to embody the gospel, come close to Gnosticism. Likewise, in failing to apply their faith holistically, in radically separating what they claim to believe on Sunday from what they do their workaday week, countless Western churchgoers betray their having succumbed unwittingly to a Gnostic script. If Christian revelation is only a subcategory of a more comprehensive system of knowledge called science, then science itself is the *pleroma*, the highest god to which even Jesus Christ must bow. For Irenaeus, the formation of a thoroughgoing Christian worldview was not an option; it followed logically and necessarily on the heels of the incarnation.

I suspect that Irenaeus would also be puzzled not only by our post-Enlightenment tendency to see the Bible primarily as a sourcebook of information but also by our unsettling abhorrence of mystery. Perhaps the contemporary crisis in preaching arises not from improper technique but, quite the contrary, from the stultifying obsession with the *gnosis* of technique in preaching. The same quest for and promise of *gnosis*, made plausible by the scientific epistemology, is often implicit in how the contemporary Western church instructs its members in building a better marriage,

leading family devotions and sharing one's faith. In attempting to be helpful and take the mystery out of such disciplines, perhaps we have taken out
too much mystery—perhaps we have taken out the person of God. Eventually, the depersonalization of the encounter with Scripture will eventuate
in a functional *gnosis*, whereby a certain metanarrative (justification by
faith, freedom, self-fulfillment, family values) becomes a default gospel behind and above the Gospels, evacuating the unique force of the biblical
texts at hand. In some ways, the importing of modern metanarratives may
be averted by deeper appreciation of the historical context of Scripture. But
we must be careful. As readers of the Bible, we must also look for more
than what the Bible meant and be open to encountering biblical truth in
inscrutable ways through nondiscursive discourse.

If Irenaeus were alive to object to the Gnostic proclivities of post-
Enlightenment Christianity, he might also have a few words for the *soi-disant*
postmoderns among us. While the emergent church has rightly intuited
the Gnostic proclivities of much of the unemerged church, there are certain respects in which this movement may also fall prey to Gnostic tendencies. The Gnostics, Irenaeus charged, were "always looking for the truth,
but never finding it." Although McLaren decries relativism in *A Generous
Orthodoxy*, his broad appreciation for so many traditions, although in many
ways salutary, reflects an approach to ecumenism that out-moderns the
moderns. While ecumenism demands mutual respect between traditions,
no theological tradition, if it is truly Christian, can be weighed by a piece-
meal appreciation of its individual parts. Approaching the spectrum of
theological options as one approaches a meal at an international buffet (a
little Mexican food here, a little Italian there, a little Chinese here) is itself
a deeply Gnostic move. Irenaeus considered the *regula* of faith as inextri-
cable from the community, which preserved the *regula* and was preserved
by it. Thus Irenaeus would say, "If you really want to appreciate French cui-
sine, don't go to a restaurant. You must go and live in Provence." By abstracting discrete theological ideas from the local narrative knowledge of
the indigenous tradition, we are in danger of reverting into—to use Guy
DeBord's perjorative description of postmodernity—the "society of the
spectacle."

While both radical Western individualism (of which McLaren may be an example) and Gnosticism tend toward a never-ending conversation among a collage of ideas, incarnational Christianity is deeply self-committing. In taking on flesh, Jesus Christ committed to participating fully in a particular social, historical and theological trajectory. As for Irenaeus, because the Word was made flesh, because Christian faith was as much a social reality as a theological reality, allegiance to a certain set of beliefs carried with it an allegiance to a certain social-historical trajectory. It is only the Gnostics who sought to present a Christ who transcended his particularity, who stood aloof to identifying with a particular people and their traditions.

Undoubtedly, Irenaeus's critique of Gnosticism, which finds contemporary leverage through the insights of Lyotard, forces us to assess the epistemic assumptions of our post-Enlightenment church on two fronts. If Irenaeus weighed Gnosticism and found it wanting in its doctrines of creation and incarnation, the same judgment may be leveled against numerous post-Enlightenment methodologies regularly employed in lectern and pulpit. The bishop never once countenanced the possibility that the epistemology of his Gnostic adversaries was morally neutral. Neither should we. Like the ancients, we too must be prepared to be chastened in our Gnostic tendencies. Neither the moderns nor the postmoderns appear to have first dibs on Irenaeus, but perhaps if we begin with his paradoxical understanding of the four Gospels, the bishop of Lyons can lead us on a path between the two.

PART THREE

The Social Practices of
the Early Church

Missional Witness

7

Hospitality

Ancient Resources and Contemporary Challenges

Christine D. Pohl

Because they are hidden from view, seem difficult to unwrap or appear outdated, wonderful gifts are sometimes overlooked. Like an unopened Christmas present buried in a corner, the ancient Christian tradition has been neglected by many of us. Discovering its treasures has been an important part of recent evangelical scholarship, and recovering its wisdom has been crucial to my personal and academic journey.

For these reasons, I have chosen to begin with a brief description of my experiences in discovering the resources of the ancient tradition of Christian hospitality. As a young adult with deep evangelical commitments, I knew the importance of the Scriptures for my life and my communities. The study of Scripture formed, challenged and defined the campus ministries, churches and small groups to which I belonged. With a good grasp of the Bible, a personal relationship with Jesus and dependence on the Holy Spirit, we were ready to do whatever God asked. We did not find it strange to assume that God would speak directly through the Scriptures to us individually or in our Bible studies or small-group meetings. We wanted to live like the church in the book of Acts, and we worked to model ourselves after the shared life of the first Christians. I cannot remember ever wondering if we were missing anything by skipping over the next fourteen hundred years of church history. If we were attentive to church history at all, it was when some theological commitment from the Protestant Reformation was occasionally acknowledged. For my communities, and for me, it was almost as if nothing had happened between the first century of the church and our own day.

This perspective was not particularly unusual for American evangelicals between the late 1960s and end of the 1980s. We did not have much time for history; the communities to which I belonged were active in making a place for refugees, engaging in racial reconciliation, working with urban poor and elderly people and those with disabilities. It was an extraordinary time of combining evangelistic outreach and social ministry. We discovered that in making a place for those the world overlooked, in offering them welcome, we were doing something countercultural, kingdom-oriented and deeply life-giving. But my evangelical coworkers and I also found ourselves swamped with the complex realities of such ministry.

We did not have an explicit theological vocabulary or moral framework to describe or interpret what we were doing. It was ministry, but it was a form of ministry in which our lives were closely intertwined with the lives of those we were assisting or accompanying. Together we discovered the joy of multicultural congregations that shared worship, the power of Scripture as it was lived out in community, the beauty of friendships that crossed significant social boundaries and the presence of God in the midst of shared meals. Through the experiences of the people among whom we ministered, we also felt the humiliation of being dependent on social service agencies and the risks of being unfamiliar with the assumptions and expectations of the surrounding culture.

The challenges of ministry eventually drove me to seminary and to the study of ethics. A new world opened up there—one rich with historical tradition, biblical studies and moral and theological frameworks. But my substantive engagement with the ancient church developed late in graduate school when I was doing research for my dissertation. Because I had been well trained as an evangelical seminary student, I found many doctoral-level ethical discussions about inclusion, voice, power, justice, community and rights surprisingly weak in terms of biblical and theological foundation. Although the overall program was theologically strong, the discussions of these particular issues were much more frequently framed in the language of political and social theory than in theological or biblical categories. But within these discussions were located key questions for my faith and experience in ministry. And so I wondered if, in its prior history, the church had not encountered concerns about addressing social differences, crossing social and economic boundaries or working out ethnic tensions. Surely these issues had come up in congregational life and ministry before the last decades of the twentieth century.

From experiences in ministry with refugees and people with disabilities, I had seen the power of welcome and of being welcomed and the significance of being "with" people. Intentional Christian communities had demonstrated to me how compelling the gospel was when it was embodied in a small community and in generous welcome. I knew that the New Testament church had dealt with tensions between Jews and Greeks and rich and poor believers and that the first Christians had not always gotten their practices right. The biblical texts showed that Jesus had made a place for socially marginalized persons in his ministry and that Paul had addressed questions of unity and diversity in very specific ways. From the biblical accounts, it seemed as if the issues often came to the surface as people gathered for meals and met together in homes. And so I began to wonder if issues of membership, voice, community, recognition and distribution of wealth and power had been addressed in earlier times in discussions about hospitality and welcome.

So, as a budding ethicist with good training in biblical interpretation but little in the methods of historical research, I dove into the ancient church documents to figure out what had been written about hospitality. I worked to discern whether or not the church of the first five centuries had used the language and lens of hospitality for addressing social issues in its day. Doing research felt much like being on a treasure hunt, complete with the occasional exhilaration of following clues down unexpected paths. The materials were far more accessible than I had imagined, despite some wooden translations and bad indexes. I came to the writings of the ancient church with particular questions that had arisen in the rough and tumble of ministry—and I could hardly believe how much material was relevant and interesting.

Because social ministry and justice concerns had shaped my questions, I tended to find the most help in sermons and commentaries written by the church fathers, when they were addressing issues that arose in congregational life. Their reflections arising out of pastoral engagement rather than their treatises on doctrinal questions proved most helpful for my particular work. As they dealt with challenging their wealthy parishioners to share with those who were hungry or in need of housing, as they addressed complacency and disrespect in the midst of God's generosity and as they struggled with the early consequences of the institutionalization of care, I found their arguments and insights spoke directly to contemporary concerns. Their biblical commentaries were helpful because both my questions and their insights worked out of a common biblical text that was expected to speak relevantly and authoritatively to our particular situations even though our contexts were socially and culturally very different.

There are, nevertheless, some complexities in attempting to retrieve or recover an ancient tradition or practice. We are always engaged in a selective retrieval of material, and a researcher risks whitewashing or ignoring the parts of the tradition that are inconvenient or embarrassing. But for the tradition to be helpful, the retrieval must be truthful. Also, the corpus of some of the writers is enormous, and if one's interest is topical, it is not always possible to read comprehensively in any one writer, and it is quite possible to miss related but significant discussions. To keep us from misreading or misrepresenting texts or persons, we are dependent on the secondary sources prepared by specialists in a period or a person. The footnotes in these secondary sources become crucial maps leading to important but more obscure materials.

Additionally, whose writings are preserved and available, and which topics are addressed, are tied to prevailing cultural values, power dynamics and ecclesial concerns. For example, in the history of hospitality, gender issues are complex. Women were regularly commended for their hospitality, but it takes additional effort to find their own stories or insights, even when they were deeply involved in the practice. In fact, we do not know much about the hospitality practices of ordinary Christians, male or female, because they did not often write the accounts, and their lives were rarely the subject of biographies or eulogies. So any retrieval of ancient wisdom and experience will be incomplete and complex because we are attempting to have conversations across centuries, continents, cultures and very diverse communities. But even when incomplete, the conversations can be challenging and fruitful.

At the start of my research, my primary question was whether or not hospitality had been a significant part of the church's life and reflection throughout some or all of its history—and, if it had been, how hospitality was practiced and understood in each period. Several years later, I could say with some certainty that indeed hospitality had been important to the church from its first days well into the eighteenth century.[1] However, within the ancient materials, there were more treasures to be found.

A Distinctively Christian Understanding of Hospitality

Writers during the first five centuries of the church drew together a number of biblical passages to form what became a normative understanding of Christian hospitality. They used that understanding to challenge the church of their day, and that same interpretation was subsequently employed to challenge and to guide the church's ministry for the next thousand years.

In those fruitful first five centuries of the church, Lactantius, Jerome, John Chrysostom and others articulated a distinctively Christian understanding of hospitality. Although hospitality was important in almost every culture of that period, these writers framed their understanding of hospitality in contrast with conventional views. Christian hospitality, they argued, was distinguished by its welcome to those whose appearance suggested that they were among "the least." On the basis of several biblical texts, these writers maintained that what made Christian hospitality different was that it was not offered in order to gain some advantage; instead, hospitality involved intentionally welcoming those who seemed to have little to offer.

The story of Abraham and Sarah and their hospitality to the three

---

[1]After the first centuries, I dealt only with understandings and practices of hospitality in the Western church. This was for two primary reasons: the literature was enormous and I wanted to trace out an entire history, and it was the Western church that had most influenced the contemporary American context with which I was particularly concerned. See Christine D. Pohl, *Making Room* (Grand Rapids, Mich.: Eerdmans, 1999). Much remains to be done in recovering other traditions for which hospitality was an important practice.

strangers/angels (Gen 18) and Jesus' identification of himself with hungry, homeless, sick and imprisoned persons, or the "least of these" (Mt 25:31-46), were especially important. In addition to these two passages, Jesus' words in Luke 14 regarding welcome into the kingdom and his recommendation that guest lists for dinner parties particularly include the sick, poor and broken shaped a distinctive understanding of the practice of welcome. This view was forged partly in continuity with Old Testament commitments and partly in contrast to Greek and Roman views of benevolence that stressed formal reciprocal obligations between benefactor and beneficiary. Because in the Greek and Roman traditions, a response of gratitude by the beneficiary was central to the ongoing relationship, emphasis was placed on the worthiness and goodness of the recipients rather than on their need. Such relations were often calculated to benefit the benefactor.[2] Christian views explicitly challenged this practice.

Lactantius, tutor to the son of Constantine, wrote that "whatever a man has bestowed upon another, hoping for no advantage from him, he really bestows upon himself, for he will receive a reward from God." Echoing Jesus' words from Luke 14:12-14, Lactantius argued that when Christians hosted a feast, they were to invite those who could not invite their hosts in return. While recognizing that this did not mean a person was "debarred from intercourse with his friends or kindness with his neighbors," Lactantius explained the full significance of such hospitality. He noted that while giving hospitality to friends, family and neighbors was part of the blessing and relations of ordinary life, providing welcome to those who could not give anything in return was "our true and just work," our work that related to God. He particularly criticized attitudes toward hospitality that saw it as a way of gaining the favor of leaders and thus as a way of gaining power and influence, and he called such hospitality "ambitious" and characterized by evil intention.[3]

---

[2]See Stephen C. Mott, "The Power of Giving and Receiving: Reciprocity in Hellenistic Benevolence," in *Current Issues in Biblical and Patristic Interpretation,* ed. Gerald F. Hawthorne (Grand Rapids, Mich.: Eerdmans, 1975), pp. 60-72.

[3]Lanctantius *The Divine Institutes* 6.12, in *The Ante-Nicene Fathers,* ed. Alexander Roberts and James Donaldson (Edinburgh: T & T Clark, 1867-1872), 7:176-77.

In 394, Jerome wrote about the duties of the clergy and offered a similar warning: "Avoid entertaining the worldly at your table, especially those who are swollen with office. You are the priest of a crucified Lord, one who lived in poverty and on the bread of strangers." Jerome urged instead, "let poor men and strangers be acquainted with your modest table, and with them Christ shall be your guest."[4] Similarly, John Chrysostom repeatedly stressed the importance of welcoming those who did not command much attention or respect. "By how much the brother may be least, so much the more does Christ come to thee through him. For he that receives the great, often does it from vainglory also; but he that receives the small, does it purely for Christ's sake."[5]

For these writers and for other leaders of the ancient church, hospitality was an important practice for transcending the status boundaries of the surrounding culture and for working through issues of recognition and respect. It was crucial to meeting human needs—especially the physical needs of impoverished believers—and it made sense in the economy of God. Generous hosts, though not seeking gain, would find themselves blessed in the hospitality relationship. By offering hospitality to someone in need, one both ministered to Christ and responded to God's generous hospitality. John Chrysostom pointed out the disproportionate generosity of God that stands behind all of our acts of hospitality. In a homily on the book of Acts, he explained that we receive Jesus into our homes, but he receives us into the kingdom of his Father; in responding to a hungry person, we take away Jesus' hunger, but he takes away our sins; we see him a stranger and he makes us citizens of heaven; we give him bread, but he gives us an entire kingdom to inherit and possess.[6]

In a similar vein, Augustine argued that acts of kindness fit into a net-

---

[4]Jerome *Letter* 52, "To Nepotian," in *Select Letters of Jerome,* trans. F. A. Wright, Loeb Classical Library (Cambridge, Mass.: Harvard University Press), pp. 217-19. See also Owen Chadwick, ed., *The Rule of Benedict,* chap. 53:1, 6-7, 15, in *Western Asceticism,* Library of Christian Classics 12 (Philadelphia: Westminster Press, 1958).

[5]John Chrysostom, Homily 45 on Acts in *A Select Library of the Nicene and Post-Nicene Fathers,* first series (New York: Christian Literature Co.), 11:275-76 (Nicene and Post-Nicene Fathers, first series, hereafter cited as NPNF).

[6]Ibid., p. 276.

work of need. Both giver and recipient were in need before God, and although God needed none of a person's goods, God had, in kindness, been willing "to be hungry in His poor." Quoting Matthew 25:35, Augustine reminded his parishioners of Jesus' words, "I was hungry" "and ye gave Me meat."[7]

Christian hospitality was thus a response to God's overwhelming generosity and welcome. It was also to be remedial; its practice among Christians was to counteract the social stratification of the larger society by providing a modest and equal welcome to everyone. High social status was not to be honored with special recognition; in fact, to welcome persons who had few needs was not true hospitality, the ancient church leaders argued. Hospitality was most centrally to be viewed as kindness to strangers. The focus, however, was on strangers in need, the "abject and lowly," those who on the first appearance seemed to have little to offer. Ministry to them was categorically different from hospitality to "illustrious" guests who could further one's own position in the world.[8]

Though often honored in the breach, it was to these understandings of hospitality that later Christian writers referred even through the time of the Protestant Reformation. While we might find the language of "ambitious" hospitality quaint, the concern that stands behind it remains fully relevant to us. Our greatest temptation in recovering hospitality is that we will use it instrumentally, to get something or to gain some advantage. Our versions of ambition are different, but we are prone to ask what hospitality will accomplish, how it will further our plans or projects and whether it will produce measurable results.

Additional Gifts of the Ancient Tradition

Writers from the early centuries of the church, particularly John Chrysostom, provided the words and the pastoral wisdom that helped me articulate why hospitality had been so important in my life and moral re-

---

[7]Augustine *Sermon* 10, NPNF 6:294; see also *Sermon* 210, "For the Lenten Season," in *Sermons on the Liturgical Seasons,* trans. Mary Sarah Muldowney, Fathers of the Church 17 (New York: Fathers of the Church, 1959), p. 107.
[8]Lactantius *The Divine Institutes,* p. 176.

flection.[9] Through their insights and the record of their practice, it became possible to locate acts of welcome in a larger context or tradition that suggested why hospitality was such a potent form of social witness and resistance. Many people today—including committed Christians—have very limited understandings of hospitality: it is coffee and doughnuts after church, the task of greeters and potluck committees or something nice that "ladies" do if they have the time. Alternately, people think of the commercial expressions of hospitality—the hospitality industry of resorts, hotels and restaurants—a service to be purchased when traveling for business or recreation.

The importance of having a story or tradition within which to locate our acts of care and welcome became clear one day during a presentation to Salvation Army officers. Few communities do more than the Salvation Army to welcome the "least" of the world, through their shelters, food programs, daycare and congregational life. After an extended discussion of biblical, historical and current understandings of hospitality, an older officer came up to me and said, "You mean all those beds and breakfasts meant something?" It was an extraordinary comment. He knew that his many years of providing shelter and breakfasts for homeless men was important for them, but he had little sense that it meant something in a larger tradition or that it fit into something the church has, at times, cared about deeply. Up to that point, no one had suggested to him how much hospitality mattered to God or that his particular work had a place in a long tradition of faithfully following Jesus.

Becoming familiar with the ancient writers was like finding new friends, conversation partners and colaborers. It was strangely comforting to know that people had always worried about being used, that they had struggled with how to offer help without humiliating the recipient and that sixteen hundred years ago Christians had wondered whether they ought to give money to the homeless person they passed on the street. But it was even more helpful to learn how Christians of earlier times had dealt

---

[9]In materials from the later centuries of the church, I found the writings of John Calvin and John Wesley to be particularly illuminating and helpful.

with such concerns while continuing a robust, theologically rooted practice of welcome.

For example, there are many discussions within the tradition concerning to whom aid should be given and how it should be distributed. Faithful Christians struggled with questions about whether it was right to distinguish between "deserving" and "undeserving" poor, and with questions about whether help should be offered indiscriminately or by using certain criteria. These are the same questions with which we struggle. How many of us wonder whether we ought to make sure the person to whom we give a dollar will use it well or, at least, that they will not use it for drugs or alcohol? How many times have we volunteered at a homeless shelter or food pantry and felt a little uncomfortable about asking people to prove their need for a loaf of week-old bread, a brick of government cheese or a cot in an overcrowded gymnasium?

John Chrysostom's warning to his congregation speaks to us about our rigorous needs tests: that it is the height of stinginess "for one loaf [of bread] to be exact about a man's entire life." While insisting on the importance of offering enthusiastic, generous and cheerful hospitality to strangers and to poor persons within the community, he also recognized concerns that imposters might take advantage of indiscriminate generosity. He acknowledged that if one knew they were imposters, it was appropriate not to receive them into one's house, "but if thou dost not know this, why dost thou accuse them lightly?" In any case the risk is in the giver's favor, because "greater are the benefits we receive than what we confer." He reminded his parishioners that Abraham and Sarah had enthusiastically welcomed three strangers to their home without knowing they were angels. He further challenged his congregation when they hesitated to offer hospitality even though they knew from Matthew 25 that in welcoming strangers they were receiving not just angels but Christ himself.[10]

Among the most compelling discussions of hospitality are Chrysostom's insights about the risk of shaming recipients while providing them with assistance. He repeatedly warned against having a grudging spirit in the ex-

[10]John Chrysostom Homily 21 on Romans, NPNF Series 2, 11:505; Homily 45 on Acts, p. 277.

ercise of hospitality, describing such an attitude as "cruel and inhuman."[11] Holding together respect and assistance is difficult—there is, as Philip Hallie has written, "a way of helping people that fills their hands but breaks their hearts."[12] Chrysostom understood how easy it could be for those with resources to "think themselves superior to the recipients and oftentimes despise them for the attention given them."[13] The antidote was deeply biblical and theological—remembering the generous welcome we had received in Christ and recognizing that in offering welcome to one in need we were somehow offering welcome to Jesus.[14]

Another gift of the ancient tradition that becomes available on close examination is an indication of the settings in which the practice of hospitality is most transformative. In the first centuries of the church, Christian households were a primary site for congregational gatherings and worship. Hospitality was crucial in that context. Congregations were hosted, and poor people, traveling leaders, and Christian refugees were cared for in the same condensed familial setting. Here persons from very different backgrounds were formed into a new kind of family. Later, hospitality was a vital if complicated practice in monasteries; these were communities that also drew into a single entity both household and church. It is the overlap of household and church that throughout Christian history provides the most important location for hospitality and suggests why small groups, house churches, Alpha programs and the like remain crucial to today's discipleship, growth and outreach.[15]

Hospitality had a central role in the early church as believers forged a new identity in a hostile culture. As Christians shared meals and resources, and as they opened their lives and homes to strangers, they formed communities that transcended and changed conventional understandings of households and expressed new understandings of social relations and po-

---

[11]John Chrysostom Homily 21 on Romans, p. 502.
[12]Philip Hallie, *Tales of Good and Evil, Help and Harm* (New York: HarperCollins, 1997), p. 207.
[13]John Chrysostom Homily 41 on Genesis, in *Homilies on Genesis 18-45*, trans. Robert C. Hill, Fathers of the Church 82 (Washington, D.C.: Catholic University of America Press, 1990), p. 413.
[14]John Chrysostom Homily 41 on Genesis, p. 408, 416; Homily 45 on Acts, p. 276.
[15]See Pohl, *Making Room*, pp. 39-58, for fuller discussion of the significance of the location of hospitality.

litical identities.[16] The outside world noticed and wondered about this odd assortment of people who claimed to be—and acted as if they were—family.

As Robert Webber has so powerfully observed, what is compelling for people today is to find a place in a welcoming community in which they are introduced to a loving and hospitable God.[17] This is the power of hospitality, well understood by the ancient church and still available to us. People are hungry for relationships that are grace-filled and not instrumental, for shared meals that bring physical strength and social reconciliation, and for communities in which they can contribute and find personal healing.

When hospitality was a more central practice, church leaders had to deal with the difficulties that arose. They found ways to protect hospitable communities from abuse, and they put structures in place that allowed communities to preserve their identity and practices while they welcomed strangers. This is evident in the sixth-century *Rule of Benedict*, with its strong commitments to offering hospitality to strangers and to monastic separation.[18] Such insights help us in reflecting on how to maintain a valued identity while offering generous welcome to persons from outside the community.

In opening the gifts of the ancient tradition, we also open up a shared heritage. These are the writers who helped to form the theologians of later centuries—whether Thomas Aquinas, John Calvin or John Wesley. This shared tradition, rooted in the Scriptures, opens up a wider space for conversations among Protestant, Roman Catholic and Orthodox Christians, and between mainline and evangelical believers. Such conversations offer new avenues for growth as we learn from the different theological emphases and spiritual disciplines that have formed practitioners in these traditions.

A final gift that the ancient tradition offers is the ease with which early Christians assumed that a mundane practice of providing food and shelter

---

[16]See, for example, Aristedes *Apology* 15, Ante-Nicene Fathers 9:277; Justin Martyr *First Apology* 14, Ante-Nicene Fathers 1:167.

[17]Robert E. Webber, *Ancient-Future Faith* (Grand Rapids, Mich.: Baker, 1999), p. 72.

[18]*The Rule of Benedict*, chap. 53.

was infused with God's presence. It is startling to recognize the frequency with which leaders spoke of welcoming the stranger or person in need and of having Jesus for one's guest. They understood the mystery at the heart of Christian hospitality: far more was going on than sharing food and a roof. Like practitioners today who talk about finding themselves on holy ground, ancient church writers understood the reality of God's presence in acts of hospitality, and that works of mercy were a means of grace.[19]

Interestingly, ancient writers understood the mystery, without letting their discussion or practice become abstract or detached from the needs of actual human beings. Today there is some use of the language of hospitality in philosophical, theological and ethical reflection that is disturbingly abstract. Extended discussions about welcoming "the other" or "otherness" can go on without any real attention to others with whom our lives intersect. The tradition, however, provides an orientation that simultaneously recognizes the rich mystery within hospitality and its human practicality, difficulty and importance.

The tradition helps to sensitize us to the glimpses of God's kingdom that are present in simple acts of giving and receiving welcome. Because of this we are better able to see hospitality as a way of life that gives life to all involved. Tendencies to reduce hospitality to a burdensome task are challenged when we are able to recognize the grace, goodness and beauty in the practice.

In fact, the tradition helps us see that the mystery of the gospel is distilled in the practice of hospitality. Jesus comes as our host and our guest, and, in his broken body, even as our food. This extraordinary mystery stays close to the physicality of human life while expressing the deepest realities of transcendence and incarnation. Hospitality connects the table of the Eucharist with the tables in our homes and reminds us that in some miraculous, mysterious way, at both we are eating and drinking with Jesus.

---

[19]See also John Wesley, Sermon 98, "On Visiting the Sick," sec. 1 in *Works of John Wesley*, vol. 3: *Sermons 3:71-114* (Nashville: Abingdon, 1986).

8

Crumbs from the Table

Lazarus, the Eucharist and the Banquet of the Poor in the Homilies of John Chrysostom

George Kalantzis

You say: "What I have heard is clear to me; but this
is hidden from me—why God willed precisely this pathway for our
redemption." Brother, this ordinance is buried from the eyes of everyone
whose intellect has not matured within the flame of love.

DANTE, *PARADISO*

As the new year 388 (or 389) dawned, John Chrysostom, still a priest in the church of Antioch, took the opportunity of the feast of the Saturnalia to inaugurate a series of sermons on Luke 16:14-31, the parable of Lazarus and the rich man. Chrysostom delivered his sermons probably within the span of the year, interrupting his schedule in order to accommodate the liturgical year, the various feasts of saints and martyrs or the "occasional" natural catastrophe, such as a devastating earthquake that hit Antioch between his fifth and sixth sermons. Throughout his preaching career in Antioch as well as in Constantinople, the homilies of Chrysostom are dominated by his care for the poor and their plight, and the responsibility of the rich, especially those within the church, to give alms generously and without distinction. Blake Leyerle reminds us that Chrysostom's picture of the poor is "always set against the prosperous marketplace of late antiquity,"[1] a picture that accentuated the chasm between the classes and the social distinctions profoundly present in the city.

The Seven Homilies

John Chrysostom follows in a great line of early writers who exhorted Christians, especially wealthy Christians, to pay more attention to their souls and divest themselves from attachments to material wealth. Throughout the patristic period, the argument was made again and again that it is the attitude one has toward wealth and poverty, not wealth itself, that marks a rich person. What seems to be of utmost concern to most writers is not wealth or poverty as such, but the venality and unreliability of wealthy Christians.[2] This attitude, of course, is not without parallels in popular philosophical systems of the time—Stoicism, in particular—and in the biblical prescriptions (1 Cor 6:12; 7:29-31; Phil 4:11-12; 1 Jn 2:15-16), which taught that freedom from passionate at-

---

[1] Blake Leyerle, "John Chrysostom on Almsgiving and the Use of Money," *Harvard Theological Review* 87 (1994): 29.

[2] Cf. Clement *Who Is the Rich Man That Shall Be Saved?* 7, 11-12, 14-15, 20. It is interesting to see the change in Cyprian's attitude toward wealth and wealthy Christians before and after the Decian persecution (249-251). In *On the Dress of Virgins,* written before the persecution, the newly installed bishop of Carthage—himself of wealthy background—warns wealthy women who had taken oaths of virginity in the name and service of Christ that they should adorn themselves in a manner appropriate to their vocation of chastity and service (5, 9). In the years that followed, however, during and after the persecution, Cyprian saw the harsh reality of attachment to one's wealth as one of the primary reasons for the financial difficulties of the church. Wealthy Christians seemed to be less moved by the plight of their poor brothers and sisters than the bishop had anticipated. Therefore, in *On the Lapsed* and *On Works and Alms,* Cyprian turned in much harsher tones to condemn those within the church who had turned their backs to the poor (*On the Lapsed* 7-9, 15-17; *On Works and Alms* 5, 6, 8, 11-14, 18-19, 26). Rebecca Weaver notes that during this time, Cyprian "characterized the Roman oppression of the church as God's judgment on the laxity and greed of its members, and he attributed the failure of many of the lapsed to their enslavement to their possessions. They had feared the loss of riches more than the loss of Christ. Moreover, once the persecution had ended, rather than lamenting their sin and engaging in heartfelt medicinal penance . . . they had continued to pamper themselves in self-indulgence and luxury." See Rebecca H. Weaver, "Wealth and Poverty in the Early Church," *Interpretation* 41, no. 4 (October 1987): 373.

tachments, including material possessions, was part of the ideal life.[3]

To be sure, Chrysostom develops similar themes in these homilies. In the first sermon, based on Luke 16:19-21, he lays out the plan for the series and invites his audience to explore the lives of the two men with the backdrop of the Saturnalia that the city had just celebrated in extravagant form. Throughout the sermon Chrysostom draws parallels between the lives of the two protagonists and those of his audience, and he brings into focus the moral character of the two men in his characteristically vatic style. The second sermon focuses on Luke 16:22-24 and concentrates on the death of the protagonists in which the true character of each is revealed. Throughout this sermon Chrysostom encourages his audience to move beyond the surface read of a dichotomy between rich and poor—even healthy and sick—in the "earthly" condition of the two, and search for the depth grammar, the spiritual meaning of the story. There, it becomes clear that, as Catharine Roth puts it, "private property is not a Christian idea, however valid it is in the law," and that the rich "must hold their property as stewards for the poor, and must share their wealth without regard to the moral qualities of those who are in need."[4] As one moves through these sermons one must bear in mind that in fourth-century Antioch, as in our time, this was not an easy argument to make or one that resonated well with the affluent members of Chrysostom's audience.

The next two homilies also follow closely the divisions in the biblical narrative: the third concentrating on Luke 16:24-26, the rich man's first petition that Lazarus bring him a drop of water and the fourth on the second petition, Luke 16:27-31, that Lazarus visit his brothers. The last three sermons move away from the Lukan account but still deal with issues of class differentiation, wealth and poverty, returning to the theme of Lazarus and the rich man in the seventh and final sermon through the text of Matthew 7:13-14, "Enter through the narrow gate" and the occasion of what

---

[3]For an excellent short essay, see Weaver, "Wealth and Poverty," pp. 368-81.

[4]John Chrysostom, *On Wealth and Poverty*, trans. and introd. Catharine P. Roth (Crestwood, N.Y.: St. Vladimir's Seminary Press, 1999), p. 12. In this essay I will use Roth's translation of John's homilies, and the page numbers refer to her edition.

John calls "the satanic spectacles of the races." Here, the preacher repri-
mands his audience for their prurient attitude and reminds them that Lazarus entered God's rest and blessedness through the narrow path, while the
rich man, who took the easy route, ended up in "the inexorable judgments,
that unquenchable fire, and the undying worm" (Mk 9:48).[5]

Stewardship and God's Gift

The first sermon, then, deals with the lives of the two men. Following the
biblical narrative, Chrysostom juxtaposes the luxury of the one and the
poverty of the other, the life of self-indulgence (the true unrighteousness
in this story) against the life of patient suffering. Chrysostom is careful
to note that there is nothing intrinsically evil or unrighteous or vile in
wealth, or righteous and good in poverty, as such. He is careful not to
trivialize one or vulgarize the other. On the contrary, he insists that both
states are neutral—one is not a sign of divine favor, the other of divine
punishment. For Chrysostom, it is how one responds within the condition one finds oneself that truly matters: "Many people admire [Lazarus]
for this reason only, that he was poor, but I can show that he endured
chastisements nine in number, imposed not to punish him, but to make
him more glorious; and indeed this came about."[6] The same held true for
the rich man who by his indifference to the plight of his poor neighbor
"became hard-hearted and more reckless even than that unjust judge who
knew neither fear of God nor shame before man."[7] This is a theme Chrysostom continues in the second homily: "Let us learn from this man not
to call the rich lucky nor the poor unfortunate. Rather, if we are to tell
the truth, the rich man is not the one who has collected many possessions
but the one who needs few possessions; and the poor man in not the one

---

[5]Ibid., p. 125.

[6]Ibid., p. 29. And he enumerates them: "He was poor, he was ill, he had no one to help him. He remained in a house which could have relieved all his troubles but he was granted no word of comfort.
He saw the man who neglected him enjoying such luxury, and not only enjoying luxury but living in
wickedness without suffering any misfortune. He could not look to any other Lazarus or comfort
himself with any philosophy or resurrection. Along with the evils I have mentioned, he obtained a bad
reputation among the mass of people because of his misfortunes. Not for two or three days but for his
whole life he saw himself in this situation and the rich man in the opposite" (p. 37).

[7]Ibid., p. 21.

who has no possessions but the one who has many desires."[8]

Now, in this second homily, the time has come for Chrysostom to move to the heart of the matter, having seen the "virtuous disposition" of his audience. It was in death that the veil of confusion, of temporality, of self-imposed ignorance and deceit was finally lifted and the true character of each was revealed. The Evangelist is clear: in this new and eternal condition, freed from pretense and oppression, the rich man became a suppliant to the poor man: "Father [Abraham], have mercy on me, and send Lazarus to dip the tip of his finger in water and cool my tongue" (Lk 16:24). The conclusion is clear, says Chrysostom; "the situation was reversed, and everyone learned who was really the poor man."[9]

But for Chrysostom this trope of irony is not a jubilant eschatological moment of social reversal or a call for the overthrow of the *ordo civilis*. As he follows the biblical narrative, the preacher is aware that he ought not pander to the factions within his congregation by making either poverty itself salvific or wealth a reason for eternal damnation. Chrysostom neither lingers voyeuristically on the suffering Lazarus nor delights in the plight of the rich man. On the contrary, John will be quick and careful to anticipate the objection: Why should the rich man suffer such a terrible fate? What is his crime? Did he do something evil to Lazarus? Did he steal from him? Did he oppress, punish, or abuse him? Is he condemned only because he is rich, or is God a respecter of persons, for Abraham, too, was a wealthy man.

All these objections, argues Chrysostom, miss the point of the story: "Indeed Lazarus suffered no injustice from the rich man; for the rich man did not take Lazarus' money," but his offense was much greater: it was the crime of indifference. For though he did not take Lazarus's money, he failed to share his own: "see the man and his works," he says, "indeed this too is theft, not to share one's possessions."[10] Chrysostom introduces God in *propria persona* to pass judgment: "I sent the poor man Lazarus to your gate to teach you virtue and to receive your love [and] you ignored

---

[8]Ibid., p. 40.
[9]Ibid., p. 46.
[10]Ibid., pp. 49ff.

[him]."[11] Unlike the righteous Abraham, who was proactive in generosity and quick to extend hospitality, who "hunted out those who were going past and brought them into his own house," the rich man of our story overlooked even the one who was lying inside his own gate. Chrysostom alludes to Malachi 3:8-10 to find support for his case: "Accusing the Jews through the prophet, God says, 'The earth has brought forth her increase, and you have not brought forth your tithes; but the theft of the poor is in your houses.' Since you have not given the accustomed offering, he says you have stolen the goods of the poor."[12] Not sharing one's own possessions is indeed theft.

Like Israel of old, each of us, individually, as well as the church as a community, are called to be stewards—the image Chrysostom uses is that of the imperial *oikonomos*—of God's wealth, God's provisions, and distribute it to those in need: "For our money is the Lord's, however we may have gathered it. . . . This is why God has allowed you to have more: not for you to waste on prostitutes, drink, fancy food, expensive clothes, and all the other kinds of indolence, but for you to distribute to those in need"[13] without distinction or limitations.[14]

"The rich must hold their property as stewards for the poor," says Roth.[15] But what does it mean to be stewards for (not of) the poor? To be sure, for Chrysostom, in the late fourth century, such stewardship included patronage and almsgiving, but it did not stop there. That was merely the beginning, for as Leyerle has shown us so clearly:

> Against the ostentatious display that was both the basis and the articulation of status [in fourth-century Antioch, as it is in our time] . . . Chrysostom sketched an alternative economic system in which the rich had to acknowledge their indebtedness precisely to those who were poor and insignificant in the eyes of the world. His message was one of mutuality. He obtained this mutuality by investing the very poor, who had previously been excluded

---

[11]Ibid., p. 48.
[12]Ibid., p. 49.
[13]Ibid., pp. 49-50.
[14]Cf. Leyerle, *John Chrysostom*, pp. 30-43, on Chrysostom's views.
[15]John Chrysostom, *On Wealth and Poverty*, p. 12.

from patron-client relations because they had nothing to contribute [like Lazarus], with a valuable commodity, namely, special access to God.[16]

A Reorientation: From Patronage to *Philia*

A reorientation was necessary. Yet, history tells us that this reorientation was very hard for Chrysostom's audience to accept. Throughout his life—as a priest in Antioch and as a bishop in Constantinople—wealthy Christians found it difficult to be around him, for he always challenged them to take care of the poor. Chrysostom's prodigious energy was not limited to elegiac warnings against the antithetical practices of the wealthy of his time. He insisted that action be taken, and his own life as monk, priest and, eventually, bishop exemplified this reflective purgation he demanded of others.

But we do not live in fourth-century Antioch. Bracketed by utopian dreams on the one hand and apocalyptic nightmares on the other, we find ourselves in unrelenting flux, outside the social and ecclesial customs of Chrysostom's time. We accept without question that the axes that oriented Greco-Roman society, that made up the fabric of late antiquity, namely, the ties of *clientela*, are foreign to us. Yet here we are. "Most people," Steve Long proposes to us, "still seem to have some orientation to their lives; we are not simply spinning on a little blue ball ride through a vast nothingness. . . . While the space and time of modern life are not so structured as to orient us to the end of Christ [which was Chrysostom's ultimate end], our lives are [nonetheless] routinely oriented."[17] Not by ominous or phantasmagoric eccentricities but by commodities of satisfaction and self-indulgence (religious as well as economic), by indolence, always oriented on the axis of the fundamental distinction of "us" and "them."

Most often, our orientating is not much different from that of the rich man in the story. His life, John tells us, was also oriented by indifference: he would step in and out of his house, perhaps many times during the day, and yet he would not even notice Lazarus lying at his doorstep. As such,

---

[16]Leyerle, *John Chrysostom on Almsgiving*, p. 41.

[17]D. Stephen Long and Tripp York, "Remembering: Offering Our Gifts," in *The Blackwell Companion to Christian Ethics*, ed. Stanley Hauerwas and Samuel Wells (Malden, Mass.: Blackwell, 2004), p. 333, referring to Nietzsche's *Untimely Meditations*.

his orientation was one of not simply indifference but a self-referential, blind indifference: "If we suppose that he passed the man by on the first day, he would probably have felt some pity on the second day; if he overlooked him even on that day, he surely ought to have been moved on the third or the fourth or the day after that, even if he were more cruel than the wild beast. But he felt so such emotion."[18]

Throughout these sermons, the preacher invites us to see the daily routine of this man; to see him stepping over the threshold of his courtyard where the suppliant Lazarus would lay incapable of uttering the customary words to entreat for the alms that never came, to go to the marketplace, even perhaps the temple to offer sacrifices for his sins, to put his alms in the box of the poor (though Chrysostom is certain that the latter would never happen, since he did not take care of the one who was at his doorstep) and come back to his home, after a day full of social and religious observance, to walk past Lazarus once more and enter his house "clean" and "satisfied," ready for another lavish banquet, "communion" with his friends. The rich man, Chrysostom argues in these homilies, is not simply a heuristic device—he is us.

But such a telling of the story can be seen a bit unfair to this unnamed rich man and, by extension, to us too. For in the commonly accepted understanding and practice of patronage of his time he could raise an objection and argue that he had no obligation to take care of Lazarus. Lazarus had nothing to offer back. Lazarus could not be a true client. The relationship was broken because the sick and dying Lazarus, due to his sickness and his inability to follow and offer loyalty, praise and prestige to his patron, had already broken the bonds of *clientela*—there is no reciprocity.

It is quite obvious that such an objection is not limited to the realm of antiquity. Our ambivalence toward the poor is often guided by the same expectations of reciprocity. The "get-your-self-up-by-your-bootstraps," "worthy" poor is privileged over the "helpless," who is looked upon with contempt. And though exceptions sometimes are made for the mentally ill, even ecclesial institutions will be deeply affected by these wisps of "wor-

---

[18]John Chrysostom, *On Wealth and Poverty*, p. 21.

thiness" and "unworthiness." We usually frame the discussion in terms of "most profitable use of limited resources," not by the language of "gift," "grace" and "abundance."

John's prescription for the care of the poor springs out of the latter rather than the former. He exhorts us to give without the imposition of limitations on those who receive. He notes that Abraham did not ask an account of the strangers' life, nor did he require them to change their ways. "He simply welcomed all who were passing by. For if you wish to show kindness, you must not require an accounting of a person's life, but merely correct his poverty and fill his need."[19] And he concludes, "The almsgiver is a harbor for those in necessity: a harbor receives all who have encountered shipwreck, and frees them from danger; whether they are bad or good or whatever they are who are in danger, it escorts them into its own shelter. So you likewise, when you see on earth the man who has encountered the shipwreck of poverty, do not judge him, do not seek an account of his life, but free him from his misfortune."[20] This is the idiosyncratic Christian move from "reciprocity" to "gift" and from "patronage" to *philanthropia*.

The Gift: *Philia* with God

In their excellent essay on the character and proper understanding of the "gift"—the "gift" in our case would be the care of the poor—D. Stephen Long and Tripp York explore this theme of reciprocity and make clear the need for its reinterpretation for the Christian community. While most of antiquity would agree with concepts of gifts as contracts, as gift exchanges, based on and perpetuating the memory of debt that obligates reciprocity ad infinitum—for that is what the Roman system of patronage truly was— few in Chrysostom's time would question the efficacy of such a system. After all, such was the basis of the Roman religious system: *do ut des,* "I give that you may give," a principle of reciprocity, contractual at its core, between the divine patron and the human client, which often led to the stoning of the temples of the gods who received the sacrifice but failed to de-

---

[19]Ibid., p. 52.
[20]Ibid.

liver prosperity, health, a good harvest or protection from the enemy.[21]

To break out of such a system of obligation and indebtedness one would have to break out of the political system that accepts it as a first principle and become estranged from the *polis*. Alternatively, as Jacques Derrida proposes, "The absoluteness of duty and responsibility presume that one denounce, refute and transcend at the same time, all duty, all responsibility, and every human law. It calls for a betrayal of everything that manifests itself within the order of universal generality."[22] In which case, Long and York tell us, inevitably, "ethics assumes a singularity, an unconditioned givenness, that refuses everything that has come before, everything that has been measured, ruled, generalized into a law or tradition. Heresy becomes dogma."[23]

Chrysostom does not see this escapism as a valid alternative. On the contrary, he understands the divine mandate to be the new axis of orientation for the church: "I sent the poor man Lazarus to your gate to teach you virtue and to receive your love."[24] Long and York note that such an understanding of the relationship we have with each other will inevitably "lead us more fully into the life of one another while also fulfilling my own life," because in this case "virtues are not grounded in competitive practices where one person's excellence can only be had at the expense of another, but virtue implies a 'cooperative social practice' where one person's achieving or fulfilling her proper function helps the other fulfill her excellence as well."[25]

Chrysostom will find this new reciprocity, this new orientation, in a meal, in God's banquet set for us: the Eucharist. Unlike the bacchanals the rich man of the story set for his flatterers and clients, only an earshot away from the dis-

---

[21]In the Greek East, the Roman insistence on class and power differentiations between patron and client was almost never expressed in those terms. For the Greeks the emphasis was on the ideal of friendship, *philia*, even if between unequals. This model of *philia* was true not only for the common, everyday interactions in the Greek *polis* but held especially true in regard to the imperial system of patronage, making, for example, imperial demands less objectionable and the bonds of friendship much stronger and long-lasting. See also Peter Brown, *Power and Persuasion in Late Antiquity* (Madison: University of Wisconsin Press, 1992).

[22]Jacques Derrida, *The Gift of Death*, trans. David Wills (Chicago: University of Chicago Press, 1994), p. 66.

[23]Long and York, "Remembering," p. 339.

[24]John Chrysostom, *On Wealth and Poverty*, p. 48.

[25]Long and York, "Remembering," p. 340. The latter section echoes the argument by Alasdair MacIntyre, *After Virtue* (Notre Dame, Ind.: University of Notre Dame Press, 1984).

tressed Lazarus, John will look at the banquet that Jesus set and note that it was indeed within the context of that meal that the Lord told those who had gathered around him that they were no longer servants but chosen friends (Jn 15:14-15).[26] A new banquet, a new meal "filled with social meaning, a meaning discovered by those who can read the message [it] contain[s]."[27]

For Chrysostom, the Eucharist is not a narrow, localized event but a new polity based on the bread, the wine, the gathered, the gathering, the community that partakes and those who bear witness; a new order of things in which we transverse the "expected" roles of the banquet, the roles that forge and simultaneously reveal the lines of *clientela* and become part of a holy Banquet, a divine liturgy, now based on our *philia*, our "patronal friendship" with God.

Eucharist: The Economy of Manna

Michael Sherwin points out that "two signs of patronage were eating at the patron's table and wearing the patron's style of clothing."[28] Both of which, Chrysostom explains to the catechumens of his church, are subverted and reinterpreted by Christ as he becomes the food they eat, the drink they drink, the garment they wear. This full identification with Christ opens God's spiritual banquet to them as friends of God.[29]

Chrysostom's instruction does not stop with the newly baptized, however. He turns to his whole congregation and insists that the Eucharist is the paradigmatic banquet of (not for) the poor. Unlike the rich man or earthly kings, God does not hesitate to invite the poor to fill his vestibules and be his honored guests at his spiritual Table. He makes them partakers of that feast, which for Chrysostom is indeed *sub specie aeternitatis*. John turns to warn his congregation:

> See that we suffer not the same with the rich man formerly. He disdained
> even to look upon Lazarus, and did not allow him to share his roof or shelter,
> but he was without, cast away at his gate, nor was he even vouchsafed a word

---

[26]See also Gordon T. Smith, *A Holy Meal* (Grand Rapids, Mich.: Baker Academic, 2005), pp. 9-18; and Geoffrey Wainwright, *Eucharist and Eschatology* (New York: Oxford University Press, 1981).

[27]Michael Sherwin, "Friends at the Table of the Lord: Friendship with God and the Transformation of Patronage in the Thought of John Chrysostom," *New Blackfriars* 85 (July 2004): 394.

[28]Ibid., p. 396.

[29]John Chrysostom *Instructions to Catechumens* 1-2, Patrologia Graeca 49:233.35.

from him. But see how, when fallen into straits, and in want of his help, he failed to obtain it. For if we are ashamed of those of whom Christ is not ashamed, we are ashamed of Christ, being ashamed of His friends. Let your table be filled with the maimed and the lame.[30]

After all, it was Jesus himself who instructed us:

When you give a luncheon or a dinner, do not invite your friends or your brothers or your relatives or rich neighbors, in case they may invite you in return, and you would be repaid. But when you give a banquet, invite the poor, the crippled, the lame, and the blind. And you will be blessed because they cannot repay you, for you will be repaid at the resurrection of the righteous. (Lk 14:12-14)

This is indeed an economy of abundance, an economy of manna, where plenty and grace overflow, precisely because "they cannot repay you." Amid the prevailing economy of this world, the economy of fear, of scarcity and anxiety, the maddening futility of self-preservation and self-interest is supplanted by the Lord's invitation to see ourselves as coparticipants in Christ's giving of himself:

In this act we become Christ's body, which, once it is in us, cannot be contained but must be shared. For it is not conformed to us, but we are conformed to it. To remember this gift as a gift-exchange is to participate in the divine economy whereby Christians are taken into the life of the triune God and become Christ on earth.[31]

In the Eucharist, then, the expected self-referential social norms are reoriented toward the truly other: the triune God. Here, at the Table, our eyes are opened to recognize the one with whom we have been traveling all the way from Jerusalem, and the myopic preoccupation with the ornamental finally has a chance of being redeemed. Here, in the breaking of the bread, it is not only our lives that are transformed but also our affections: "Were not our hearts burning within us" (Lk 24:13-34). The only possible response is, like Cleopas and his companion, to run back and proclaim the

---

[30]John Chrysostom *On First Thessalonians* homily 11; Patrologia Graeca 62:468, Nicene and Post-Nicene Fathers 1-13, 375.
[31]Long and York, "Remembering," p. 343.

good news "and how he had been made known to them in the breaking of the bread" (Lk 24:35).

Thus, in receiving the body of Christ and being conformed to it, it ought not to come as a surprise that the church is charged now to be the body of Christ at work in the world. In this economy of manna, our affections are liberated to notice Lazarus and engage in true fellowship. In this economy the Gnostic ideals of "secret" and "personal" salvation and spirituality are constantly challenged by the profoundly communal: Lazarus who demands our attention. In this new economy of abundance, "attention," as Simone Weil puts it, "is the rarest and purest form of generosity." Only now it flows freely from the Table.

The lesson from the story is clear: We do not need to look beyond the walls of the city (where only the gods and beasts survive) to find the stranger in need—for he is not a stranger after all. He is Lazarus; he lies at our doorstep; we pass him by every day as we go work, as we go to church, as we gather around the Table. The dominical exhortation creates a new topography, the kingdom of God:

> Come, you that are blessed by my Father, inherit the kingdom prepared for you from the foundation of the world; for I was hungry and you gave me food, I was thirsty and you gave me something to drink, I was a stranger and you welcomed me, I was naked and you gave me clothing, I was sick and you took care of me, I was in prison and you visited me. (Mt 25:34-36)

To this the church adds a seventh admonition: we also serve Christ when we take care to bury the dead.[32] In the process, we become the "sheltering" harbor John calls us to be.

---

[32]The burial of the dead was added to the list of six works of mercy, as they are found in Matthew 25:31-46 (feed the hungry, give drink to the thirsty, welcome the stranger, clothe the naked, visit the sick, visit the prisoner) as early as the third century, making the seven collectively known as the seven corporal works of mercy. Traditionally, to the corporal works are added another seven, the spiritual works of mercy, which include instructing the ignorant, counseling the doubters, admonishing sinners, bearing wrongs with patience, forgiving enemies willingly, comforting the afflicted and praying for all. Though not exhaustive, these works of mercy bear witness to the particularity of the church as a community of redeemed persons who are truly the body of Christ in the world.

9

"They Alone Know the Right Way to Live"

The Early Church and Evangelism

Alan Kreider

The ancient church was growing. From several thousands on Pentecost, the Christian movement spread rapidly, east to Syria and into the Persian Empire, south to Egypt and across North Africa, north and west to Asia Minor and to what we call Europe. As it spread geographically, it grew numerically. By the time of Constantine I's accession to the throne in the early fourth century, the Christian communities within the Roman Empire, scattered unevenly, had come to comprise approximately six million people—one tenth of the imperial populace. According to one scholar, this represents a growth, on average, of approximately 40 percent per decade.[1] Christianity was an illegal cult, subject to an imposing variety of disincentives, so its early growth is formidable and question posing. Why did the early church grow?

It is easy to compile a list of reasons for church growth that might seem obvious to us but then to observe that, alas, most of these good ideas do not occur in the sources for early Christianity. The early Christians did not engage in public preaching; it was too dangerous. There are practically no evangelists or missionaries whose names we know. Missionaries are not

---

[1]Rodney Stark, *The Rise of Christianity* (Princeton, N.J.: Princeton University Press, 1996), p. 6.

listed among the church's clergy or functionaries.[2] The early Christians had no mission boards. They did not write treatises about evangelism. In the surviving sermons and catechetical materials there are, to my knowledge, no examples of leaders urging the believers to be evangelistic. The Great Commission, so central in the missionary movement in late Christendom, was hardly mentioned by the Christians in the early centuries.[3] Prayers for the conversion of pagans occur occasionally in the early centuries, but generally as prayers in obedience to Jesus' command to pray for enemies and persecutors.[4] The worship services of the early Christians: were they seeker-sensitive, attempting to interpret the gospel to the pagans who attended? Alas, even this does not fit our modern templates. After Nero's persecution in the mid-first century, the churches in the Roman Empire closed their worship services to visitors. Deacons stood at the churches' doors, serving as bouncers, checking to see that no unbaptized person, no "lying informer," could come into the private space—the "enclosed garden"—of the Christian community.[5]

And yet the church was growing. Officially it was a *superstitio*. Prominent people scorned it. Neighbors discriminated against the Christians in countless petty ways. Periodically the church was subjected to pogroms, and three times it underwent empire-wide waves of persecution. It was hard to be a Christian. Christians knew that by becoming believers they had embraced a demanding life, which made them marginal rather than respectable. And still the church grew. Why?

The church grew in its early centuries, I believe, because it was attractive. People were fascinated by it, drawn to it as to a magnet. The disincentives that I have just rehearsed were real; any potential convert would take them into account. Nevertheless, non-Christians were attracted by

[2]Reidar Hvalvik, "In Word and Deed: the Expansion of the Church in the Pre-Constantinian Era," in *The Mission of the Early Church to Jews and Gentiles*, ed. Jostein Ådna and Hans Kvalbein (Tübingen: Mohr Siebeck, 2000), p. 270.

[3]Norbert Brox, "Zur christlichen Mission in der Spätantike," in *Mission im Neuen Testament*, ed. Karl Kertelge (Freiburg-im-Breisgau: Herder, 1982), pp. 194-97.

[4]Alan Kreider, *Worship and Evangelism in Pre-Christendom*, Alcuin/GROW Joint Liturgical Studies 32 (Cambridge: Grove Books, 1995), p. 7n.

[5]Athenagoras *Legatio* 1.3; *Didascalia Apostolorum* 2.39; Gregory of Pontus *Canonical Epistle* 11; *Testament of Our Lord* 1.36; Cyprian *Epistle* 73 [74].11.

Christians who by the very nature of things could not give witness in the public square. The Christians assembled in private. They met in apartments in tenement blocks, or in self-standing private houses or in clusters of conjoined flats forming "inconspicuous community centers" that were nevertheless private in their appearance.[6] But the Christians themselves, though private, were everywhere. People met them, often without knowing they were Christian, in workplaces. It was in an inconspicuous workshop that a pagan aristocrat found an uneducated Christian telling other workers that the Christians "alone know the way to live."[7] What insolent, insubordinate rubbish! Or, if not in workshops, then in the women's quarters of houses, or in stairways in their apartment buildings or in the streets. There, where Christians were in their typical mode—face-to-face communication—relationships began, friendships developed and people discovered that Christians were attractive and intriguing.

What was it about the Christians that attracted the pagans? One of these attractions was spiritual power. Non-Christians observed that the Christians, even at their weakest, embodied a power that could be construed as divine. In 202, in the amphitheater in Carthage, the soldier Pudens was assigned to oversee the execution of Christians on the emperor's birthday. But Pudens realized, the Christians reported, "that we possessed some great power within us"; shortly thereafter Pudens became a believer.[8] This power manifested itself in the Christians' inexplicable strength under torture and persecution. This power was evident in healings, which were rumored to take place in Christian circles. This power was also evident in exorcisms. Many people in the Greco-Roman world felt themselves in bondage to fate and imprisoned by demonic powers. In the Christian churches there were gifted people—healers, exorcists—who prayed that people would be "liberated from bondage."[9] The Christians' prayers for healing, Tertullian pointed out, were not like the treatments in

---

[6]Richard Krautheimer, *Rome, Profile of a City, 312-1308* (Princeton, N.J.: Princeton University Press, 1980), p. 33.
[7]Origen *Against Celsus* 3.55.
[8]*Passio Perpetuae* 9, 21.
[9]Origen *Against Celsus* 7.17.

the shrines of the pagan healing god Asclepius; they were free, without charge![10] Further, Irenaeus added, the Christian prayers were effective and led to conversion: "those who have been cleansed from evil spirits frequently both believe [in Christ], and join themselves to the church."[11] When conversations took place in workplaces, they often had to do with spiritual power: "I'm sorry your son is ill; we have people who can pray for him. May we help you?"[12]

A second attraction was the distinctive behavior of the Christians, who had question-posing ways of addressing common problems in society. Consider babies, for example. The Christians were committed to the sanctity of life and opposed killing in all forms—abortion, war, gladiatorial games and capital punishment.[13] This is also true in the culturally acceptable custom of discarding unwanted babies. Not only did the Christians refuse to discard their own babies, even when their families were large, they also went to the dumps and rescued unwanted babies of pagan parents, whom they proceeded to raise as their own children.[14] These rescued babies, often girls, are one reason that the proportion of females was extraordinarily high in Christian communities.[15]

Consider also the matter of burial. Ancient people were concerned to be buried with dignity, so they founded burial societies such as the Athenian Association of Iobacchi, the worshipers of Dionysius. This Iobacchic society provided monthly banquets and, when its members died, promised suitable obsequies. If, however, a member was unable to pay the dues, then the member (the society's rules said) "shall be excluded from the gathering"

---

[10]Tertullian *Apology* 37.9. For comment on early Christian healing, see Wolfgang Reinbold, *Propaganda und Mission im ältesten Christentum*, Forschungen zur Religion und Literatur des Alten und Neuen Testaments 188 (Göttingen: Vandenhoek & Ruprecht, 2000), p. 322.

[11]Irenaeus *Against Heresies* 2.34.4.

[12]Ramsay MacMullen, *Christianizing the Roman Empire (A.D. 100-400)* (New Haven, Conn.: Yale University Press, 1984), p. 41; Peter Brown, *The World of Late Antiquity* (London: Thames and Hudson, 1971), p. 55.

[13]E.g., Athenagoras *Legatio* 11, 35; Origen *Against Celsus* 3.7; Lactantius *The Divine Institutes* 5.18; 6.20. See also Alan Kreider, "Military Service in the Church Orders," *Journal of Religious Ethics* 31, no. 3 (2003): 415-42.

[14]O. M. Bakke, *When Children Became People* (Minneapolis: Fortress, 2005), p. 110.

[15]Stark, *Rise of Christianity*, p. 99. Another reason for the disproportionate presence of women in the churches is that women were freer there than elsewhere in ancient society (pp. 109-10).

and get no obsequies.[16] The Christian churches, in contrast, from an early date provided burial—free burial—for all members, even the poorest.[17] This was the purpose of the catacombs. The Christians did not dig the catacombs to provide secure places to worship in times of persecution; instead, they dug them to provide a dignified burial for all Christians, regardless of their economic means.[18] When conversations took place in workplaces, the Christians might say, with the authority of an intriguingly behaving community behind them: we "alone know the right way to live."[19]

Or consider the plague. For eight months in 250 to 251, Christians for the first time were subjected to an empire-wide persecution. Many Christians apostasized, and there was chaos in many churches. Within a few months after the persecution ended with the death of the emperor Decius, a new enemy appeared: the plague, possibly measles. This disease, Cyprian of Carthage reported, "attacks our people equally with the heathens."[20] Wealthy residents, including pagan priests, were leaving the city for the purer air of the countryside. What should Christians do? Cyprian called the Christian community together and urged them not to leave the city but, on the basis of Matthew 5:43ff., to love their enemies—those who had recently persecuted them—as well as their spiritual siblings by providing elementary nursing to all: food, water, visits.[21] And what if the Christians were to die? This, Cyprian admonished, would be no cause for mourning, for the Christians, unlike the pagans, had no reason to fear; there is a "departure to salvation for God's servants."[22] At stake, said Cyprian, was the integrity of the Christian witness. We Christians must not give occasion "to the Gentiles for them deservedly and rightly to reprehend us, that we

---

[16]Ramsay MacMullen and Eugene N. Lane, eds., *Paganism and Christianity, 100-425 C.E.* (Minneapolis: Fortress, 1992), p. 70.

[17]Aristeides *Apology* 15.7; Tertullian *To Scapula* 3.1.

[18]Vincenzo Fiocchi Nicolai, Fabrizio Bisconti and Danilo Mazzoleni, *The Christian Catacombs of Rome* (Regensburg: Schnell & Steiner, 1999), pp. 13ff.; Wolfgang Wischmeyer, *Von Golgatha zum Ponte Molle*, Forschungen zur Kirchen- und Dogmengeschichte 49 (Göttingen: Vandenhoeck & Ruprecht, 1992), p. 160.

[19]Origen *Against Celsus* 3.55.

[20]Cyprian *Mortality* 8.

[21]Pontius *Life of Cyprian* 9.

[22]Cyprian *Mortality* 15.

mourn for those, who, we say, are alive with God. . . . There is no advantage in setting forth virtue by our words, and destroying the truth by our deeds."[23] Led by their bishop, Cyprian, Christians in Carthage stayed in the city and nursed their enemies, as well as other Christians.[24] This question-posing behavior led not only to the missional integrity of the church but also to its numerical growth.[25]

A third attraction was the Christians' common life as resident aliens.[26] The early Christians knew that they were residents; they were like their neighbors in many ways—they wore similar clothing, they ate similar food, they observed the same customs. But they knew that they were aliens; they lived in a microsociety whose values were deviant. This meant that they could be at home anywhere ("Every foreign land is their fatherland"), but that they would be fully at home nowhere ("Yet for them every fatherland is a foreign land").[27] This identity as resident aliens gave the early Christians a catholicity that was countercultural. The Christians, more than their pagan neighbors, had a sense of translocal belonging. The Christians were more mobile than most of their contemporaries; their involvements in trade and emigration were major means by which the church grew globally.[28] So wherever the Christians went, they found nongenetic sisters and brothers who provided hospitality for them, and they maintained relationships across long distances, which they nourished with an astonishing number of letters. Their catholicity was also a product of their deepest theological convictions. Many second-century Christians were confident that God was in the business of reconciliation, that God was going to restore—*recapitulate* was their word—*all* things in Christ. They believed that God had sent Christ "for the reconciliation and restoration of the hu-

---

[23]Ibid., 20.

[24]In the plague of 260, the bishop of Alexandria, Dionysius, led the Christian community there in a similar approach, supported by a similar rationale. See Eusebius *Ecclesiastical History* 7.22.

[25]Stark, *The Rise of Christianity,* chap 4.

[26]For microsociety, see Larry Miller, "The Church as Messianic Society: Creation and Instrument of Transfigured Mission," in *The Transfiguration of Mission,* ed. Wilbert R. Shenk (Scottdale, Penn.: Herald Press, 1993), p. 137; for resident aliens, see Rowan A. Greer, *Broken Lights and Mended Lives* (University Park: Pennsylvania State University Press, 1986), chap. 6.

[27]*Letter to Diognetus* 5.

[28]Reinbold, *Propaganda und Mission,* p. 310; Wischmeyer, *Von Golgotha zum Ponte Molle,* p. 61.

man race."[29] Therefore the Christians' identity was far greater than race or empire. As Tertullian put it, "One state we know, of which we are all citizens—the universe."[30]

The Christians also had an extraordinary sense of local catholicity. Their insistence that poor as well as rich could be buried with dignity was an indicator of their countercultural sociological inclusiveness. Unlike the adherents of other religions, the Christian communities were made up of all sorts and conditions of people. There were women as well as men (and it was, then as now, often women who brought the men); there were illiterates as well as literates; there were people of a wide range of crafts and occupations. In the social pyramid of the time, all parts of the pyramid could be found in the churches except the apex: the aristocratic males, who controlled the economic life and the pagan cults, were absent from the churches. In the Christian microsociety, the richer shared with the poorer—food in Eucharists and agapes, and clothing in church storehouses. Further, many congregations had common funds through which the rich engaged in a "limited material equalization" with the Christian poor.[31] Indeed, conversion to Christ at times could involve a wealthy candidate intentionally simplifying his or her lifestyle. Such was the story of Cyprian, the mid-third-century Carthaginian rhetorician whom we have already met. Cyprian was attracted to the Christian community's freedom from competitive conspicuous consumption. As a pagan, Cyprian dressed elegantly, ate the finest of foods and was surrounded by fawning adherents. Cyprian despised this lifestyle—he called it "gilded torment"—but he also was addicted to it.[32] Cyprian wondered: could he, like the Christians, know the right way to live? Could he be free to live simply, to share? Through friendship with the Christian Caecilianus who became his sponsor, Cyprian became a catechumen. While undergoing catechesis he prac-

---

[29]Irenaeus *Against Heresies* 4.14.2; Justin Martyr *First Apology* 23; Eric Osborn, "Love of Enemies and Recapitulation," *Vigiliae Christianae* 54 (2000): 12-31.
[30]Tertullian *Apology* 38.3.
[31]Peter Lampe, *Die stadtrömischen Christen in den ersten beiden Jahrhunderten*, Wissenschaftliche Untersuchungen zum Neuen Testament, 2. Reihe, 18 (Tübingen: J. C. B. Mohr [Paul Siebeck], 1987), pp. 113-14.
[32]Cyprian *To Donatus* 3.

ticed actions that "loved the poor,"[33] and through a "wondrous" experience in baptism, Cyprian discovered "what I had thought difficult began to suggest a means of accomplishment."[34] For Cyprian, conversion involved downward mobility into the shared life of a community of resident aliens, and this downward journey prepared him for his martyr's death.

All of these things attracted pagans to Christianity. Despite disincentives and persecution, people were drawn to churches in which there was spiritual power, question-posing behavior and a combination of catholicity with community. But what was it that formed Christians and Christian communities so that they would embody these qualities that attracted outsiders? Two community-forming realities stand out: catechesis and worship.

I have already noted that an outsider could not come into a Christian Eucharist unless he or she had been baptized, and at least from the second century believers were not baptized until they had gone through a lengthy process of catechesis. In the early fourth century, in Spain, catechesis could last five years; the *Apostolic Tradition,* probably from the previous century, stated that catechesis could last three years—except when the candidate "is keen, and perseveres well . . . [then] the time shall not be judged, but only [the candidate's] conduct."[35] According to the *Apostolic Tradition,* this had to do with the candidate's treatment of the disadvantaged and weak: "Have they honored the widows? Have they visited the sick? Have they done every kind of good work?"[36] These are questions about question-posing behavior characteristic of a catholic microsociety. Teachers and sponsors taught the candidates a new way of living and of viewing the world.[37] The teachers imparted new narratives—the stories of the Bible, which replaced the traditional narratives of the culture, and gave the candidates biblical texts to memorize—key passages that expressed the Christian community's beliefs and that reinforced its values of economic sharing and nonvi-

---

[33]Pontius *Life of Cyprian* 6.

[34]Cyprian *To Donatus* 4.

[35]*Canons of Elvira* 11; *Apostolic Tradition* 17.

[36]*Apostolic Tradition* 19.

[37]For the content of catechesis, see Kreider, *Worship and Evangelism,* pp. 21-25; idem, *The Change of Conversion and the Origin of Christendom* (1999; reprint, Eugene, Ore.: Wipf & Stock, 2007), pp. 26-32.

olence.[38] Justin reported that the teachers in Rome assisted the candidates to confront, as Cyprian did, their addictions and spiritual bondages and to be liberated from the lures of fornication, the magic arts, materialism ("taking pleasure in the means of increasing our wealth and property") and violence (hating and killing enemies and "people from different tribes").[39] In these catechetical sessions the candidates at times dramatically encountered the power of God; as the catechist Origen put it, exorcistic experiences "lead many people to come to faith."[40] Further, the teachers taught the candidates how Christians live. They taught by their own example; their catechumens were their apprentices in the faith. But they taught also by overseeing the candidates' progress in forms of behavior that were characteristic of the Christian community—care of the poor, works of mercy, nonviolence. When candidates' sponsors could vouch that the candidates were living like Christians, then the candidates underwent the final baptismal preparations: they memorized the Christian creed ("hear the gospel") and learned its meaning; they were given the Lord's Prayer and taught how to pray it; they were exorcized repeatedly, to make sure that all vestigial rule of the evil one was named and dethroned; and, finally, they were baptized in a ritually imposing ceremony.[41]

Why, we may wonder, all this emphasis upon catechesis? After all, in the New Testament, baptism seems to have taken place immediately on a converting experience (e.g., Acts 2:41; 8:37; 10:47; 16:33); why this dithering? The reason goes to the heart of the early Christian approach to mission. The Christians did not offer the world intellectual formulas; they offered a way of life rooted in Christ.[42] The Christians were not mute—they were "talkative in corners," workplaces and face-to-face relationships. But in general their verbal witness grew out of the attractive, distinctive qualities of their

---

[38]Andy Alexis-Baker, "*Ad Quirinum* Book Three and Cyprian's Catechumenate," M.A. thesis, Associated Mennonite Biblical Seminary, April 2007.

[39]Justin Martyr *First Apology* 14. The similarity of Justin's list to Richard Foster's "money, sex and power" indicates the durability of these as areas of human addiction.

[40]Origen *Homilies on Samuel* 1.10.

[41]*Apostolic Tradition* 20-21.

[42]Robert L. Wilken, *The Christians as the Romans Saw Them* (New Haven, Conn.: Yale University Press, 1984), p. 82.

lifestyle. The Christians commented on this. "Beauty of life," Minucius Felix wrote around 200, "causes strangers to join the ranks. . . . We do not preach great things; we live them."[43] Nothing, the Christian leaders knew, could more undercut the mission of the church than baptized Christians who did not embody the message but who instead lived by the same values as pagans. As the catechist Justin put it in Rome: "Those who are found not living as [Christ] taught should know they are not really Christians, even if his teachings are on their lips."[44] Catechesis shaped character; catechesis thereby shaped witness. The *Canons of Hippolytus*, an early fourth-century church order, stated this explicitly: the new believers—catechized and baptized— should "shine with virtue, not before each other [only], but also before the Gentiles so they may imitate them and become Christians."[45]

How then did worship fit in with the church's witness? The church's evangelism and mission were inconceivable without the church's life of worship.[46] The church assembled in worship glorified God; their actions of worship also edified Christians who, formed by worship, lived the question-posing life of God in the world.[47] The offering, for example, of money and goods that believers brought to worship services replenished the church's common fund and redistributed wealth within the community. The sermons reminded believers of the teachings of Jesus and of the Christians' vocation to live these in their lives, for outsiders were watching. One preacher pointed out that it was fine for the believers to talk about a cardinal value of the Christian communities—loving the enemy—but the believers must also love each other. If they do not, the observant outsiders will say that the Christian faith "is a myth and a delusion."[48] The kiss of peace, which Christians in many places practiced weekly, enabled Christians to express their love and unity and, where they were at odds with each other, to make peace

---

[43]Minucius Felix *Octavius* 31.7; 38.5. A century later Lactantius wrote (*The Divine Institutes* 5.20): "We do not entice, as they say; but we teach, we prove, we show."

[44]Justin Martyr *First Apology* 16.

[45]*Canons of Hippolytus* 19.

[46]For an initial exploration of this point, on which there is no detailed study, see Kreider, *Worship and Evangelism* (passim).

[47]For Cyprian's statement of this relationship, see *To Quirinus* 3.26.

[48]*2 Clement* 13.

and experience reconciliation.[49] This peacemaking rite had missional effect. In the amphitheater, just before the Christians were beheaded, the kiss of peace on several occasions was their last act of witness.[50] And in less extreme circumstances, according to the *Didascalia Apostolorum,* it was those who were peaceable who could be missional; those whose peace had been made in worship through the kiss could "convert and tame those who were wild and bring them into her midst."[51] Corporate prayers were the Christians' "greater sacrifice."[52] When the believers gathered together, according to Tertullian, they wrestled with God. We can see them, standing in the posture of the *orans,* hands raised, eyes open, concentrating intensely. These are people who faced difficult circumstances: urban crowding, persecutions, robbers, dangers in travel, poverty, temptations, epidemics, insecure jobs and scornful workmates. We can see the believers "massing our forces to surround him [God]." As the Christians prayed, according to Origen, they sensed that they were joining angelic powers; through this prayer "the Power of Our Lord and Savior Himself" came upon the gathered saints, enabling them to live filled with faith in situations that they could not control.[53] Finally, the Eucharist: as the first three centuries go by, this emerges as central to the worship life of the Christian communities. By the third century, in some places Christians were not only communicating in their Sunday services; daily they ingested consecrated elements, and some people sensed that these elements contained the fiery presence of God, which enabled disciples to shed their blood for Christ.[54] As the martyrs of Abitinia in North Africa put it in 304, "We cannot go without the Lord's Supper."[55]

So in the early centuries, the growth of the church was the product of

[49]Eleanor Kreider, "Let the Faithful Greet Each Other: The Kiss of Peace," *Conrad Grebel Review* 5 (1987): 29-49; Michael Philip Penn, *Kissing Christians* (Philadelphia: University of Pennsylvania Press, 2005).

[50]*Acts of Perpetua* 21; *Martyrdom of Shamuna, Guria and Habib* (Ante-Nicene Fathers 8:701).

[51]*Didascalia Apostolorum* 2.53-54.

[52]Cyprian *The Lord's Prayer* 23.

[53]Origen *On Prayer* 31.5.

[54]Cyprian *The Lapsed* 26; *The Lord's Prayer* 18; *Epistle* 55 [58].1; Andrew McGowan, "Rethinking Agape and Eucharist in Early North African Christianity," *Studia Liturgica* (2004): 133-46.

[55]*Acts of the Abitinian Martyrs* 12 in *Donatist Martyr Stories,* ed. Maureen A. Tilley, Translated Texts for Historians 24 (Liverpool: Liverpool University Press, 1996), pp. 36-37.

the distinctive life of the people, which grew out of their catechesis and was nourished by their worship. Already in the third century, some observers sensed that things were deteriorating—the church's growth in numbers lessened its discipline and affected its witness. In the 240s, Origen, catechizing in Caesarea, spoke wistfully about an earlier period when "the catechumens were catechized in the midst of the martyrs and in the midst of the deaths of those who confessed the truth unto death."[56] In the rest of the third century, numbers—despite three waves of empire-wide persecution—continued to grow. The large numbers changed the character of the church. So also did the advent of imperial approval. From his arrival in Rome in 312 onward, Constantine the Great made a difference for the Christians. Constantine removed the disincentives that Christians had faced, made it legal for Christians to worship as long as they wanted on Sunday (hitherto Christian morning gatherings had to be relatively brief, before the Christians went to work) and gave powerful incentives in the form of financial subsidies and royal approval. In 320, Constantine exempted the Christian clergy from taxation for a reason that was explicitly missional: "That the churches' assemblies may be crowded with a vast concourse of peoples."[57] Constantine especially made Christianity attractive to the aristocratic males who hitherto had been notably absent in the Christian churches. From Constantine's accession, Christianity, which had grown by attraction, began to grow by a new means—advantage. As the fourth century progressed, aristocratic males emerged as leaders in the church, which by the century's end constituted approximately half of the population of the empire.[58] But it was not enough for Christians to have equal status with other religions in a pluralist empire: the architects of the civilization called Christendom agreed with Ambrose of Milan that "there [should] not be a place where Christ was denied."[59] So in the last two decades of the century, the Christian emperor Theodosius I issued two rescripts: the first, of 380, closed down the assemblies of "heretical" Chris-

---

[56]Origen *Homilies on Jeremiah* 4.3.
[57]*Codex Theodosianus* 16.2.10.
[58]MacMullen, *Christianizing the Roman Empire*, p. 83.
[59]Ambrose *Epistle* 40.8.

tians, whom it called "demented and insane"; the second, of 392, prohibited pagan worship, private or public.[60] In various parts of the empire, armies and militant monks smashed pagan temples and looted their treasures.[61] So the Christian church, which before Constantine had grown by attraction and since Constantine had grown by advantage, began to grow in numbers by a third means—compulsion. In 529, the emperor Justinian I brought this compulsory growth of the church to conclusion with a rescript that required the entire populace of the Roman Empire to be baptized.[62] The ancient church offers us three models for church growth.

The result of this growth is the civilization that since the seventh century has called itself Christendom. It has lasted in Europe and in other countries settled by Europeans for fifteen hundred years. Christendom assumes a special relationship between the church and empire—a Christian empire; it presupposes an equivalence between civil population and church membership—the church is society, not a microsociety. And the Christendom church achieved these goals by modulating the positions of the church on key issues to fit in with the values of the wider society, including those of the aristocratic males, and by altering the method of evangelism—from attraction to compulsion.

So, from the late fourth century onward, as Christendom took shape in the West, Christians had power and control, but some people felt that Christians had lost the plot. What has happened to Christianity when a pagan, being urged to convert to Christianity, points to the Christians he knows and says, "Do you want me to be like that so-and-so, or the other one?"[63] Something has mutated, and the church was no longer able to grow by its earlier methods, including the attractive quality of the believers' lives. When Christians become rich and conventional, when they coerce

---

[60] *Codex Theodosianus* 16.1.2; 16.5.42.
[61] W. H. C. Frend, "Monks and the End of Greco-Roman Paganism in Syria and Egypt," *Cristianesimo nella Storia* 11 (1990): 469-84.
[62] For the changes in the Christians' means of growth within the fourth century, see Alan Kreider, "Violence and Mission in the Fourth and Fifth Centuries," *International Bulletin of Missionary Research* 31, no. 3 (2007): 125-33; idem, "Beyond Bosch: The Early Church and the Christendom Shift," *International Bulletin of Missionary Research* 29, no. 2 (2005): 59-68.
[63] Augustine *Sermon* 15.6.

and persecute—for the best of reasons, even "love"—they are engaged in what one might call a false mutation, which has made them different from the Christians of the earlier centuries and different from Jesus Christ. This has had huge consequences for the church's life and evangelism.

One person who observed this happening was John Chrysostom. In the 380s, preaching in Antioch, John asserted, "There would be no heathen . . . if we kept the commandments of Christ." Instead, he observed, Christians had become worldly. They were afraid of death, in love with money and mesmerized by power. God's power was no longer evident in miracles.[64] In the past, when Christians had lived distinctively, pagans had been intrigued. But now, with Christians living just like everybody else, pagans were recalcitrant in their paganism.[65]

That was sixteen hundred years ago. But today, in the West, the Christian church is living in the shadow of Christendom, and conditions are similar. We American Christians live in a society that has unprecedented material wealth. We spend billions of dollars on cosmetics and cat food. In 2005, our government alone spent 43 percent of the world's military expenditure.[66] Nevertheless, our society is full of discontent and dread. Many Christians are afraid, not only concerning their own safety or for their children's well-being but also that the church in the United States is losing momentum as it has done in Europe. People sense that the prognosis for Christianity in the United States is unpromising—unless Christians in the United States learn how to be evangelistic.

But what shape should evangelism in the United States take? Diagnoses differ. Does the ancient faith offer us wisdom for the church's future? I believe that the early church—especially the early church prior to the late fourth century when Theodosius I made Christianity the only legal religion—has much to teach us.

Faith-sharing, today as in the early church, happens in the context of

---

[64]E.g., Ambrose *The Sacraments* 2.15.
[65]John Chrysostom *Homilies on 1 Timothy* 10.
[66]"US Military Spending vs. the World," *Center for Arms Control and Non-Proliferation*, February 5, 2007 <www.globalissues.org/Geopolitics/ArmsTrade/Spending.asp#InContextUSMilitarySpending VersusRestoftheWorld>.

friendship. Faith-sharing is not primarily the product of evangelistic programs; it is a byproduct of face-to-face relationships in which there is no program and no goal—simply the communication of people who value each other and can share what is central to their lives, while all parties listen. If the gospel is precious to us Christians, if God is at work in our lives and our churches and our world, we Christians will speak about it to the people we care about.

It is all right to live without being in control. The evangelist Paul tell us that God's power is made perfect in weakness (2 Cor 12:9), and the early Christians whom we have been studying would tell us that encounters with God's reality in prayer and worship—and experiences of the manifestations of divine power—take place not when Christians are in control but when Christians are needy and therefore are dependent on God. "Prayer," missiologist Jonathan Bonk has written, on the basis of his experience of Christians from many countries, "is the resort of weak, overwrought, desperate people whose life circumstances call for resources beyond their own."[67] And when God answers their cry from a place of weakness, when God heals, supplies, protects and comforts, the world takes note and people come to faith.

Jesus calls us to live in ways that are unconventional, and these question-posing ways are interesting to outsiders—far more interesting than culturally conventional ways of living smothered by Christian rhetoric. What are today's equivalents of the early Christians' babies, burial and response to the plague? These equivalents can be unostentatious: a Christian lawyer who, responding to the biblical practice of Jubilee, quietly gives to the poor his entire earnings for his forty-ninth year. These equivalents can be deeply counterintuitive. In October 2006, a lone gunman broke into an Amish school in Nickel Mines, Pennsylvania, shot to death five Amish schoolgirls and then shot himself. To this the Amish response was one of reflexive forgiveness—forgiveness for the killer, forgiveness for his family. "Do not leave this area," the Amish delegation told the family of the murderer.

---

[67]Jonathan J. Bonk, *Missions and Money*, American Society of Missiology series 15, rev. ed. (Maryknoll, N.Y.: Orbis, 2006), p. 94.

"Stay in your home here. We forgive this man."[68] The response to this, globally, was remarkable. Within two weeks of the shootings, four thousand news stories worldwide were written about the Christian virtue of forgiveness and about the kind of Christian community in which forgiveness was reflexive behavior.[69] This was an example of lived apologetics. Today, as in the early centuries, when Christians do what Jesus says in areas that touch their security, the world takes notice. And outsiders ask questions: "Is *this* what Christianity is about? Why don't Christians do this kind of thing more often?"

The Christian church is a social reality that is called to embody the gospel. Wherever we find ourselves as Christians, we face the challenge of being both resident and alien. One characteristic way that we Christians can be resident aliens is through affirming our calling to be catholic, by sharing a primary identity with Christians who live on the other side of the world and in other periods of history and by sharing a common life locally with Christians of every stratum of society with whom we will share time and wealth. When we as Christian churches live this vision, the watching world asks of us, as they asked of the early Christians, with curiosity, admiration, irritation and envy, "What is it that those people have in common? They seem to love each other. Why?"

We Christians do not learn these gospel ways from the wider culture, even from a professedly Christendom culture; instead we learn these gospel ways and are reflexed to live them when our faith communities model and teach them. Today, a growing number of Christians are aware how deeply we are all catechized by the media, peer pressure and advertising. We are aware that we are offered not only many things to fear but also many panaceas that advertisers and politicians promise will salve our insecurities and deliver security, longevity and beauty. We are coming to realize that if we Christians are to have an alternative to this seductive Western obviousness, we will need to *be* an alternative to this obviousness. And the

---

[68]Quoted by Joan Chittister, "What Kind of People Are These?" *National Catholic Reporter,* October 9, 2007.

[69]Donald B. Kraybill, Steven M. Nolt and David L. Weaver-Zercher, *Amish Grace* (San Francisco: Jossey-Bass, 2007).

only way that we can become this alternative and embody a vision that we can offer to non-Christians will come through a renewal of catechesis—apprenticing—in our churches which forms, resocializes, re-reflexes Christians to be disciples of Jesus Christ.[70] Some of our churches catechize before baptism (in the believers baptism traditions); others catechize after baptism (in the pedobaptist traditions); many of our churches catechize lightly or not at all. Whatever our approach, it is vital that we undertake catechesis seriously and unhurriedly, as the third-century *Apostolic Tradition* did; further, that we ponder, as Cyprian did in Carthage, how Christ is formed within us so that we Christians will be free to live riskily.

Worship: a renewal of worship is essential to Christians who want to share the gospel of Jesus Christ. Many Christians today think about the relationship between worship and mission. Some think primarily in terms of culture. They are convinced that for Christians to become evangelistically effective, our churches' worship services must break through a "culture barrier" so that we will employ "the language, music, style, architecture, and art forms of the target population."[71] Others concentrate on the worshipers' experience. What matters is not what is culturally relevant or what "multisensory" things we do in worship, but rather "how our hearts worship the Lord."[72] Both of these approaches have something to offer. I am suggesting, however, that we are more likely to move forward in evangelism if we allow the early Christians to stretch our imaginations. Remember: in the early Christian centuries, the churches did not allow outsiders into their worship services, and deacons stood at the door to keep the unbaptized out! The churches' worship services were not designed to be evangelistic. Nor were their services designed to move the hearts of the worshipers. The churches' acts of worship rather were designed to glorify God and to form the worshipers into attractive, intriguing disciples of Jesus Christ and their congregations into communities that embodied the

---

[70]Alan Kreider, "Baptism and Catechesis as Spiritual Formation," in *Remembering Our Future*, ed. Andrew Walker and Luke Bretherton (Milton Keynes, U.K.: Paternoster, 2007), pp. 170-206.

[71]George G. Hunter III, "The Case for Culturally Relevant Congregations," in *Global Good News*, ed. Howard Snyder (Nashville: Abingdon, 2001), p. 98.

[72]Dan Kimball, *Emerging Worship* (Grand Rapids, Mich.: Zondervan, 2004), p. 112.

ways of Jesus. So let us go to our churches' worship services expecting to meet God, to pray passionately, to be renewed by God's story told and God's Word proclaimed, to be fed at the Lord's Table. And through all this let us ask God to empower us to be people who question society's values of violence, wealth, security and control and who have the freedom and imagination necessary to experiment with alternatives.

How will this affect our evangelism? Non-Christians will look at our communities and us and be offended or intrigued. In the tradition of the early Christians, we might begin by inviting our non-Christian friends not to church services but to work with us in tasks that are expressions of our Christian discipleship. Let them join us in renovating a house in our run-down neighborhood or in learning the disciplines and skills of victim-offender reconciliation or in feeding poor people in a soup kitchen or in eating regular communal meals in our homes. In these settings our friends can find out what the lordship of Jesus Christ means in practice; they can experiment with this in hands-on ways; and they can converse seriously about the faith of the Christian church. These activities build friendships. And when the time is right, our non-Christian friends will come to Christian worship, where they will encounter not a service that is designed for them but a service that is the believing community's offering to God. In this service, believers encounter the reality of God and are empowered to take part in God's mission in the world, and inquirers will take Christian worship seriously because they have come to believe, on the basis of the evidence that they have seen, that God is real and transforms the lives of those who believe. It is people who encounter God in worship and who in worship are renewed in a deviant story of what it is to be fully alive as humans, who will be able, in conversations with non-Christians, to say "we alone know the right way to live." And, if the wisdom of the ancient church is relevant today, the outsiders will be fascinated by the integrity of their Christian friends and the vitality of their communities and will want to know more.

PART FOUR

Theology of
the Early Church

Worship, Christology and Politics

10

Embodying the Wisdom
of Ancient Liturgical Practices

Some Old-Fashioned Rudimentary Euchology
for the Contemporary Church

John D. Witvliet

When my students and I approach the ancient church, we are on a quest for liturgical wisdom. As practical theologians we are ultimately interested in discovering wisdom to ground and inspire faithful liturgical practice to-day.[1] One of the most robust veins of wisdom we have discovered is located in the outlines, structures and patterns of ancient intercessory prayers. At first blush, structures and patterns seem to have more to do with order than mystery, the charisma of the early church that is so attractive to a variety of postmodern audiences. But as with the Old Testament Psalms and the New Testament Pauline letters, early church liturgical texts are essentially contextualized improvisations on established patterns. And those patterns are chock full of theological and pastoral significance.

In the heyday of nineteenth- and twentieth-century liturgical move-

---

[1]This search for wisdom is similar to Kevin Vanhoozer's discussion of phronesis and sapiential approach to theology and ministry. See his *The Drama of Doctrine: a Canonical-Linguistic Approach to Christian Theology* (Louisville: Westminster John Knox Press, 2005), pp. 329ff. See also Valerian John Odermann, "Interpreting the Rule of Benedict: Entering a World of Wisdom," in *American Benedictine Review* 35, no. 1 (1984): 25-49. This wisdom can be sharpened through attention to exemplary and nonexemplary, common and idiosyncratic practices.

ment scholarship, the patterns of prayers, especially eucharistic prayers, were a primary object of study, as scholars drew upon methods sharpened in higher-critical studies of Scripture and in textual criticism of many documents from patristic and medieval sources.[2] Evangelicals were introduced to the fruits of this work, in part, by Robert Webber. Already in *Worship Is a Verb* (1985), Webber argued for the theological significance of form, contrasting biblically grounded worship with—instructively—the kind of agnostic formlessness of *Waiting for Godot*. Attention to the large patterns of worship subsequently became a hallmark of many of Webber's writings.

One of Webber's enduring pedagogical moves was to distinguish between the content, the form and the style of worship. This simple move was designed to take seriously the stylistic concerns of his audience, but also to protect space for consideration of other topics. It was Webber's way of insisting that there is more to worship and its study than concern for the style or technique of preaching and songwriting.[3]

In general, evangelicals have done well at energizing and deepening discussions about Webber's first category, the content or theology of worship, producing numerous studies and sermons on various worship-related scriptural texts and a continuing stream of books on the theology of baptism, preaching, music and the Lord's Supper. But evangelicals have given much less attention to the form or pattern of worship. There are, to be sure, many persistent patterns in various streams of evangelical worship—inevitably so. In a revival the altar call comes after the sermon. In a seeker service the situation-in-life drama comes before the sermon. In praise and worship the "worship time" comes before the "teaching time," and a song sequence that begins in "praise" ends in "worship," a journey from exuberance to intimacy. Children, youth workers and even seminary students are

---

[2]See, for example, Anton Baumstark, *Comparative Liturgy* (London: A. R. Mowbray, 1958), and Josef A. Jungmann, *The Mass of the Roman Rite* (New York: Benziger Brothers, 1959). With some exceptions, more recent historical scholarship has focused on moving beyond analysis of texts alone and giving more attention to the genetic history of textual development, rather than their pastoral significance.

[3]See Robert Webber, *Ancient-Future Faith: Rethinking Evangelicalism for a Postmodern World* (Grand Rapids: Baker, 1999), in which chap. 12 bears the title "Recovering the Theology and Order of Worship"; and his *Worship Is a Verb* (Waco, Tex.: Word Books, 1985), in which chap. 2 bears the title "The Order of Worship."

often taught to balance a prayer by using the acronym ACTS (adoration, confession, thanksgiving, supplication). In other congregations what is utterly predictable is that the service will contain no feeling of predictability; surprise and variety become protected species. So evangelicals certainly have forms or patterns in worship, but not necessarily a lot of practice in assessing what those forms mean, what they highlight or obscure and how adequate they might be.[4]

One of the primary reasons for evangelicalism's failure to accord serious attention to form, I suspect, is evangelicalism's longstanding ambivalence about ritual, habit and pattern. In the last two decades it has become quite acceptable for evangelicals and Catholics to work together on common social issues and even to gently probe doctrinal comparisons. But evangelicals still love to critique formalism. The very thought that something might become ritualistic is enough to quench emerging fires of enthusiasm for most patterned activity, even if that activity is cloaked in the language of "spiritual disciplines." And this persistent concern about formalism fuels persistent worries about form itself.[5]

Yet matters of form are not only inevitable; they are also significant, both theologically and pastorally. For one, different forms are good at doing different things. Consider forms in music, for example.[6] Theme and variation form, for example, is especially good at giving a composer the opportunity to demonstrate creativity, and giving an audience the delightful experience of trying to listen for the main theme through (usually) an ever-growing complexity of harmony, countermelody and rhythm. Symphonic form rests on the

---

[4] Barry Liesch's *The New Worship* (Grand Rapids, Mich.: Baker, 1996) is one of the few books to reflect on the structure of worship.

[5] We need constant reminders that the most acerbic critique in the Old Testament is not a critique of form and ritual but rather formalism and ritualism.

[6] On the significance of form in art and music generally, see Suzanne Langer, *Feeling and Form: A Theory of Art* (New York: Scribner's, 1953); *Philosophy in a New Key: A Study in the Symbolism of Reason, Rite and Art* (Cambridge, Mass.: Harvard University Press, 1942); and *Problems of Art* (New York: Scribner's, 1957). Langer's influence among liturgical scholars is evidenced in the frequent use of the term *significant form* in recent writings by liturgists. See Don Saliers, *Worship as Theology: A Foretaste of Glory Divine* (Nashville: Abingdon, 1994), p. 214; Gordon Lathrop, *Holy Things: A Liturgical Theology* (Minneapolis: Fortress Press, 1993), p. 206; Graham Hughes, *Worship as Meaning: A Liturgical Theology for Late Modernity* (Cambridge: Cambridge University Press, 2003), pp. 160-65; A. G. Martimort, "Structure and Laws of the Liturgical Celebration," in *The Church at Prayer: An Introduction to the Liturgy* (Collegeville, Minn.: Liturgical Press, 1985).

assumption, now generally proven by modern psychologists, that we respond favorably to music we recognize. So after introducing a melody to its audience, symphonists take their audience on a journey through various subsidiary melodies and keys, all of which—in part—set up the return of the opening melody, inviting audiences to experience that familiar melody in new and compelling ways. The moment of recognition of the original melody is often a moment of significant musical satisfaction or surprise. Symphonies that don't achieve that satisfaction or surprise are often quickly forgotten.

Forms also matter in worship music. Repetitive Taizé choruses (music from the Taizé community in France, which has been sung worldwide) as well as some contemporary worship songs are well suited to capturing an emotion and then helping worshipers dwell in or "center" on that feeling over time. In contrast, a ballad, whether in a contemporary song or narrative hymn, is good at telling a story. A traditional multiple stanza hymn, in turn, is effective at presenting the development of a theological idea, unpacking the beauty of a metaphor or juxtaposing multiple ideas or metaphors in ways that create new insight. Michael Hawn offers one of the best analyses of liturgical forms to date, unpacking the value of both cyclical and sequential musical forms for the life of faith.[7] His point is that forms carry meaning. They both highlight and obscure certain specific emphases.

Briefly stated, this chapter is designed to develop some old-fashioned (trusting older methods of scholarship), rudimentary (covering only the most basic structural points) euchology (the study of prayer) for the contemporary church (unapologetic about the use of history in this way). It will offer a series of basic observations about the patterns of three prominent early church types of liturgical prayer, along with a summary of the wisdom they embody.

Analysis: Case Studies in Ancient Euchology

Exhibit A: Intercessory prayer litanies. For our first example, consider Eastern and Western intercessory prayer litanies from the third to fifth centu-

---

[7]Michael Hawn, "Form and Ritual: Sequential and Cyclic Musical Structures and Their Use in Liturgy," in *Gather into One* (Grand Rapids: Eerdmans, 2003) pp. 224-40.

ries. When we study these documents we join Martin Bucer and John Calvin, among others, whom we should really think of as patron saints of the "ancient-future" worship movement because of the way they studied texts like these and then worked to restore similar approaches to corporate intercessory prayer in their Reformation liturgies.[8]

These prayers come from one of three spots in emerging structures of worship: (1) near the opening of worship, usually in a litany built around the refrain *Kyrie eleison* (Lord, have mercy), (2) after the reading and preaching of Scripture and before the Lord's Supper, a typical place for the "prayers of the people" in many churches even today, and (3) near the conclusion of the eucharistic prayer, after the thanksgiving for salvation history.[9] These intercessory prayers differ in detail in many interesting and provocative ways, but they also would strike modern readers as being remarkably similar in form.

Limitations of space permit me to cite just one example, the intercession from the fifth-century Gelasian sacramentary.[10]

> The Litany *(deacon):* Let us all say, Lord, hear and have mercy. Father Unbegotten, and Son of God Begotten not made, and Holy Spirit of God, the breath of the faithful, we pray, *Kyrie eleison.*
>
> • For the spotless church of the living God, constituted throughout the whole world, we entreat the riches of divine gifts, *Kyrie eleison.*
> • For holy priests and ministers of the Mighty God, and all people worshiping the true God, we pray Christ our Lord, *Kyrie eleison.*
> • In particular, for all teaching rightly the Word of Truth, the manifold Wisdom of the Word of God, we pray, *Kyrie eleison.*

---

[8]Calvin's liturgy, after all, was titled "Form of Church Prayers After the Use of the Ancient Church." As Hughes Oliphant Old concludes, "The prayer of intercession is one of the clearest examples of the Reformer's use of patristic literature in their liturgical reforms. With the help of Ambrose, Augustine, Tertullian, they were able to restore to their worship an important form of prayer which had been lost from the Roman Mass" (*The Patristic Roots of Reformed Worship* [Zurich: Theologischer Verlag, 1975], p. 250).

[9]See W. Jardine Grisbrooke, "Intercession at Eucharist: I.," *Studia Liturgica* 4 (1965): 129-55.

[10]Gelasian Sacramentary, as translated in Marion J. Hatchett, *Seven Pre-Reformation Eucharistic Liturgies: Historic Rites Arranged for Contemporary Celebration* (Sewanee, Tenn.: University of the South, 1973), pp. 48-49. The text has been formatted in such a way as to help students perceive the structure of the text more quickly.

- For those who keep themselves chaste in mind and body for the sake of the Kingdom of heaven, and exert themselves in spiritual labors, we pray for plentifulness of spiritual gifts, *Kyrie eleison.*
- For all religious rulers and their soldiers, who prize justice and right judgment, we implore the Power of the Lord, *Kyrie eleison.*
- For agreeable weather and opportune rains and caressing vital winds and the prosperity of divers times rightly ordered, Lord of the world, we pray, *Kyrie eleison.*
- For those who for the first time into the name of Christian are initiated, whom now the desire for heavenly grace inflames, we pray for mercy to Almighty God, *Kyrie eleison.*
- For those who are involved in the weakness of the infirmities of humanity, in envy of spiritual wickedness or various errors of the world, we implore the mercy of the Redeemer, *Kyrie eleison.*
- For those who are of necessity traveling, or are oppressed by the powers of iniquity, or are vexed by hostile hardships, we pray the Lord the savior, *Kyrie eleison.*
- For those deceived by heresy or superstition, we pray the Lord of Truth, *Kyrie eleison.*
- For doers of good works, and those who assist in the necessary labors of brotherly charity, we pray the Lord to have mercy, *Kyrie eleison.*
- For all within this holy House of the Lord, that they may be turned to religious hearers and devout pray-ers, we pray the Lord of Glory, *Kyrie eleison.*
- For the cleansing of our souls and bodies, and forgiveness of sins, we pray the merciful Lord, *Kyrie eleison.*
- For refreshment of faithful souls, particularly of priests of the Holy Lord, who preside over this catholic church, we pray the Lord the spirit and judge of all flesh, *Kyrie eleison.*
- Mortification of sins of the flesh and quickening of the life of faith, *Grant, Lord, grant.*
- Holy fear and love of truth, *Grant, Lord, grant.*
- A pleasant ordering of life and a creditable end, *Grant, Lord, grant.*
- An angel of peace and holy consolation, *Grant, Lord, grant.*
- Hear, Lord, the voice of your family who cry for preservation.

First, the pattern intentionally covers a wide range of topics. This prayer text, like nearly all the examples we have of similar texts, offers relatively few words about a lot of topics, instead of a lot of words about a few topics. This concern for breadth is grounded in biblical injunctions to pray prayers for those in authority (1 Tim 2:1-8), enemies (Mt 5:44), laborers in the vineyard (Mt 9:38), the afflicted, rain (Jas 5), the needs of the church (Phil 4), and the needs of fellow Christians (Eph 6). It is similar to the sixteenth-century prayer prepared by Thomas Cranmer with the title "Prayer for the Whole State of Christ's Church Militant Here on Earth." The point is to help us get beyond the inevitable limitations of our personal prayers to pray with a very large scope of concern.

This breadth of concern suggests a robust understanding of the scope of divine activity in both human lives, institutions and in creation itself. A prayer for God to act in a given arena is, in fact, a veiled statement of confession that God can act in that arena (intercessory prayers are not likely, then or now, to be offered for something that the prayer does not believe God can or will do).

This breath of concern is also marked by a balance of global and local concern. These texts view the world through both a wide-angle and zoom lens. The typical pattern is to begin with the world, narrow to the world-wide church and after a time to zoom in on the local assembly and its needy ones.

Second, these prayers reflect a high ecclesiology, especially when viewed from the context of North American evangelicalism. They give significant attention to clergy. They establish the relationship of the local clergy with the clergy of the worldwide, catholic church, as well as the link between the local congregation and the worldwide, catholic church. They convey the sense that the church is called to vicarious prayer for the needs of the world. The prayer is, we might say, a liturgical outworking of the Nicene confession in "one, holy, catholic and apostolic church."

Third, the use of a refrain in these prayers conveys the importance of the assembly's participation in worship. The presider speaks no more than twenty words before the congregation is asked to declare its assent.

In sum, ancient patterns of prayer challenge us to pray (1) for a wide range of creation, global, ecclesial and local needs, (2) with acute awareness of the breadth of divine activity in each of these arenas, (3) with a clearly articulated view of the local and catholic church, and (4) with congregational assent as part of a genuinely corporate prayer. We could phrase this wisdom in proverb form:

> Wise is the church whose prayer life stretches to match the full range of divine activity, gives balanced attention to both local and global concerns of the world and the church, and encourages communal participation and assent.

These types of prayers may also, of course, obscure important features of prayer. They do not dwell for long on a given topic. As finished texts they don't appear to be flexible enough to accommodate unique and unforeseen circumstances, though it may well be that in practice these texts were more like a guide to an improvisatory prayer than a straightjacket of a set text. But these caveats do not detract from the wisdom we find in them or from the force with which that wisdom might interrogate our present practices.

How might we embody this wisdom today? The answer depends a lot on the context.

Congregations in traditions that self-consciously use these ancient patterns today (Orthodox, Catholic, Episcopalian, Lutheran, certain streams of Reformed/Presbyterian and Methodist churches) might begin by simply calling attention to the wisdom of the way they already practice prayer. Sometimes we think something is good simply because it is old, but it may also be true that it is old because it is so good. Liturgical catechesis that explores its intrinsic wisdom may redirect and deepen how typical worshipers experience it.

That wisdom may well also continue to help these traditions in the process of liturgical renewal. Vatican II called for the restoration of "elements which have suffered injury through accidents of history . . . to be restored to the vigor which they had in the days of the holy Fathers, as may seem useful or necessary."[11]

---

[11]*Constitution on the Sacred Liturgy*, p. 50.

Congregations in other Christian traditions are likely to imagine quite different possibilities for embodying this wisdom. One emergent evangelical church, for example, created a form for intercessory prayer that "prayed through the Sunday newspaper": each Sunday the pastor took the Sunday newspaper headlines, projected them for the congregation to see, offered an improvised prayer in response to each one and invited the congregation to respond with "Amen." The result features the same breadth of concern and a pattern of common assent that these early texts demonstrate. In this case, the proverb-like wisdom distilled from an ancient pattern became the springboard for innovation that was more deeply rooted than might otherwise have been the case.

Churches in all traditions, then, can be prompted by an encounter with these ancient practices to grow in grace and knowledge.

Exhibit B: The collect. For our second example, we will consider arguably the most recognizable traditional liturgical prayer form, the collect.[12] At minimum, the collect form dates back to fifth-century Roman texts for the entrance rite, as found in the Leonine and Gelesian sacramentaries.[13] It became a staple of Anglican prayers in the sixteenth century, and today is found in literally hundreds of prayer books for personal use published in nearly every Christian tradition, including evangelical devotionals that are used by people who otherwise may actively resist the use of set prayers in worship.

Many recently published liturgical manuals and textbooks take time to describe a simple outline of a collect. It consists of

- a statement of address to God
- a description of God in terms of a specific attribute or action
- a petition for divine action

---

[12]Collect prayers gain meaning from a lot more than their form. In the structure of the liturgy as a whole, the collect can serve to make common what has been private (literally "collect the prayers of the people"). For an introduction to the history of this prayer form see the excellent introduction in A. Corrêa, *The Durham Collectar* (London: Boydell Press, 1991), and Martin Dudley, *The Collect in Anglican Liturgy: Texts and Sources, 1549-1989* (Collegeville, Minn.: Liturgical Press, 1994).

[13]However, prototypes of this pattern can easily be found in, among other sources, Acts 4:24-30, *Didache* 9—10, the scattered prayers of blessing in the *Apostolic Constitutions* as well as in Psalm collects for use at the daily office that date back to the fifth century.

- a statement of result

- a statement of mediation, such as "through Jesus Christ our Lord"

This simple form gives us some of the most recognizable prayers in the history of worship, such as this collect for purity:

> Almighty God, to you all hearts are open, all desires known and from you no secrets are hid: cleanse the thoughts of our hearts by the inspiration of your Holy Spirit, that we may perfectly love you and worthily magnify your holy name, through Christ our Lord, Amen.

Millions of Christians have offered prayers in this form. Some have so internalized this form that when they pray extemporaneously, they end up improvising a collect. But while this form is frequently used and described, much less attention has been given to what this form means, to what it highlights and what it obscures.

First, prayers in this form address God in personal terms, reflecting what Emmanuel Levinas, Ninian Smart and Graham Hughes call the "vocative dimension of worship."[14] This is not a form of prayer as introspective contemplation. It is a prayer of personal address that most often conveys in the address a sense of divine transcendence.

Second, prayers in this form usually give relatively significant attention to divine attributes and mediation. A lot of time in the prayer is spent simply getting it started and ended, naming God (parts 1 and 2) and naming the mediation (part 5) on which the prayer depends. A modern student could feel the force of this by replacing a typical five-minute extemporaneous prayer with praying a set of ten or so collects. The concluding statement of mediation "through Jesus Christ, our Lord" (or its longer trinitarian version "through Jesus Christ our Lord, who lives and reigns with you and the Holy Spirit, one God, now and forever") is particularly significant as a source of trinitarian piety and formation. In A.D. 393, the Synod of Hippo mandated that the opening collect of worship be addressed to the Father, with a statement of mediation that acknowledged the work of the

---

[14]See Graham Hughes, *Worship as Meaning: A Liturgical Theology for Late Modernity* (Cambridge: Cambridge University Press, 2003), p. 282.

Son and Spirit.[15] This prayer then offers explicit acknowledgment of a trinitarian theology of worship as a graced event. And it is this prayer form that offers the historical basis for James Torrance's influential, *Worship, Community and the Triune God of Grace.*[16]

Third, collect prayers balance and interconnect praise and petitions. Parts (2) and (3) are almost always about the same length. And they are almost always shaped in response to each other. The genius of the collect lies in the apt pairing of attribute and petition, with the acknowledgment of a past action of God grounding a petition for similar future action. The things God has done in the past are linked with what we pray for in the future. As such, this prayer form is an expression of divine constancy: God is trusted to act in ways that are consistent with past divine activity. In contrast, the ACTS acronym works to rebalance prayer, but not necessarily to help us think about the best flow or connection between one part and the others.

The logical correlative of this linkage is that the form or pattern of the prayer offers resistance to some intercessions. Those who pray collects are not likely to pray for God to do something for which no precedent can be found. In the words of Swiss liturgical theologian J. J. von Allmen, "Christian prayers must not express any statement or wish, but should be controlled by what we know of God's will revealed in Jesus Christ."[17] The form is thus an outworking of the logic of Psalm 68:28: "Show us your strength, O God, as you have done before." Petition is always grounded in praise. Prayers for God's future work begin with a look back to the past.

For prayers based on specific biblical texts and events, this pattern of interconnections also fosters a theocentric hermeneutic which resists any supersessionism—a way to pray Scripture that bears some resemblance in this way to lectio divina and "composition of place." When they follow Scripture, these little prayers foster a theocentric hermeneutic (drawing

---

[15]Josef A. Jungmann, *The Early Liturgy* (Notre Dame, Ind.: University of Notre Dame Press, 1959), pp. 295-97.

[16]James B. Torrance, *Worship, Community, and the Triune God of Grace* (Downers Grove, Ill.: InterVarsity Press, 1997).

[17]J. J. von Allmen, "The Theological Meaning of Common Prayer," *Studia Liturgica* 10 (1974-1976): 129.

our attention to what God is doing in the text) with the assumption that what God has done in a particular scriptural account, God may well do again.[18]

Fourth, the prayer generates a kind of eschatological momentum. It gives a relatively significant amount of attention to ultimate results or outcomes. We are forced to say why we want so-and-so to be cured from disease. We find ourselves adding clauses like "so that they may witness to your kingdom" or "so that we may truly be a blessing to those with whom we work."

In sum, we could look at patristic collects and conclude that it would take most of a college-level systematic theology curriculum to prepare us to form robust collects:

- The doctrine God or theology proper prepares us for the address.
- The doctrines of revelation, incarnation and atonement (among others) shape our ways of naming divine attributes and actions in fulsome and balanced ways.
- The doctrine of sanctification helps us make sure our petitions are far-reaching enough.
- The doctrine of eschatology helps us clarify our ultimate aspirations.
- The doctrine of the Trinity helps us end the prayer so that we find ourselves still praying to the Christian God.

All of this embodies significant pastoral wisdom about prayer. We could phrase this wisdom in proverb form:

> Wise is the congregation who prays with a vivid awareness of divine splendor and of the trinitarian dynamics of prayer. Wise is the congregation who perceives past and potential future divine action to be of a single, united whole. Wise is the congregation whose prayer is filled with explicit longing for the coming kingdom of God.

Here too there are weaknesses to identify. For one, the form can become

---

[18]This is not unlike the "grammar" for preaching suggested in Paul Scott Wilson, *Four Pages of the Sermon: A Guide to Biblical Preaching* (Nashville: Abingdon, 1999). Indeed, there are few more clarifying actions for a preacher than preparing a collect around a preaching text. That simple action interprets the text, with awareness of God's activity both in past and present, in the context of an eschatological trajectory.

too neat and tidy, especially when yoked with one kind of rhetoric. For another, the form could potentially be stronger if it weren't so brief. For example, if the praise of God would happen by naming both an attribute and action of God, it certainly would avoid the mistaken dualism that sometimes creeps into Christian piety and prayer when divine actions and attributes are separated too much. Still, all things being equal, these are prayers that embody wisdom that, apart from their regular use, few Christian communities arrive at on their own.

How might contemporary Christians learn from and embody this wisdom? Once again, churches that regularly use texts in these ancient patterns can begin by simply becoming aware of the particular wisdom they practice. The value of these patterns is not limited to the fact that they happen to be ancient.

Churches that don't practice these patterns can "try them on." With new awareness of their theological and pastoral value, preachers in these churches might practice the discipline of writing an apt collect to follow each sermon, youth leaders and church educators might generate innovative ways to teach this form to children and youth.

Even if a congregation resists praying prayers in collect form, they could well contemplate the wisdom these collects reflect and use that as a springboard for further innovation.

Exhibit C: Cosmological timeline eucharistic prayers. With these relatively modest examples behind us, consider now our third example, the most robust and fulsome of all the ancient prayers, the great prayers of thanksgiving prayed at celebrations of the Lord's Supper. The following extensive example is a text from the *Apostolic Constitutions*, a fourth-century church order from Antioch.[19]

The grace of almighty God and the love of our Lord Jesus Christ and the

---

[19]Translated from *Prayers of the Eucharist: Early and Reformed*, ed. R. C. D Jasper and G. J. Cuming, 3rd ed. (Collegeville, Minn.: Liturgical Press, 1990), with notes added in brackets to help readers sense the structure of the prayer. See also W. E. Pitt, "The Anamneses and Institution Narrative in the Liturgy of Apostolic Constitutions Book VIII," in *Journal of Ecclesiastical History* 9 (1958): 1-7; and Raphael Graves, "The Anaphora of the Eighth Book of the Apostolic Constitutions," in *Essays on Early Eastern Eucharistic Prayers*, ed. Paul F. Bradshaw (Collegeville, Minn.: Liturgical Press, 1997), pp. 173-94.

fellowship of the Holy Spirit be with you all.

All: And with your spirit.

The bishop: Up with your mind.

All: We have it with the Lord.

The bishop: Let us give thanks to the Lord.

All: It is fitting and right.

The bishop: It is truly fitting and right . . .

[Creation and Providence]

to praise you before all things, essentially existing God, existing before created things, from whom all fatherhood in heaven and on earth is named, alone unbegotten, without beginning, without lord or master, lacking nothing, provider of all good things, greater than every cause and origin, always being in one and the same mode, from whom all things came into being as from a starting point.[20] For you are knowledge, without beginning, eternal vision, unbegotten hearing, untaught wisdom, first in nature, alone in existence, too great to be numbered. You brought all things from non-existence into existence through your only-begotten Son, the Word, God, living wisdom, the firstborn of all creation, the angel of your great purpose, your highpriest [and notable worshiper], king and lord of all rational and sentient nature, who was before all, through whom are all.

For you, eternal God, made all things through him, and through him you vouchsafe a fitting providence over everything. Through him you granted existence, through him also a good existence; O God and Father of your only-begotten Son, through him before all things you made [the heavenly powers], the cherubim and the seraphim, the ages and the hosts, virtues and powers, principalities and thrones, archangels and angels; and through him after all these things you made this visible world and all that is in it.

For you are he who set out heaven as a vault, and stretched it out as a screen, and established the earth on nothing by your sole intent; you fixed the firmament, and arranged night and day; you brought light out of your treasures, and by its contraction you brought on darkness (to give) rest to the living things that move in the world. You appointed the sun in heaven to be-

---

[20]Note the combination of apophatic/cataphatic phrases and communicable/incommunicable attributes in this section.

gin the day and the moon to begin the night, and you inscribed the chorus of the stars in heaven to the praise of your magnificence.

You made water for drinking and cleansing, life-giving air for breathing in and out, and for the production of sound through the tongue striking the air, and for hearing which is aided by it to receive the speech which falls upon it. You made fire for comfort in darkness, for supplying our need, that we should be warmed and given light by it. You divided the ocean from the land, and made the one navigable, the other fit to be trodden by our feet; you filled the one with creatures small and great, the other tame and wild; you wove it a crown of varied plants and herbs, you beautified it with flowers and enriched it with seeds. You constructed the abyss and set a great covering on it, the piled-up seas of salt water, and surrounded it with gates of finest sand; now you raise it with winds to the height of the mountains, now you level it to a plain; now you drive it to fury with a storm, now you soothe it with a calm, so that it gives an easy journey to travelers in ships. You girdled the world that was made by you through Christ with rivers and flooded it with torrents, you watered it with ever-flowing springs and bound it round with mountains as an unshakable and most safe seat for the earth. For you filled the world and adorned it with sweet-smelling and healing herbs, with many different living things, strong and weak, for food and for work, tame and wild, with hissing of reptiles, with the cries of variegated birds, the cycles of the years, the numbers of months and days, the order of the seasons, the course of rain-bearing clouds for the production of fruits and the creation of living things, a stable for the winds that blow at your command, the multitude of plants and herbs.

[Theological Anthropology]

And not only have you fashioned the world, but you have also made man in it, the citizen of the world, displaying him as the ornament of the world. For you said in your wisdom, "Let us make man in our image and likeness, and let him rule over the fish of the sea and the birds of the air." So also you made him from an immortal soul and a perishable body, the one from what is not, the other from the four elements. And you gave him in respect of the soul, logical reason, discernment between godliness and ungodliness, observance of right and wrong, and in respect of the body, the five senses and the power of motion. For you, almighty God, planted by Christ a garden eastward in

Eden with adornment of every kind of plant for food, and in it, as in a costly home, you placed man; and in making him you gave him an inborn law, that he might have in himself and of himself the seeds of the knowledge of God. And when you had brought him into the paradise of delight, you allowed him authority to partaker of everything, and forbade him the taste of one thing alone, in the hope of better things, that, if he kept the commandment, he should receive immortality as a reward for that.

[Fall]

But when he neglected the commandment and tasted the forbidden fruit, by the deceit of the serpent and the counsel of the woman, you justly drove him out of the paradise; but in your goodness you did not despise him when he was utterly perishing, for he was the work of your hands, but you subjected creation to him, and granted him to provide food for himself by his own sweat and labors, while you caused everything to shoot and grow and ripen. And in time, after putting him to sleep for a short while, you called him to rebirth by an oath; and after destroying the limit of death, you promised him life after resurrection.

[Old Testament Historical Narrative]

Nor was this all, but you poured out his descendents to a countless multitude; you glorified those who remained faithful to you, and punished those who rebelled against you; you accepted the sacrifice of Abel as being a righteous man, and rejected the gift of Cain, who slew his brother, as being a man accursed; and in addition you received Seth and Enosh, and translated Enoch.

For it is you who fashion men and provide life and fill need and give laws and reward those who keep them and punish those who break them; you brought the great Flood upon the earth because of the multitude of the ungodly, and saved righteous Noah from the Flood in the ark with eight souls, the end of those who dwelt there, but the beginning of those who were to be; you kindled the terrible fire against the five cities of Sodom, and turned a fruitful land into salt for the wickedness of those who dwelt in it, and snatched holy Lot from the burning. It was you who rescued Abraham from the godlessness of his forefathers and made him inheritor of the world; and revealed your Christ to him; you chose Melchizedek to be high-priest of your service; you declared your long-suffering servant Job to be the victor over the serpent, the origin of evil; you made Isaac the child of promise; you made Jacob the father of twelve sons, and his descendants to become a multitude, and brought him into Egypt with seventy-five souls. You, Lord, did not despise Joseph but, as a reward of his chastity for your sake, gave him the rule over the Egyptians. You, Lord, because of your promises to their Fathers, did not despise the Hebrews when they were oppressed by the Egyptians, but you rescued them and punished the Egyptians.

And when men destroyed the law of nature and taught that the Creation had created itself, or honored it more than they should, making it equal to you, God of all, you did not allow them to go astray, but revealed your holy servant Moses and through him gave them the written law in aid of nature, you showed that the Creation was your work and expelled the error of polytheism. You glorified Aaron and his descendents with the honor of priesthood, you punished the Hebrews when they sinned, and received them when they turned back.

You avenged them on the Egyptians with the ten plagues, you divided the sea and led the Israelites through, you drowned and destroyed the pursuing Egyptians. You sweetened the bitter water with wood, you poured water from the precipitous rock, you rained manna from heaven, and quails as food from the air. (You set up) a pillar of fire for light by night and a pillar of cloud for shadow from the heat by day. You declared Joshua to be leader, you destroyed through him the seven nations of the Canaanites, you parted Jordan, you dried up the rivers of Etham, you laid walls low without machines or human hands.

For all things glory be to you, almighty Lord. You are worshipped [by every bodiless and holy order, by the Paraclete, and above all by your holy child Jesus the Christ, our Lord and God, your angel and the chief general of your power, and eternal and unending high priest,] by unnumbered armies of angels, archangels, thrones, dominions, principalities, powers, virtues, eternal armies. The cherubim and the six-winged seraphim with two wings covering their feet, with two their heads, and with two flying, together with thousands of thousands or archangels and myriads of myriads of angels say unceasingly, never resting their voices:

All the people say: Holy, holy, holy (is the) Lord of Sabbath; heaven and earth are full of his glory; blessed (is he) for ever. Amen.

[Life of Jesus]

The bishop continues: Truly you are holy and all-holy, most high and exalted above all for ever.

Holy also is your only-begotten Son, our Lord and God Jesus the Christ, who ministered to you, his God and Father, in all things, in the varieties of creation, and in appropriate forethought. He did not despise the race of men as it perished; but after the law of nature and the warnings of the Law and the reproofs of the prophets and the guardianship of the angels, when they were violating the natural and written law, and casting out of memory the Flood, the burning (of Sodom), the plagues of the Egyptians, and the slaughter of the Palestinians, and were all about to perish as never yet, by your counsel it pleased him who was maker of man to become man, the law-giver to be under the law, the high-priest to be the sacrifice, the shepherd to be a sheep.[21]

And he propitiated you, his own God and Father, and reconciled you to the world, and freed all men from the impending wrath. He was born of a virgin, God the Word made in the flesh, the beloved Son, the firstborn of all Creation, according to the prophecies spoken beforehand by him concerning himself, from the seed of David and Abraham, of the tribe of Judah. He who fashions all who are begotten was made in a virgin's womb; the fleshless became flesh; he who was begotten outside time was begotten in time.

He lived a holy life and taught according to the law; he drove away every disease and every sickness from men; he did signs and wonders among the people; he who feeds those who need food and fills all things living with plenteousness partook of food and drink and sleep; he made known your name to those who did not know it; he put ignorance to flight; he re-kindled piety; he fulfilled your will; he accomplished the work which you gave him.

And when he had achieved all these things, he was seized by the hands of lawless so-called priests and high priests and a lawless people, by betrayal through one who was diseased with wickedness. He suffered many things at

---

[21]Note the recapitulation of earlier history in terms of Jesus and especially the highly paradoxical Christological formulations here.

their hands, endured all kinds of indignity by your permission, and was handed over to Pilate the governor. The Judge was judged and the Savior was condemned; he who cannot suffer was nailed to the cross, he who is immortal by nature died, and the giver of life was buried, that he might free from suffering and rescue from death those for whose sake he came, and break the bonds of the devil, and deliver men from his deceit.

And on the third day he rose from the dead, and after spending forty days with his disciples, he was taken up into heaven and sits at your right hand, his God and Father.

Remembering therefore what he endured for us, we give you thanks, almighty God, not as we ought but as we are able, and we fulfill his command.

For in the night he was betrayed, he took bread in his holy and blameless hands and, looking up to you, His God and Father, he broke it and gave it to his disciples, saying, "This is the mystery of the new covenant: take of it, eat; this is my body which is broken for many for forgiveness of sins." Likewise also he mixed the cup of wine and water and sanctified it and gave it to them, saying, "Drink from this, all of you; this is my blood which is shed for many for forgiveness of sins. Do this for my remembrance; for as often as you eat this bread and drink this cup, you proclaim my death, until I come."

Remembering then his Passion and death and resurrection from the dead, his return to heaven and his future second coming,[22] in which he comes with glory and power to judge the living and the dead, and to reward each according to his works, we offer you, King and God, according to his commandment, this bread and this cup, giving you thanks through him that you have deemed us worthy to stand before you and to serve you as priests.

[Prayer for the Holy Spirit]

- And we beseech you to look graciously upon these gifts set before you, O God who need nothing, and accept them in honor of your Christ; and to send down your Holy Spirit upon this sacrifice, the witness of the sufferings of the Lord Jesus, that he may make this bread body of your Christ, and this cup blood of your Christ;

- that those who partake of it may be strengthened to piety,

---

[22]Note here the use of the term *remembrance* to extend into the future. The term *remembrance* (Greek *anamnesis*) means, roughly, "to call to mind or contemplate an identity-shaping event." There is nothing illogical, in this sense, about remembering the future.

- obtain forgiveness of sins,
- be delivered from the devil and his deceit, be filled with the Holy Spirit,
- become worthy of your Christ,
- and obtain eternal life, after reconciliation with you, almighty Master.

[Prayer for the Life of the Church]

- Further we pray to you, Lord, for your holy Church from one end of the world to the other, which you redeemed with the precious blood of your Christ, that you would guard it unshaken and sheltered until the consummation of the age; and for all bishops who rightly divide the word of truth.[23]

- And we entreat you also for my worthless self who offer to you, and for all the priesthood, for the deacons and all the clergy, that you would instruct them all and fill them with the Holy Spirit.

- And we entreat you, Lord, for the Emperor and those in authority and all the army, that they may be peaceable towards us, that we may live the while of our life in quietness and concord, and glorify you through Jesus Christ our hope.

- And we offer to you also for all those holy men who have been well-pleasing to you from everlasting: patriarchs, prophets, righteous men, apostles, martyrs, confessors, bishops, priests, deacons, sub-deacons, readers, singers, virgins, widows, laymen, and all whose names you know.

- And we offer to you for this people, that you would make them a royal priesthood, a holy nation, to the praise of your Christ; for those in virginity and chastity, for the widows of the Church, for those in holy marriage and child-bearing, for the infants among your people, that you may make none of us a castaway.

- And we ask you on behalf of this city and those who live in it, for those in illness, those in bitter slavery, those in exile, those whose goods have been confiscated, for sailors and travelers, that you would become the help of all, their aid and support.

- And we entreat you for those that hate and persecute us for the sake of

---

[23]Note here a set of wide-ranging intercessions, that fit much of what is described in section 1 of this chapter (the formatting bullets are added to help readers sense the structure and flow of the intercessions).

your name, for those who are outside and have gone astray, that you would turn them back to good and soften their hearts.

- And we entreat you also for the catechumens of the Church, for those distressed by the Alien, and for those in penitence among our brothers, that you would perfect the first in the faith, and cleanse the second from the works of the devil, and receive the repentance of the third, and forgive them and us our transgressions.
- And we offer to you also for a mild climate and an abundant harvest, that we may partake of the good things from you without lack, and unceasingly praise you, who give food to all flesh.
- And we entreat you also for those who are absent for good cause, that you would preserve us all in piety, and gather us without change, without blame, without reproach in the kingdom of your Christ, the God of all sentient and rational nature, our King.

[Eschatological Doxology]

For [through him] (is due) to you all glory, worship, and thanksgiving, [and through you and after you to him in] the Holy Spirit honor and adoration, now and always and to the ages of ages, unfailing and unending.

And all the people say: Amen.

This type of prayer raises all sorts of questions, not the least of which concerns how much time it might take to actually pray this text in a service. When Protestants have attended to these prayers, they usually have focused their attention on their use of sacrificial imagery and the impression they give about the consecration of the eucharistic elements and the nature of Jesus' presence in the meal, key topics in Reformation debates about the Lord's Supper. However, the basic form of this prayer offers some other rather obvious lessons that often go unexplored.

A capacious, historical structure. First and perhaps most obviously, the prayer offers a recitation of salvation history. The prayer is concrete and historical rather than abstract and timeless. Like Nehemiah 9, many historical Psalms, sermons in Acts, the patristic Christian calendar and the arrangement of icons in many Orthodox worship spaces, this prayer form charts a history from creation to new creation.[24] As such, the prayer is a vivid example of just how important the concepts of narrative and story are to Christian experience. The prayer demonstrates that narrative is not only a main genre within Scripture and in Christian preaching and apologetics; it is also a main genre for prayer—a rather simple assertion often ironically neglected by even proponents of narrative theology and narrative preaching.

Along the way, the prayer speaks to so many different doctrinal concerns, with sections that correspond roughly to the Christian doctrines of creation, providence, humanity, incarnation, atonement, justification, sanctification, ecclesiology and eschatology. There is enough here so that any reader of this chapter who teaches systematic theology might well consider asking students to assess a given section of the prayer in terms of a specific doctrinal theme, and propose an pastorally contextualized version for use today. (Given the prayer's length, it may well offer enough material for a comprehensive final exam!)

Equally obvious is the grand scale of the prayer. The scale is not primarily a matter of length of the text but rather the breadth of its themes. This is a prayer of wide-angle vision. It offers praise for creation, for God's providence in guiding the people of Israel and for the birth, life, death and resurrection of Jesus. Then it offers petition for the work of the Spirit in the life of the church and expresses longing for the full coming of God's kingdom. It is a fourth-century version of *A Brief History of Everything*. N. T. Wright once observed, "the whole point of Christianity is that it offers a story which is the story of the whole world."[25] This prayer is a vivid illustration of exactly that.

Theologically, this prayer offers worshipers a large horizon in which to place their most pressing concerns and their interpretation and appropriation of any particular biblical text or theme. In liturgy, this large horizon

---

[24]See Louis Bouyer, *Liturgical Piety* (Notre Dame, Ind.: University of Notre Dame Press, 1955), p. 116; Robert Wilken, *The Spirit of Early Christian Thought* (New Haven, Conn.: Yale University Press, 2003), pp. 34-36; and Nicholas Wolterstorff, "The Remembrance of Things (Not) Past: Philosophical Reflections on Christian Liturgy," in *Christian Philosophy*, ed. Thomas P. Flint (Notre Dame, Ind.: University of Notre Dame Press, 1990), pp. 118-61.

[25]N. T. Wright, *The New Testament and the People of God* (Minneapolis: Fortress Press, 1992), pp. 41-42.

plays a particularly important role, in light of the inevitable limitations of preaching. Thomas Long, for example, argues that while "preaching, of necessity, is selective . . . the sacrament works to place the particularities of preaching into the context of the whole mystery of resurrection faith."[26] Like the recitation of a historic creed, like the Apostles' or Nicene, these Lord's Supper prayers direct the attention of worshipers to the full scope of God's activity in creation, redemption history and eschatological fulfillment.

The obvious point of comparison here for current evangelical readers is the work over the past generation on the importance of comprehensive worldview for Christian belief, a theme explored by Francis Schaeffer, Arthur Holmes, James Sire, David Naugle, Al Wolters, Charles Colson and David Wells, among others. Among the main themes in this discussion are the need for both individual believers and congregations to approach the world with an understanding of overarching biblical themes and to internalize a gospel-shaped perspective on space, time, good, evil, personhood, salvation, creation and final redemption. Craig Bartholomew speaks for many when he calls for a worldview that is "Christocentric, utterly comprehensive, and communal."[27]

My suggestion, which feels rather easy to make in light of this capacious prayer printed, is that there are few better models for what this can look like than the fully-orbed eucharistic prayers that emerge in the fourth century. They present a theological vision of space, time, good, evil, personhood, salvation, creation and final redemption—all compressed into a prayer that is open to eternity and to the mystery and beauty of God's being.

---

[26]Thomas Long, "Reclaiming the Unity of Word and Sacrament in Presbyterian and Reformed Worship," *Reformed Liturgy and Music* 16 (1982): 17. In addition to its breadth, one specific strength of a prayer this long is that it offers room for multiple metaphors and poetic imagery drawn from the Scriptures. It describes the atonement, for example, as an act of propitiation, reconciliation and freedom. See David Power, *The Eucharistic Mystery: Revitalizing the Tradition* (New York: Crossroad, 1994), p. 97.

[27]Craig Bartholomew, "A Christian World-view and the Futures of Evangelicalism," in *The Futures of Evangelicalism: Issues and Prospects,* ed. Craig Bartholomew, Robin Parry, and Andrew West (Grand Rapids, Mich.: Kregel Academic and Professional, 2003), p. 199. On the liturgical studies side of this larger point, see Frank Senn, *New Creation: A Liturgical Worldview* (Minneapolis: Fortress Press, 2000).

To modern readers this can be thought of as first-order systematic theology, but done in a vocative (and evocative) mood. And there is much to be gained by the fact that all of these wide-ranging theological assertions are offered in the form of a prayer, a demonstration that vital piety and precise theological thinking need not be in any way opposed to each other. So let me suggest, quite simply, that future discussions of Christian worldview among evangelicals could very helpfully move in the direction of what models of praying might best embody the worldview we hope to hone.

Integrating contemplative, apophatic piety into historical, cataphatic structures. This prayer finds room, inside an overarching structure of historical narrative, for expressions of praise that are mystical, that focus on divine incommunicable attributes and that fit an apophatic approach to theology (an approach to God that focuses on what may not be said of God). The prayer includes phrases such as "you are alone unbegotten, without beginning, without lord or master, lacking nothing," which reflect proper concern for divine ineffability. This comes to one climax at the singing of the *Sanctus*, which has a long history of use associated with mystical worship.[28] In short, there is room here for respectful, confessional statements of transcendence, mystery and wonder.

At the same time, those statements are integrated into a prayer that is historical in orientation, with a clear sense of the past and future, and with clear cataphatic assertions about divine character. Without this framework, apophatic praise and the *Sanctus*—like labyrinths, solitude, centering prayer and other disciplines inspired by patristic practice—can rather easily be used in a deistic, unitarian way. Even the *Sanctus* needs a narrative context, lest we define "holy, holy, holy" in terms of our own experience, and thus fashion a god of our own making. As Robert Webber and others have explained, without contemplation of God's transcendent work in history, our mystery-oriented contemplating can quite easily end up as something that plumbs the depths not of divine life but rather of our own inner selves.[29]

---

[28]Bryan Spinks, *The Sanctus in the Eucharistic Prayer* (New York: Cambridge University Press, 1991).
[29]Robert Webber, *The Divine Embrace: Recovering the Passionate Spiritual Life* (Grand Rapids, Mich.: Baker, 2006), pp. 51-53, see also 235ff.

This point in particular is pastorally crucial for the church today: there is great enthusiasm in some sectors of contemporary church life around a new appropriation of mystery. This is a welcomed reprieve from patterns of piety that leave far too little time to contemplate the beauty of God. Yet while many ancient orthodox liturgical practices slake our thirst for mystery, metaphor, transcendence, spaciousness, breadth and symbol, they also, however, protest our resistance to metanarrative and accountability and our attachment to certain forms of creativity, variety, celebrity and love for individual autonomy. More specifically, they protest recent enthusiasm for ahistorical mysticism. The ancient practices of spiritual life and devotion inform and sustain a vital contemporary spirituality and practice of reading the Bible by reinforcing the Bible's metanarrative, insisting on the ultimate unity of biblical themes and challenging us to pray in continuity with the kind of divine action we find there.

In sum, this eucharistic prayer embodies much patristic liturgical wisdom. Hence, my final proverb:

> Wise is the church that grounds its doxology in the history of God's actions. Wise is the church whose prayer is as wide-ranging and overarching as the Bible. Wise is the church who praises and thanks God both apophatically and cataphatically, with mystery-laden wonder and concrete and vivid descriptions of divine activity.

As with the other prayers we have studied, different traditions will appropriate this learning in different ways. Liturgical churches may reorder the church education programs to deepen understanding of current practices and (with the exception of the Orthodox) consider textual revisions to better capture this ancient wisdom.[30] Other congregations may develop new models to accomplish similar goals.

Assessment: Embodying Wisdom in Contemporary Practice

As we have seen, these three common patterns of patristic prayer embody

---

[30]For analysis of newer texts based on these ancient precedents in a variety of Christian traditions, see Frank C. Senn, ed., *New Eucharistic Prayers: An Ecumenical Study of Their Development and Structure* (New York: Paulist Press, 1987).

pastorally strategic liturgical wisdom. Even these brief encounters with ancient liturgical texts offer us some rather robust wisdom for the practice of liturgical prayer today.

Wise is the church that forms its children of all ages to pray

- for both local and global concerns
- for both the local and worldwide church
- in praise for both the attributes and actions of God
- for the whole sweep of salvation history
- with awareness of the trinitarian beauty of God's nature
- in ways that see creation and redemption as inextricably intertwined
- in ways that help us perceive coherence and beauty of Word and Spirit
- with a sense of wonder and participation in cosmic story of divine redemption
- in ways that picture God not only receiving our prayer but also prompting and perfecting it

The list could go on.

This is serviceable wisdom for pastors and youth pastors, camp counselors and theology professors. These proverbs can function quite easily as criteria for evaluating contemporary practices—even for practices that use quite different forms than we have studied.

This wisdom promises to challenge different Christian communities in different ways. In liturgical churches this study promises to offer deeper understanding of inherited patterns, insisting that catechesis attend to this wisdom rather than less consequential matters. In confessional churches, this study promises to help us understand how Reformational confessional documents, theologies and practices were shaped by awareness of patristic sources, and to imagine a euchology that is more adequate to our confessions than current practices. In free church, low church, alternative and other contexts this study promises to develop deeper criteria for grounding contemporary improvisation and for evaluating innovations. In all traditions, articulating the wisdom of ancient practices helps us to avoid a grab-bag approach to past practices, and to approach contextual ministry today with poise.

Above all, the wisdom of ancient practices can guide us as we work together to help the whole church engage more deeply and intentionally in corporate prayer. Regardless of the form that prayers take, engaged participation in public prayer is a perennial challenge for Christian laypeople. It is not easy to mean the words that someone else speaks. There are versions of the same problem in Catholic Masses, Orthodox matins, Pentecostal prayer meetings and Baptist revivals.

To overcome these inevitable challenges, pastoral leaders in all traditions need to deepen participation by deftly combining memorable teaching about prayer with effective models of prayer, by interweaving solid theological insights in prayer along with appropriate emotional engagement, by allowing for both corporate participation and priestly leadership. To this end, these patristic sources offer us challenging and inspiring models worthy of continued study.

11

Apatheia and Atonement

Cyril of Alexandria and the Contemporary Grammar of Salvation

Paul I. Kim

Contour of Contemporary Theology of Atonement:
Reversal of *Apatheia*

The age-old anathema that God suffers has become a "new orthodoxy" to many contemporary theologians.[1] In the face of the human suffering witnessed in the bloodiest of all centuries, God's *apatheia* ("divine impassibility"), the axiomatic belief held by the great fathers and doctors of the church, seems no longer tenable. An impassible God who is unmoved by human tragedy and so incapable of sympathy and love seems not just unscriptural but rightly deserves Camus's charge of an immoral "eternal bystander."[2] Daniel Day Williams called this growing theological consensus to replace the traditional doctrine of divine immutability and impassibility with a suffering God who passionately engages in human

---

[1] Ronald Goetz, "The Suffering God: The Rise of a New Orthodoxy," *Christian Century* 103, no. 13 (April 1986): 385.

[2] Albert Camus, *The Rebel* (New York: Knopf, 1954). Camus criticized what he regarded as the deceptive doctrines of "absolutist" philosophies—the vertical (eternal) transcendence of Christianity and the horizontal (historical) transcendence of Marxism—that rationalize violence as a legitimate means for forgiveness in the former and political progress in the latter.

history a "structural shift in the [modern] Christian mind."[3]

The reversal of the ancient *theopaschite* heresy that now thrives as a new orthodoxy is widespread in geographical and theological landscapes. On the European continent, Eberhard Jüngel and Jürgen Moltmann seek to reconstruct theology after the Holocaust.[4] They locate God's identity in his becoming, which by definition must eschew *apatheia*. Other theologians see *apatheia* as a Hellenistic contamination into Christian orthodoxy. The idea of divine impassibility and immutability was at best a temporary compromise of the early Christian church, which had to employ the resources of pagan philosophy to contextualize the Christian gospel. Alister McGrath, a British evangelical theologian, assesses the *apatheia* to be an epitome of "the subordination of a biblical to a philosophical view of God" in patristic Christianity.[5] The proponents of open theism in North America argue that it is overdue to clean the "residue of an obsolete metaphysics" of Greek philosophy.[6]

A number of theologians in Asia have also added their perspectives and insights to this contemporary criticism of divine impassibility along with the concern to relating God to the suffering world.[7] Kazoh Kitamori and Andrew Sung Park, prominent East Asian theologians, share a common emphasis on divine *pathos* ("suffering"). Kitamori's "theology of pain" attempts to reconstruct Christian theology by emphasizing the biblical theme of the allegedly pathetic God.[8] This Japanese theologian believes that the pain of God is a universal theme and the Japanese context can pro-

---

[3]Daniel Day Williams, *What Present-Day Theologians Are Thinking* (New York: Harper & Row, 1967), p. 172.

[4]Eberhard Jüngel, *The Doctrine of the Trinity* (Grand Rapids, Mich.: Eerdmans, 1976); Jürgen Moltmann, *History and the Triune God* (London: SCM, 1991), p. 29. "There can be no theology 'after Auschwitz,' which does not take up the theology *in Auschwitz*."

[5]Alister E. McGrath, *Iustitia Dei* (Cambridge: Cambridge University Press, 1998), p. 18. McGrath based such assessment of patristic theology on his unfiltered acceptance of Adolf von Harnack's concept of Hellenization. Cf. Alister E. McGrath, *Christian Theology* (Oxford: Blackwell, 1997), p. 343.

[6]John Sanders, *The God Who Risks* (Downers Grove, Ill.: InterVarsity Press, 1998), p. 165. "Though the tradition, with good intentions, employed immutability and impassibility in order to protect God's perfection, those traits were at times pushed so far as to leave no room for speaking of divine openness, in which God, in vulnerability, binds himself to others in love."

[7]A list of representatives would be Kazoh Kitamori, Kosuke Koyama, Jung Young Lee and Andrew Sung Park.

[8]Kazoh Kitamori, *Theology of the Pain of God* (London: SCM, 1966).

vide an effective medium.[9] Park's "theology of *han*" ("deep wound") makes a radical claim that God's *han* relieves human *han*, as he attempts to incorporate the insights of process theology within his Asian and North American contextual theology.[10] Park asserts that a Korean concept of *han* can balance the perpetrator-oriented atonement theories with a perspective from victims.

These various theologians of radical divine passibility render a variety of contemporary atonement reflections with one common premise. God as fellow sufferer will alleviate human pain from the enormous bloodshed and atrocity of the twentieth century by affirming the biblical God of compassion with an acute relevance. They claim that the discovery of suffering within God's divine nature will bring comfort and solidarity to the afflicted humanity.

Retrieving Cyril's Christology of "Impassible Suffering"

Against the reversal of two-thousand-year-old church tradition in contemporary reflection and the simplistic logic of salvation, this essay will attempt to show that the dynamic theological articulations of *apatheia* by the fathers of early church are indispensable for the theological grammar of salvation. Particularly Cyril of Alexandria's *mia* ("one-subject") Christology must be retrieved as a timely resource for contemporary discussion of redemptive suffering of God in Christ.

The fathers of the early church had a unique vision of *apatheia* as the ontological and moral foundation of the biblical view of God as Creator who is ontologically distinct from, yet immanent and active in, the creation. During the trinitarian and christological controversies of the early centuries, *apatheia* was a theological plumb line: how one reconciled the divine impassibility with christological integrity and with the passion story

---

[9]Writing from the Japanese wartime experience, Kitamori claims to recover pain as the heart of the gospel: pain penetrates God's being when God's Son is hanging on the cross, which enables God to overcome wrath.

[10]Andrew Sung Park, *The Wounded Heart of God* (Nashville: Abingdon, 1993). *Han* is a traditional Korean concept that describes imploded anger and deep wound of victims. During a recent nuclear stalemate, North Korean government claimed that its nuclear bomb test was an expression of *han* against American imperialism.

in the Gospels determined to a significant degree one's orthodoxy or heterodoxy.[11] Contrary to the contemporary assessment, most patristic theologians had a dynamic understanding of divine *apatheia* and creatively appropriated a Greek philosophical idea to articulate biblical insights of the creation and the reality of the incarnation. The doctrine of divine impassibility signifies not that God is a stranger to joy and delight but rather that his joy is permanent, clouded by no involuntary pain. The meaning of his gracious involvement in the world points to a glorious hope of humanity to participate in the triune life of perfect virtue, *apatheia*.

Among the early church fathers who employed *apatheia* to qualify divine affection apophatically (negatively) and to envision human perfection, Cyril of Alexandria achieved a "full maturity" of tradition of divine impassibility.[12] The bishop of Alexandria (c. 375-444) was the most important fifth-century Greek theologian who shaped the general dogma of the incarnation culminating in the creeds of Ephesus (431) and Chalcedon (451).[13] In the West, Cyril was declared a doctor of the church in 1882 and was the subject of papal encyclicals in 1931 *(Lux Veritatis)* and 1944 *(Orientalis Ecclesiae)*. In the East (at least, west of the Euphrates) he has always been regarded as one of the greatest of the doctors—"the seal of the Fathers," as Anastasius of Sinai (d. 700) called him.

Few periods in the history of Christian thought have received more attention than the christological debates in the fifth century. By then, everyone, including Nestorius, the principal opponent of Cyril, firmly held the Nicene Christology of *homoousia*, the full divinity of the Son—the Son is God as the Father is God. Thus, the first truth of the incarnation was defined. The second major refinement came through the condemnation of Apollinarius of Laodicea (c. 315-392), who denied a human soul in Jesus.

---

[11]Paul L. Gavrilyuk, *The Suffering of the Impassible God* (Oxford: Oxford University Press, 2004).

[12]Norman Russell, *The Doctrine of Deification in the Greek Patristic Tradition* (Oxford: Oxford University Press, 2004), p. 13.

[13]John A. McGuckin, *St. Cyril of Alexandria: The Christological Controversy* (New York: E. J. Brill, 1994), p. 1. "Cyril of Alexandria was not only one of the finest Christian theologians of his day, he also stands out in the ranks of the greatest patristic writers of all generations as perhaps the most powerful exponent of Christology the church has known and, after Athanasius, the writer who has had the greatest historical influence on the articulation of this most central and seminal aspect of Christian doctrine."

As the full humanity of the Son was affirmed, the final debate on the incarnation arose during the Nestorian controversy. How could the Son of God actually become human without impinging on the integrity of his full divinity or his full humanity? What was the proper theological language to unlock the true ontological nature of the incarnational becoming and the ensuing ontological union between the divinity and humanity?

While everyone attempted to answer the unresolved implications of Nicene Christology in different ways, the common tenet of their theological discourse was still the *apatheia* of God. The fifth-century christological debate was not just an innovative shift from the relationship of the Son to the Father to the relationship of the Son to humanity but a fuller Christian articulation of divine impassibility.[14] It was Cyril of Alexandria whose exposition surpassed the limitation of usual apophatic language about divine impassibility with crucial implications for Christian life: he grasped the most decisive significance of *apatheia* in the hypostatic union of Christ.[15] Locating *apatheia* in the incarnation and passion of Christ, Cyril construed his one-subject Christology in the mystery of "impassible suffering" of the Son: the coexistence of divine (impassible) and human (passible) natures in the one person of the Son achieves salvation for humanity.[16] As Cyril augmented the christological axiom of *apatheia* as the

---

[14]John O'Keefe argues that the driving force behind the christological debates of the fifth century was not the humanity of Jesus but the impassibility of God. See John J. O'Keefe, "Impassible Suffering? Divine Passion and Fifth-Century Christology," *Theological Studies* 58 (1997): 39. "Most textbook accounts of the fifth-century Christological debates suggest that the humanity of Jesus was the primary concern of the Antiochene theologians. From this perspective, Alexandrian Christology, represented by Cyril, appears to have fundamentally misunderstood the meaning of the Incarnation . . . The primary theological concern of the debate was the impassibility of God. Thus, the Alexandrians, rather than the Antiochenes, are shown to have defended more faithfully the humanity of the Son of God."

[15]Athanasius, Cyril's theological champion, located the mediating work of the Logos not solely in his divinity but in his incarnate state. Cyril not only inherited this insight but also deepened it with a clear understanding of a human soul in Christ. Long before the debate with Nestorius, his commentary on John already recognized the human soul of Christ to be an ontological and soteriological factor that articulates the passions of Christ.

[16]Cyril did not use *mia physis* in the sense of one quiddity that Christ is compositionally united but in the sense of one entity that affirms the continuing presence of the Logos in full humanity. Quoting the Anathasian expression that "the Word did not come in a man" but "the Word became a man," he asserted that this ontological union of Christ with humanity explains the "great exchange" between the immutable Word and the impoverished humanity.

ontological and soteriological certitude of divine love, he rendered a coherent way to articulate the redemptive suffering of Christ without either transmuting divinity or absorbing humanity.

To understand Cyril's epoch-making Christology, it is helpful to remember three interwoven threads in his theological tapestry: his unique expression of the impassible suffering, his consistent exegetical motifs of Christ based on divine economy and his employment of the *communicatio idiomatum* with its anthropological implication.

Cyril consistently described the suffering of Christ as "impassible suffering" *(pathoi apathos)* in his writings. Between the outbreak of the *theotokos* controversy in 428 and the Council of Ephesus of 431, he composed a short treatise titled "On the Right Faith" for Eudocia, the wife of the emperor Theodosius II, and his sister, Pulcheria. In this letter, he coined a unique expression of "impassible suffering." By that he meant that Christ experienced suffering but was not changed by the experience.

> It would be consistently fitting also for the Word to fear death, to look upon danger with suspicion, to weep in temptations, and in addition to learn obedience by what he suffered when tempted. Nevertheless, I think it completely foolish either to think or say this, since the Word of God is all powerful, stronger than death, beyond suffering, and completely without a share in fear suitable to man. But though he exists this way by nature, still he suffered for us. Therefore, neither is Christ a mere man nor is the Word without flesh. Rather united with a humanity like ours, he suffered human things impassibly . . . in his own flesh. Thus these events became an example for us in a human fashion . . . so that we might follow in his steps.[17]

The catchiness of the expression was typical of Cyril's apologetic style, and as with other catch phrases such as "two-Sons approach" (to characterize Nestorius's position) he chose terms that most shockingly set out the lines of his thought while flatly contradicting the main premises of his opponents. Cyril's theological language of paradox came from his immersion

---

[17]Cyril of Alexandria *On the Right Faith* 163, trans. Rowan A. Greer (unpublished), p. 33; Patrologia Graeca 76:1393B.

in biblical studies.[18] As a biblical theologian, the bishop of Alexandria was not original, as was Gregory of Nyssa, or creative, as was Origen, but he was "tedious, repetitious, and verbose . . . handling the Bible with a high degree of theological sophistication."[19] He took the typology of Adam and Christ further than did any major Father, including his champion, Athanasius. His descriptions of Christ as "the New Man," "Second Adam" and "the Heavenly Man" not only inherited Athanasian notions of "double scope" of the incarnation but also deepened with his exposition of a human rational soul in Christ. Origen first recognized a "rational or human soul" in Christ but did not develop that idea fully. Athanasius did not take a notice of a human soul in Christ. Augustine also had the idea of two stages of Christ, as illustrated in his Christmas sermon "Two Births of Christ." But Augustine did not elaborate how two aspects of Christ are integrated into one person. Cyril developed Irenaeus's idea of recapitulation further with ontological acumen. While Nestorius spoke of two-nature and two-subject Christology, Cyril insisted only on two-stages Christology: one apart from the incarnation and the other within the incarnation. His affirmation of *apatheia* in Christ was a way of protecting the truth that the incarnate one was truly God. According to Thomas Weinandy, the contribution of Cyril is that for the first time, the attributes were predicated not of the natures but of the person, taking on a new manner or mode of existence.[20]

One unarguable fact is that Cyril was no docetic who denied the reality of Christ's sufferings. On the contrary, he pointed to the whole experience of incarnation as adding a unique aspect to the divinity: the personal experience of human suffering and death. In his later complete work, *On the Unity of Christ*, Cyril explained the meaning of "impassible suffering" to an

---

[18]O'Keefe, "Impassible Suffering," p. 44: "From the time of his ordination to the episcopacy in 412 until the eruption of the conflict with Nestorius in 428, Cyril's works reveal no sense of Christological crisis. During this time he composed massive commentaries on the Bible and several doctrinal works. Cyril's immersion in the biblical text during this period provided him with a basic Christological perspective that would mature under the pressure of his debate with the Antiochenes."

[19]Robert L. Wilken, *Judaism and the Early Christian Mind* (New Haven, Conn.: Yale University Press, 1971), p. 222.

[20]Thomas G. Weinandy, *Does God Suffer?* (Notre Dame, Ind.: University of Notre Dame Press, 2000), p. 200.

international audience after the Council of Ephesus. When someone asked, "How can the same one both suffer and not suffer?" Cyril answered with the traditional analogy of iron in fire.

> He suffers in his own flesh, and not in the nature of Godhead. The method of these things is altogether ineffable.... Yet following these most correct deductions ... we do not deny that he can be said to suffer, but this does not mean that we say that the things pertaining to the flesh transpired to his divine and transcendent nature. No as I have said, he ought to be conceived of as suffering in his own flesh, although not suffering in any way like this in the Godhead.... It is like iron ... when it is put in contact with a raging fire. It receives the fire into itself, and when it is in the very heart of the fire, if someone should beat it, then the material itself takes the battering but the nature of the fire is in no way injured by the one who strikes. This is how you should understand the way in which the Son is said both to suffer in the flesh and not to suffer in the Godhead.... The force of any comparison is feeble.[21]

Another way to understand Cyril's Christology of impassible suffering would be a brief review of his debate with Nestorius. The initial point of their contention was about Mary's being *theotokos*. When Nestorius's teaching began to influence some monks in Egypt, Cyril suspected that the bishop of Constantinople was dangerously relapsing into the Arian mistakes. Quoting Athanasius in his *Against the Arians,* Cyril reminded the monks that the Scripture "contains a two-fold declaration concerning the Savior." He "always was God" and "for our sake, by taking flesh from the Virgin Mary, the Mother of God, he became man."[22] Cyril argued that to deny the *theotokos* is logically same as Arianism. Those who negate Mary to be the mother of God do not confess the fullness of the Son's participation with humanity, just as the Arians discounted the fullness of the

---

[21]Cyril of Alexandria, *On the Unity of Christ,* trans. John A. McGuckin (Crestwood, N.Y.: St. Vladimir's Seminary Press, 1995), pp. 130-31. Although Cyril employed other metaphors and this one was a quite commonly used analogy, the metaphor was often misused as an exact model to conceive the hypostatic union. See Weinandy, *Does God Suffer,* pp. 182-83.

[22]Cyril of Alexandria, *On the Unity of Christ,* p. 16; *Against the Arians* 3.29. "Therefore the mark and characteristic of Holy Scripture, as we have often said, is this that it contains a twofold declaration concerning the Savior, that he both always was God and that he is the Son, being the Word and brightness and wisdom of the Father, and that afterwards, for our sake, by taking flesh from the Virgin Mary, the Mother of God, he became man."

Son's participation in God. For Cyril, Nestorius was too concerned about protecting the impassibility of God that he missed the entire point of the incarnation—God really became a human for the sake of redemption. The bishop of Constantinople not only evacuated the meaning of *kenosis* but also jeopardized the indispensable unity of Christ.[23]

Cyril was swift and strong in his condemnation of Nestorius's failure and lack of conceiving an ontological union between the divinity and humanity of Christ so that he finally brought forth twelve anathemas in the *Third Letter to Nestorius* (430). Other than a real personal union, he called any manner of relation of two natures in Christ such as "conjunction" or "juxtaposition" completely heretical. Among twelve anathemas, the last one was most succinct and central.

> If anyone does not confess that the Word of God suffered in the flesh, and was crucified in the flesh, and tasted death in the flesh, and became the firstborn from the dead, since he is life and life-giving as God, let him be anathema.[24]

Throughout the twelve anathemas, one could see Cyril's obsession with the language of "one flesh" *(mia physis)* which he repeated to accentuate the "concrete, fleshed-out reality" of the Word of God. Without this enfleshed reality of Christ, there is no single subject of the incarnation event and humanity has no real Savior. In the summer of 431, Cyril, under house arrest, was asked to provide the holy synod with a clearer explanation of his previous twelve anathemas. On the twelfth one, Cyril articulated the soteriology of the impassibly suffering Christ.

The Word of God the Father is impassible and immortal, for the divine and

---

[23]Cyril of Alexandria, *On the Unity of Christ*, p. 22. "Now there are some who cut the one Lord Jesus Christ in two, that is, into man and into the Word of God the Father. They say that the one born of the Holy Virgin submitted to the emptying. . . . Let them prove that in form and in equality he is considered and, in fact, is from the Father, in order that he might submit to the manner of emptying himself, to which very position he had not attained. But there is no creature . . . which is equal to the Father. How, then is he said to have emptied himself, if, being man by nature, he has been born like us from a woman? And tell me the nature of the higher eminence greater than that of human from which he descended to be man? Or how might he be considered to have taken the form of a servant, which he did not have to start with, who by nature belonged to the class of servants and lay under the yoke of servitude?"

[24]Cyril of Alexandria *Letter* 17.19.

ineffable nature is above all suffering. . . . Yet even though the Word of God the Father is so by his own being, he made his own the flesh which is capable of death so that by means of this . . . he could assume sufferings for us . . . and so liberate us all from death and corruption by making his own body alive, as God, and by becoming the first fruits. . . . He who endured the noble cross for our sake and tasted of death was no ordinary man conceived of as separate and distinct from the Word of God the Father but it was the Lord of Glory himself who suffered in the flesh, according to the scriptures (1 Peter 4:1).[25]

For Cyril, "the impassible suffering" is an essential Christian conception to connect the divine *apatheia* with divine *agape* for two reasons: first, it preserves the inviolability of the divine in the hypostatic union; and second, it demonstrates Christ's transformation of human nature. Cyril saw an inseparably double significance of the incarnation of the divine Word that the hypostatic union of two natures in Christ was not only real but also necessary for the healing of human sins. In order for Christ to free us from death, the Word must be both divine (impassible) and must genuinely experience suffering and death (passible) in the conquering process. Cyril understood Christ's conquest of death through the divinization of human nature in terms of the *communicatio idiomatum:* the incarnated Word communicates the incorruptibility of his divine nature to corruptible human nature.

Cyril held that *kenosis* does not mean Logos's emptying of his intrinsic nature, such as impassibility and transcendent power. Rather, *kenosis* refers to the problem and limitation of humanity, which the Word takes on himself. During the incarnation, Cyril asserted, the divine nature of the Word retained its immutability. Christ's immutability was shown in his preservation of his impeccable obedience to the Father. The reason that Christ overcame temptation was because he was "irrevocably fixed on the good." "Jesus' intuitive grasp of the good can be attributed only to his divinity; for the divine nature is ever inaccessible to wickedness."[26] The way that Christ

---

[25]Cyril of Alexandria, *Explanation of the Twelve Chapters, Anasthematism 12,* in McGuckin, *St. Cyril of Alexandria,* pp. 292-93.

[26]Cyril of Alexandria, *Commentary on Isaiah* 1.4, trans. Norman Russell (London: Routledge, 2000), 74-75; Patrologia Graeca 70:205B. "And it [divine nature] repudiates the ways of viciousness, for it is not put to the test from that quarter, nor does it experience any annoyance, for it rejects wickedness by virtue of its nature."

did not succumb to the human instincts for self-preservation was through the strength of his divine will. According to Cyril, Jesus controlled the impulses of his baser appetites by the power of *thymos*, the spirited faculty of the soul. One of Cyril's key passages was Hebrew 2:18, "For because he himself has suffered and been tempted, he is able to help those who are tempted": he read that Jesus, far from being weakened under temptation, became stronger and perfected as a result of suffering. "For 'he endured the cross, despising the shame' entirely by the good pleasure of God the Father so that he might make us bold, taken by the hand to follow in his steps."[27] Christ's revelation of transforming human fear into glory and virtue is not a mere example for his disciples to imitate, but his impassible suffering creates in their souls the necessary virtue, courage, to endure their own persecutions and suffering for the faith. Cyril calls humanity sanctified by the impassible suffering *(pathoi apathos)* of Christ the "New Adam," which includes all of Adam's race. In the hypostatic union of Christ, our frail human nature was given the vision and power of impassible suffering from the divine nature that we have the capacity for joy, glory and freedom from bodily corruption.

> The effect of the indwelling of the divine in us ("in Christ") is our sanctification, which is accomplished in dialectic between purgation and illumination. . . . "For when Christ has come to be within us he lulls to sleep the law that rages in the members of the flesh. He rekindles our reverence toward God, while simultaneously causing the passions to atrophy." As the soul is reoriented toward God in due reverence, the passion cease to have a hold upon us.[28]

The impassible suffering of Christ is indispensable for Cyril to explain the "great exchange" of the incarnation between the immutable Word and impoverished humanity. Cyril's use of the *communicatio idiomatum* clearly expounds the anthropological and soteriological implications of his oneness Christology. John McGuckin notes the significance of Cyril's articu-

---

[27]Cyril of Alexandria, *On the Right Faith*, p. 30.

[28]J. Warren Smith, "Suffering Impassibly: Christ's Passion in Cyril of Alexandria's Soteriology," *Pro Ecclesia* 11 no. 4 (2002): p. 479.

lation of Christian vision of transformed and transcendent humanity:

> The Lord became, for Cyril, the epitome of all that was truly human, but humanity defined on a new premise—a transfigured humanity that came alive in its communion with God, and was "made personal" precisely in and through that communion. . . . Christian anthropology, under the twin stimuli of philosophical thought and biblical exegesis had, until Cyril's time, moved uneasily between the two. It was Cyril's ultimate achievement to present the blueprint for a final resolution of a definitive Christian anthropology—one that was wholly re-defined in terms of the incarnation, and which synthesized the biblical and Hellenistic insights.[29]

Reflecting on the Tradition-Based Grammar of Salvation for Today

As I attempt to show that the contemporary theological concern to situate God's presence in human suffering can be more coherently incorporated in Cyril's oneness Christology, I find three crucial contributions of Cyril's Christology for contemporary reflections on grammar of salvation. First, the single-subject Christology of Cyril preserves the irreducibility of God's redemptive suffering with the mystery of the apathetic suffering of the Son. The fact that there has been no official dogma of the work of Christ corroborates the ongoing mystery of the person of Christ, which always creates an indelible impact in every particular context. The universal efficacy of Christ's atonement is best illustrated by a theological approach, which cherishes the irreducible mystery of God's grace in Christ.[30] That is what the bishop of Alexandria achieves in his oneness Christology by retaining and elucidating the scandal of Christian gospel, namely, the atoning death of God in human flesh on the cross.

Second, Cyril's Christology not only protects the mystery of atonement of Christ but also preserves the theological integrity of the biblical trini-

---

[29]McGuckin, *St. Cyril of Alexandria*, pp. 224-25.

[30]Henri de Lubac, *The Discovery of God* (Grand Rapids, Mich.: Eerdmans, 1996), p. 117. "Infinite intelligibility—such is God. The deeper we enter into the infinite, the better we understand that we can never hold it in our hands. . . . The infinite is not a sum of finite elements, and what we understand of it is not a fragment torn from what remains to be understood . . . it [intelligence] in no way diminishes it [mystery], it does not 'bite' on it; it enters deeper and deeper into it and discovers it more and more as a mystery."

tarian scheme. Contemporary theologians who base their atonement theories on radical divine passibility tend to blur the traditional distinction between the imminent Trinity and economic Trinity. A prime example would
be Moltmann's interpretation of the cross of Christ as an intra-trinitarian
event in which the Father experiences the pain of abandoning the Son and
the Son the pain of being abandoned. Together they suffered a divine rup-
ture for human redemption.[31] According to David Coffey, Moltmann subordinates the mystery of the Trinity to the metaphorical matrix of penal
substitution, which justifies "a real separation of the Father from the Son
on the cross."[32] While Moltmann attempts to advance Karl Rahner's dic-
tum that "the immanent Trinity is the economic Trinity," he forgets that
the identification of the economic Trinity with the immanent Trinity does
not have to be a collapse of the divine mystery into the human matrix but
must be a window into God's infinite welcoming of humanity. While the
economic Trinity exhibits the immanent Trinity, it does not exhaust the
mystery of God's unfathomably free love. In his later conversation with
Moltmann and others, Rahner corrects the former's rejection of divine impassibility by saying, "To put it crudely, it does not help me to escape from
my mess and mix-up and despair if God is in the same predicament."[33]
Cyril of Alexandria's two-stages Christology prevents such critical misstep
in contemporary articulation of God's suffering love. As he locates the
mystery of suffering in the hypostatic union of Christ in a concrete historical way, he elevates the incarnation of God as a transformative event while
deepening the mystery of eternal God's involvement in temporal realm.

    Third, Cyril's hypostatic union of Christ promises a better picture of
transformed humanity. To bring a genuine hope to afflicted humanity and
han-ridden victims, God's engagement with humanity in Christ must be

---

[31]Jürgen Moltmann, *The Crucified God* (Minneapolis: Fortress, 1993), p. 243. "To understand what
happened between Jesus and his God and Father on the cross, it is necessary to talk in Trinitarian
terms. The Son suffers dying, the Father suffers the death of the Son. The Fatherlessness of the Son
is matched by the Sonlessness of the Father, and if God has constituted himself as the Father of Jesus
Christ, then he also suffers the death of his Fatherhood in the death of the Son. Unless this were so,
the doctrine of Trinity would still have a monotheistic background."
[32]David Coffey, *Deus Trinitas* (Oxford: Oxford University Press, 1999), p. 113.
[33]Karl Rahner, *Karl Rahner in Dialogue*, ed. P. Imhof and H. Biallowons (New York: Crossroads,
1986), p. 126.

paired with human participation in divine life. Whereas the contemporary grammar of salvation inevitably reduces atonement to a modern theodicy of divine passibility, the holistic vision of divine transformation of human suffering evoked by *apatheia* deepens atonement as an indispensable event to advance original divine intention for humanity. The doctrine of the suffering Christ is not a psychological prop of commiseration but signifies the divine mercy, which empowers sinners with God's willingness to overcome evil with and for them.

It is a grave mistake for contemporary theologians to posit that making God passible would alleviate human suffering.[34] Such oversimplified theological thinking not only undermines a proper understanding of God but also distorts the Christian gospel. In contrast to the inadvertent disservice of the contemporary theology of passibility, Cyril's Christology presents a timely resource for today's church to rediscover and reflect on the enriching implication of *apatheia* of God that great fathers and doctors of the church held with careful qualifications and utmost convictions. To misapprehend the divine *apatheia* has anathematic significations not just in the past but more in the present, where the memory of the bloodiest century is still fresh and repeating. For the contemporary concern with suffering and evil, Cyril's hypostatic Christology with impassible suffering more fully enunciates the care and love of God for humanity.

---

[34]Weinandy, *Does God Suffer*, p. 214. "Many contemporary theologians, who posit suffering within God's divine nature, give the impression that once they have demonstrated this, they have done all that is required and significant. The soteriological import of divine suffering remains barren. It does not achieve any end other than to register that God does indeed suffer in solidarity with humankind, and so comfort can be taken from this. Why we should be comforted by a suffering God remains unclear, especially if he, like us, can now do little to alleviate it and is rendered helpless in vanquishing its actual causes."

12

Two Augustinianisms

Augustinian Realism and the Other City

D. Stephen Long

If there is one ancient thinker evangelical Protestants do not need to recover, it would be Augustine. He has always been with us, influencing both the Calvinist and Wesleyan evangelical traditions. Unlike Denys, Macarius or John Chrysostom, we may not need an Augustinian *ressourcement* to recover antiquity for an ancient-future church. Augustine led the way for evangelical renewal. In one sense, then, evangelical Protestantism is already a *ressourcement*.

Yet familiarity with Augustine may be the very thing that prevents evangelical Protestants from drawing on this ancient thinker for a future church. In fact, we need to do with Augustine what Henri de Lubac did with Aquinas. During Lubac's time, Roman Catholic theologians thought they knew Aquinas well. He gave us a two-source theory of truth, grounded in a double finality for human creatures where one of our ends was natural and one was supernatural. Those two ends were distinct from each other such that politics, economics and ethics could proceed based solely on an investigation of our natural end while the Christian life pursued the supernatural end. The result, as Lubac pointed out, was that this late medieval interpretation of Aquinas contributed to a thoroughgoing secular reading of politics, economics and ethics. Is it possible that our familiarity with Augustine has produced for us what late medieval readings of Aquinas produced for Roman Catholics—an unintended affirmation of the secular understood as a "pure nature" that does not need Christ for its intelligibility? We should not be surprised if this is the case. Lubac traced the history of the emergence of the secular to interpretations of Augustine in which his doctrine of grace supposedly set it free from the scholastic corruptions that mingled it with Aristotle. Because of original sin, our situation is so vastly different from Adam's that we can find nothing positive in natural desire per se, and we can do nothing to contribute to our redemption except receive Christ's grace in a nature that stands only in opposition to it. This makes grace so extraordinary and so opposed to nature that it left unexplained that "nature" or "creation" to which grace comes and made grace "extrinsic." Given that the "political" exists within this unexplained domain of "nature" or "creation," it too can easily become a site for a "pure nature," which we describe as if it knew nothing of Christ's victory over the principalities and powers of this world. Is this "nature" only totally depraved and therefore this ungraced nature bears only a kind of Hobbesian desire where politics is nothing but the contest of contending powers? How often does this understanding of politics find resonances in Protestant Christianity, evangelical and nonevangelical? How often does Calvin come off looking like Hobbes? Perhaps it is why Reinhold Niebuhr's work, despite its doctrinal heterodoxy, so often finds supporters in evangelical circles. It produces a political theology in which what counts as "political" is now known outside Christ's victory, and theology must correlate itself to this purely "political" nature. The result is a preoccupation with the modern state, for it alone defines what we mean by the term *political*. I fear emergent Christianity could easily reinscribe this modern preoccupation if it fails at a thoroughgoing *ressourcement* of an Augustinian theological politics.

Robert Dodaro offers such a *ressourcement*. He reminds us that for Augustine, Christ is the only source of virtue for a truly just society because he rescues us from the deep problem in every other political society. This problem is "linguistic or rhetorical in character"; it is the fact that "the lie" constitutes political society as well as our social relations.[1] Paul J. Griffiths

---

[1] Robert Dodaro, *Christ and the Just Society in the Thought of Augustine* (Cambridge: Cambridge University Press, 2004), p. 69.

has made a similar argument. He writes,

> Lies bind the fabric of every human life. We lie to our lovers when we whisper sweet nothings; we lie to the glowing screen when we process the words of our novels, poems and (especially) autobiographies; we lie to the mirror when we smooth on the subtly deceptive unguents that replace our face with someone else's; we lie to our children when we browbeat them with the image of our own imagined rectitude; . . . we obscure our creatively diverse uses of the lie from ourselves and espouse the dubious portrait of the truth-teller upon our souls with the acid of the lie denied. We are imaginatively masked, adorned with the lie, bedecked with the elegance of verbal dissimulation. To be so is the very mark of adult humanity. Or so it may seem.[2]

For Augustine, this is the fundamental problem of sin. For him, "the lie is a sin, a recursively self-defeating action that shatters the image of the Triune God in which we are made."[3] It distorts all our social relations, while it may at the same time be the basis for them.

The centrality of "the lie" for politics is especially true when it comes to religion. Plato suggested the "noble lie" as the necessary religious myth that would maintain civic order. In the *City of God*, Augustine argues that both fabulous and civic theologies perpetuate the lie, and as long as you perpetuate those theologies you can have no just society. What can save us from the lie? Dodaro provides an Augustinian answer. "Augustine argues that human beings are united to Christ when they accept in faith and humility that virtue derives from the mediation of Christ's grace. Thus united in Christ as members of his body, these believers form the just society."[4] Faith and humility, rather than desire for glory, provides the basis for this just political society. But this requires a political society that would be "truly penitential."[5] Dodaro suggests that for Augustine, "only those leaders whose church encourages them to acknowledge their sins and to seek pardon from God can hope to avoid the desire to dominate others."[6] He

---

[2]Paul J. Griffiths, *Lying* (Grand Rapids, Mich.: Brazos Press, 2004), p. 11.
[3]Ibid., p. 17.
[4]Dodaro, *Christ and the Just Society*, p. 71.
[5]Ibid., p. 112.
[6]Ibid., p. 202.

mentions three necessary features for such an Augustinian just society. First, it would "reject the concept of an autonomous moral reason." Second, it would "affirm" that the "source of virtue" is Christ alone. Finally, it would also "accept that perfect human virtue can be found only in Christ."[7] This would prevent us from seeking perfect societies outside of Christ's victory. It might also free us from the illusion of a "progressive politics" as well as its twin, "conservativism." This means that for us late moderns a proper recovery of Augustine's theological politics must be less a state project and more an ecclesia project.[8]

Augustine's importance for the emerging, future church lies in his development of a city that is other than our earthly cities. It is a transnational unity, grounded in a common and ancient worship that can affirm a single, unifying source for civic virtue in Christ and then participate without a bad conscience in the unity, commonalty and even sameness those virtues brings. This ancient reading of Augustine contrasts with modern political configurations grounded as they are on a rigid ethics of evil. The postmodern, Marxist philosopher Alain Badiou, although he is no friend to theology, nevertheless helps identify the prevailing "ethical ideology" that always subordinates truth to a liberal politics ruled by the language of rights and diversity. The language of rights requires that our political bonds are grounded in evil because we must first be victims who need protection before we can be political agents. "Diversity," "the other" and "inclusivity" merely repeat what already is in a liberal political society. This language only tells us what we know: we live in a world with people different from us. This produces a conservative, even reactionary, political agenda. As an alternative to this, Badiou seeks a politics grounded in the priority of goodness and truth. He notes that the modern political problem is not recognizing the other but "recognizing the same."[9] For this we need a strong account of truth and a fidelity to an event that will not fit into the prevailing ethical ideology. An Augustin-

---

[7]Ibid., p. 72.

[8]"Augustine is less interested than his interpreters in discussing the respective merits of a Christian or secular state" (ibid., p. 17).

[9]Alain Badiou, *Ethics*, trans. Peter Hallward (London: Verso, 2001), pp. 25-27.

ian theological politics provides such an account of truth and fidelity with a truly postmodern sensibility.

This ancient reading of Augustine also contrasts with a more contemporary one in which, consistent with the prevailing ethical ideology, Augustine's primary contribution is a doctrine of original sin. In this reading, it is "sin" that makes political society possible. This of course means no just political society is possible. We all must be fallibilists when it comes to truth, for no one truly knows the true or the good. There is nothing that does not merely repeat our present bourgeois liberalism in such a truncated Augustinian realism. In what follows, I will first trace this Augustinian realism and then contrast it with Augustine's other city in which a just order is possible. The former I will call "political theology" and the latter "theological politics."[10] These two terms define two Augustinian traditions. "Political theology" defines that tradition of Augustinian thought that begins with the assumption that we know what "the political" is without knowing Christ or his body, the church, and that we must make theology relevant to this purely natural notion of "the political." This could also be known as a politicized theology. A rereading of Augustine that emphasizes his witness to another city, I will call "theological politics." It characterizes that tradition of Augustinian thought that assumes we cannot know the true nature of the political if we do not know Christ and his church. I will also call that tradition of thought "Augustine's Other City."[11] Finally, I will relate this other city to the importance of a theology that is not in service to a civic order that finds its source in something other than Christ—as all secular civic orders must.

Augustinian Realism

Augustinian realism is a recent tradition that perhaps goes back no farther than Reinhold Niebuhr, although one might trace its lineage back to Machiavelli, Hobbes or perhaps even to the "noble lie" in Plato's *Republic*. In

---

[10]This distinction comes from Arne Rasmussen, *The Church as Polis* (Notre Dame, Ind.: University of Notre Dame Press, 1995).

[11]I do not mean to imply that everyone who uses the term *political theology* fits well within the tradition of Augustinian realism.

explaining Augustinian realism, Niebuhr began not with Augustine but with Machiavelli. He wrote,

> "realism" denotes the disposition to take all factors in a social and political situation, which offer resistance to established norms, particularly the factors of self-interest and power. In the worlds of a notorious "realist," Machiavelli, the purpose of the realist is 'to follow the truth of the matter rather than the imagination of it.'[12]

By this Niebuhr meant that any account of politics that does not take into account the inevitable power, violence and self-interest that a society must use to preserve itself is not an adequate account of politics. Niebuhr explained this in *Moral Man and Immoral Society*: "Since reason is always to some degree, the servant of interest in a social situation, social injustice cannot be resolved by moral and rational suasion. . . . Conflict is inevitable, and in this conflict power must be challenged by power."[13] This of course depends on a definition of politics similar to that of Max Weber, who stated, "The decisive means for politics is violence."[14] It also fits quite well Machiavelli's admonition to the prince that when it comes to the society for which he is entrusted, it is better to be feared than loved. For although, as Machiavelli puts it, "every prince must desire to be considered merciful and not cruel," nevertheless,

> a prince must not mind incurring the charge of cruelty for the purpose of keeping his subjects united and faithful; for, with a very few examples, he will be more merciful than those who, from excess of tenderness, allow disorders to arise, from whence spring bloodshed and rapine; for these as a rule injure the whole community, while the executions carried out by the prince injure only individuals.[15]

The prince, like the government, must preserve the common life of the nation, even if this requires noble lies, violence, perhaps cruelty and torture.

---

[12]Reinhold Niebuhr, *Christian Realism and Political Problems* (Fairfield, Conn.: Augustus M. Kelley, 1953), p. 119.

[13]Reinhold Niebuhr, *Moral Man and Immoral Society* (New York: Charles Scribner's Sons, 1932), p. xv.

[14]Max Weber, "Politics as a Vocation," in *From Max Weber*, ed. H. H. Gerth and C. Wright Mills (New York: Oxford University Press, 1946), p. 121.

[15]Niccolò Machiavelli, *The Prince* (New York: Modern Library, 1950), p. 60.

Augustinian realism takes Augustine's doctrine of original sin, reads it through Machiavelli's exhortation to the prince and argues that for the sake of any political society, the government must of necessity be willing to get its hands dirty in order to preserve the body politic. This includes the political necessity not only of executions but also of the use of deceit, violence and the possibility even of torture—all for the sake of the common good. Moreover, it also assumes, as Niebuhr assumed, that Christian doctrines must be understood primarily as "mythopoetical" and assessed by their contribution to this account of politics. This is why I called it a "political" or "politicized" theology. Politics is what we know; theology is what must make sense of the underlying political reality.

How this understanding of political realism ever became associated with the good name of Augustine is difficult for me to comprehend. But a further move intensified this kind of politicized theology. This move, as one finds in Paul Ramsey, links Augustine's earthly and heavenly cities in terms of a notion of politics mediated through Weber that suggests only one real politics exists, and it is a politics that recognizes the inevitability of mendacity, violence and a contest of powers. So Ramsey quotes Augustine in book 19, chapter 17, in order to argue that the *City of God* is "inextricably bound up with" the earthly city. He cites this reference, but as I will show in a moment, he leaves out key parts of the passage at those points where Augustine qualifies the relationship between the two cities. Ramsey quotes,

> The heavenly city, while it sojourns on earth . . . not scrupling about diversities in the manners, laws, and institutions whereby earthly peace is secured and maintained, but recognizing that, however various these are, they all tend to one and the same end of earthly peace . . . [is] so far from rescinding and abolishing these diversities, that it even preserves and adopts them. . . . Even the heavenly city, therefore, while in its state of pilgrimage, avails itself of the peace of earth, and . . . desires and maintains a common agreement among men regarding the acquisition of the necessities of life.[16]

---

[16]See D. Stephen Long, *Tragedy, Tradition, Transformism: The Ethics of Paul Ramsey* (1993; reprint, Eugene, Ore.: Cascade Press, 2007), p. 171.

From this Ramsey concludes, "Thus, a Christian in this life finds his own life and will bound up inextricably with such a common agreement among men as to the objects of their political purposes, and he is bound to foster the combination of men's wills to attain the things which are helpful to this life."[17] Ramsey makes it appear that there is only one way to be political in this life, and it is for the heavenly city to make common cause with the earthly city and use the means it deploys.

Does this follow from Augustine? What Ramsey left out in the quote he cites from the *City of God* shows that this "realist" reading of Augustine does not fit well what Augustine wrote. For Augustine did not write,

> The heavenly city, while it sojourns on earth . . . not scrupling about diversities in the manners, laws, and institutions whereby earthly peace is secured and maintained, but recognizing that, however various these are, they all tend to one and the same end of earthly peace . . . [is] so far from rescinding and abolishing these diversities, that it even preserves and adopts them.[18]

What he wrote was:

> The heavenly city, while it sojourns on earth . . . not scrupling about diversities in the manners, laws, and institutions whereby earthly peace is secured and maintained, but recognizing that, however various these are, they all tend to one and the same end of earthly peace . . . [is] so far from rescinding and abolishing these diversities, that it even preserves and adopts them so long only as no hindrance to the worship of the one supreme and true God is thus introduced.[19]

And where Ramsey cited Augustine as stating that the Christian "desires and maintains a common agreement among men regarding the acquisition of the necessities of life," he neglected to cite Augustine's second qualification, "so far as it can without injuring faith and godliness."[20] Augustine never argued that the city of God and the earthly city were inextricably bound up, that there was only one politics and that any good pol-

---

[17]Paul Ramsey, *War and the Christian Conscience* (Durham, N.C.: Duke University Press, 1961) p. 29.
[18]Long, *Tragedy, Tradition and Transformism*, p. 171.
[19]Ibid.
[20]Ibid.

itics would make common cause with the violence and mendacity of the earthly city because it promoted a common good. In fact, he argued that when the earthly city demanded anything contrary to the truthful worship of the true God, then Christians could not make common cause with it.

Augustinian realism misreads Augustine as Machiavelli. It assumes we must get our hands dirty in order to be political, which assumes that activities such as lying, deceit, manipulation and violence inescapably set the contours for politics. It assumes violence is as ontological as peace and thus repeats Greek notions of the tragic and calls this "realist" in direct opposition to Augustine's ontological priority of peaceableness. And it treats theological doctrines as mythopoetics, which is precisely what Augustine rejects in his rejection of fabulous theologies. I do not think that an appeal to the doctrine of original sin alone can make a position Augustinian, or for that matter Christian, but that is the only Augustinian doctrine on which this tradition of realism draws.

Augustine and the Other City

In *Another City: An Ecclesiological Primer for a Post-Christian World,* the Baptist theologian Barry Harvey nicely lays out a very different reading of Augustine from the one found in the realist tradition, which has great resonances with Dodaro's reading. In this reading we do not have a single politics that inextricably links the earthly and heavenly cities, but instead we have two very different politics located in two very different cities, both of which share the same space in that time known as the *saeculum,* the time between the times. Here the task of the church is not, as it is in Augustinian realism, to foster the combination of wills between the earthly and heavenly city despite what that combination requires of Christians. Augustinian realism views Christians as having a mission in the world, and the church is instrumental to the mission. For the Augustinian of the other city, as Harvey puts it, "This community was the mission."[21] Or as Stanley Hauerwas puts it, "The Church doesn't have a social ethic; it is a social

---

[21]Barry A. Harvey, *Another City* (Harrisburg, Penn.: Trinity Press International, 1999), p. 27.

ethic."[22] Here the church is the other city by which all politics is to be measured. This does not mean alliances and common causes cannot be made with those who are not members of the church; they can. We all share a common space and time and work within it. But the church also has its own sense of time, exemplified in liturgical time, and its own sense of space, found present in the Word and Eucharist. The church's political task then is to read all politics through this alternative space and time even while it exists within secular time.

This tradition of Augustinian thought tends to draw on the conclusion from book 18 of the *City of God*, which sets the stage for the discussion of the different ends of the two cities in book 19. Book 18 concludes with this:

> But let us now at last finish this book, after thus far treating of, and showing as far as seemed sufficient, what is the mortal course of the two cities, the heavenly and the earthly, which are mingled together from the beginning down to the end. Of these, the earthly one has made to herself of whom she would either from any other quarter, or even from among men, false gods, who she might serve by sacrifice; but she which is heavenly and is a pilgrim on the earth does not make false gods, but is herself made by the true God of whom she herself must be the true sacrifice. Yet both alike either enjoy temporal good things, or are afflicted with temporal evil, but with diverse faith, diverse hope, and diverse love, until they must be separated by the last judgment, and each must receive her own ends, of which there is no end.[23]

The two cities, which share the same goods and afflictions in time, have diverse faiths, hopes and loves and therefore very different ends. The one end is idolatrous and invites you to live the deceitful life of a fabulous theology. The other serves the true God and knows the supreme good, which alone should make you happy, for it is not subject to the vagaries of historical contingency. Augustinianism teaches us to be suspicious of the earthly city because its politics depends on false gods based on deceit and violence that inevitably try to absorb the other city into its false end.

---

[22]Stanley Hauerwas, *The Peaceable Kingdom* (Notre Dame, Ind.: University of Notre Dame Press, 1983), p. 99.

[23]Augustine, *City of God*, bk. 18, trans. Marcus Dodds (Grand Rapids, Mich.: Eerdmans, 1979), p. 54.

Augustine's Three Theologies and Political Ends

When Augustine begins book 19, in which he sets out the different ends of the two cities, he does so by referring to Varro and the 288 different philosophical sects on which different conceptions of the supreme good are founded. He refers to ancient philosophy and not ancient religion because he agreed early on with Varro that of the three kinds of theology practiced during his age, only natural theology or philosophy approximates what Christians mean by theology. He agreed with Varro about this but disagreed with him that ancient natural theology knew the supreme good. And for Augustine, without knowledge of the supreme good, no true politics could exist. For Augustine, politics is not grounded in evil and sin; it is grounded in the good. That is why his work can never be understood well in liberal, political societies, to which evangelical Christians remain deeply committed, even patterning our ecclesiologies after them. True politics has a name: Jerusalem, the city of peace. And for Augustine, peace both eternally and temporally is the supreme good that alone brings happiness (*City of God* 19.11). Augustine stated,

> For even the mystical name of the city itself, that is, Jerusalem means, as I have already said, "Vision of Peace." But as the word peace is employed in connection with things in this world in which certainly life eternal has no place, we have preferred to call the end or supreme good of this city life eternal rather than peace . . . it may therefore be advisable, in order that every one may readily understand what we mean, to say that the end or supreme good of this city is either peace in eternal life, or eternal life in peace. For peace is a good so great, that even in this earthly and mortal life there is no word we hear with such pleasure, nothing we desire with such zest, or find to be more thoroughly gratifying. (*City of God* 19.11)

For Augustine, only the city of God can deliver on this true end, and therefore only it is truly political. And thus theology should never be in service to some other politics; theology understood within the context of the city of God is always already political. This helps us make sense of Augustine's analysis of Varro's types of theology.

In *City of God* 6.5, Augustine discusses the types of theology as Varro laid them out. He gives them the name fabulous (mythical), physical or natural and civil. Fabulous theology is for the people; it is the theology present in the forum presented by poets and actors. (In our day you might say it is the theology that can be found on television and perhaps on the Internet.) Natural theology is theology for the academy; it is kept out of the hands of the populace, for it begins with criticism of the mythical theology. Augustine quotes Varro's criticism of fabulous theology: "For we find in it that one god has been born from the head, another from the thigh, another from drops of blood; also in this we find that gods have stolen, committed adultery, served men; in a word, in this all manner of things are attributed to the gods, such as may befall, not merely any man, but even the most contemptible man" (*City of God* 6.5). Natural theology rejects fables and myths; it deals with matters that we would call metaphysics. It does not concede the poets' fabulous theology but examines fire, atoms and numbers. Augustine sides with Varro up to this point, but Varro then goes on to distinguish natural and civil theology. Civil theology is for "citizens in the city." It is what the "priests ought to know and to administer." Varro concludes that fabulous theology is for the theater, natural theology is for the world and civic theology is for the city.

These three theologies serve different interests, the interests found in the theater, the academy and the city. In a book titled *City of God*, this should make us take note, for Augustine is also providing a theology for the city in this work, but his will be neither fabulous nor civic. In fact, Augustine questions whether Varro has truly distinguished a fabulous from a civic theology. He writes,

> But those two theologies, the first and the third—to wit, those of the theatre and of the city—has he distinguished them or united them? For although we see that the city is in the world, we do not see that it follows that many things belonging to the city pertain to the world. For it is possible that such things may be worshipped and believed in the city, according to false opinions, as have no existence either in the world or out of it. But where is the theatre but in the city? Who instituted the theatre but the state? (*City of God* 6.5)

Augustine argues that Varro's distinction between the fabulous and the civic is the right distinction to make; he needs to distance God from any political instrumentality, which is found in both the fabulous and civic theologies. A civic theology, like the fabulous, does not make it politically real. But like the theater, it is an illusion whose true interests are hidden behind fantastic images.

Varro recognizes that a kind of theology exists that is not made by human hands; it would be neither fabulous nor civic. But Varro cannot rid himself of the assumption, the all-too-Greek-and-Roman (and perhaps American) assumption that the gods must serve primarily political interests; they must serve the earthly city. So Augustine says to Varro, "Thou desirest to worship natural gods; thou are compelled to worship the civil." The difficulty with both the fabulous and the civic theology is that they serve primarily human interests, and thus the true subject matter of such theology is not God but humanity.

Nevertheless, Augustine finds that Varro opens up a space for a development of a true, rather than a fabulous, theology. He writes,

> Who then is so stupid as not to perceive that this man [Varro], by setting forth and opening up so diligently the civil theology, and by exhibiting its likeness to that fabulous, shameful, and disgraceful theology, and also by teaching that that fabulous sort is also a part of this other [civic theology], was laboring to obtain a place in the minds of men for none but that natural theology, which he says pertains to philosophers, with such subtlety that he censures the fabulous, and not daring openly to censure the civil, shows its censurable character by simply exhibiting it; and thus, both being reprobated by the judgment of men of right standing, the natural alone remains to be chosen. (*City of God* 6.9)

Varro, like all created things for Augustine, points in the direction of the one true God, who is more like the God of the philosophers than the gods of the civic and mythic religions. Augustine recognized that Christianity is not religious; it bears nothing in common with the fabulous tales and spectacles in the state-sponsored theaters that serve the interests of civic theology. Christianity is more like what the philosophers do in the academy, but unlike them, Christianity does not refuse to speak the truth about God in the forum. It makes no compromise with the civic theology, as Varro's natural theology had to do. And this is only because there is another city, a true city, that allows the truth of God to be spoken in such a way that we need not present God as simply a fabulous image of human making.

Augustine explains this when at the beginning of book 11 he makes the important move from critiquing Greek and Roman theology to presenting the theology of the *City of God*. He writes,

> We have learned that there is a city of God and its Founder has inspired us with a love which makes us covet its citizenship. To this Founder of the holy city the citizens of the earthly city prefer their own gods, not knowing that He is the God of gods, not of false, i.e., of impious and proud gods, who, being deprived of His unchangeable and freely communicated light, and so reduced to a kind of poverty-stricken power, eagerly grasp at their own private privileges and seek divine honors from their deluded subjects; but of the pious and holy gods, who are better pleased to submit themselves to one, than to subject many to themselves, and who would rather worship God than be worshipped as God. (*City of God* 11.1)

Augustinian realism, with its mythopoetic interpretation of Christian doctrine, and its a priori acceptance of the political as a site of contestation and power that cannot be ordered toward anything true or good beyond it, is not Augustinian. It is a return to the pagan fabulous and civic theologies from which Augustine's *City of God* is a remedy. What makes this a remedy is that we have with us, in time, a vision of another city that is not grounded in evil, diversity and power but in a common life, a common life based on the necessity of confession and penance for us to speak and live truthfully. For only in confession can we avoid the deceptive politics of the lie. As Paul Griffiths reminds us, for Augustine, "Confession is the only speech-act not performatively incoherent in the mode of the lie, and so confession is the ideal type of truthful speech."[24] This is of course dangerous; a common life can lead to the tower of Babel. The earthly cities grounded in deceit are God's judgment against such a false unity. But with Christ's resurrection, ascension and pouring out of the Holy Spirit, the

---

[24]Griffiths, *Lying*, p. 92.

task of the church, both future and ancient, is to share in his common unity, to have the "same mind." This mind, however, cannot be one that seeks to dominate through mendacity and violence but one where we can tell the truth about all those deceits that form the everyday basis of our family and political life. That requires listening to those who are not from our tribe about how we fail in this common life.

If there is no catholic community, transnationally united in Christ through its penitential structures, there can be no truly just society, or at least not one in terms that Augustine would recognize. For evangelicals, this produces a problem. How do we hear the witness of the common life, a common life that is both diachronic and synchronic, against us when the illuminated individual reading Scripture is the primary source of authority? How can we speak of a common life when we confess catholicity but have no genuine structures for it? Can we hear Hugo Rahner's critique of us? "It is a fact grasped not only by faith but also seen in history that all the churches who wish to withdraw from the unity of the church dogmatically first of all seek refuge with the state but soon are absorbed by the state and fall with it."[25] How can we have a truly catholic unity based on a common worship and life, drawing on the ancients, leading us into the future unity we know Christ seeks for his church?

At least these two possibilities emerge. First, we might find our way back to Rome as communions (not individuals). We will need to live in such a way that Catholics see our faith and seek a genuine unity. We will also need their ecclesial structures; for they have had the only successful transnational unity grounded in a penitential structure that did not finally depend on a modern nation-state or ethnic identity for its viability. Second, we could work toward a conciliar Catholicism that forges a common penitential structure that would include accountability in doctrine, worship and life, perhaps along the lines of the newly developing Anglican covenant. Without some such politics of sameness that unites us in the one body of Christ and asks of us obedience to something other than ourselves, then I fear that what will emerge in recent evangelical efforts to recover antiquity for the future of the church will be nothing but one more consumer

---

[25]Hugo Rahner, *Church and State in Early Christianity* (San Francisco: Ignatius, 1992), p. xvi.

option we individuals can choose to give our lives meaning. And that will be about as significant as the food court at the mall. If the emergent movement contributes to this transnational unity, it will truly be emergent, and we pray God's blessings on it. If it only seeks to be one more consumer option further fragmenting Christ's already fragmented, tortured body, then may it go the way of other commodity fetishes like Pokemon cards and hula hoops. I hope and pray it will be the former.

A Forward Glance

Emergent Christianity

13

Emerging from What, Going Where?

Emerging Churches and Ancient Christianity

Jason Byassee

It was a pleasure to teach Augustine at Wheaton College in the spring of 2007. The students were as good as I had been led to expect—hard-working, curious, spiritually serious. I did notice in many of them a certain dis-ease with the evangelicalism in which they were raised. They seemed unsure that their home churches had all the answers they once thought they did. Some simply grumbled about it—they were often in the back corner of my class, cracking jokes at things the other students took very seriously. Some took the path outlined famously by Robert Webber, of blessed memory, in *Evangelicals on the Canterbury Trail*. They now worship in Anglican churches with their ordered liturgy, apostolic succession and sacramental emphases.[1] Some were tempted to more life-changing conversions to Roman Catholic or Orthodox churches. Some, I should say, were just fine in their home churches, thank you very much. If I had to guess, most will remain in the evangelical churches that taught them Christ, baptized them and sent them to Wheaton. If asked, I counseled them that Augustine, the

---

[1]Robert Webber, *Evangelicals on the Canterbury Trail* (Harrisburg, Penn.: Morehouse, 1989).

subject of my course, would say they should do just that. Given this restlessness, I am not surprised Emergent has caught hold among such students elsewhere.

My students did not seem much interested in Emergent, though. It may be that the heat Emergent has taken from evangelicals like D. A. Carson has turned them off.[2] Most of this criticism has centered around what is perceived as Brian McLaren and friends' abandonment of "absolute truth." I do not know of serious criticism of Emergent that has not come from the theological right.

Mine today will come from the left. Not that I mean it to. I just belong to mainline liberal institutions—the United Methodist Church of my baptism and training, the *Christian Century* of my present vocation. I see Emergent as a movement of postevangelicals in search of a theology. Postevangelicals because they are reacting to the evangelicalism of their youth, though mostly trying to stay evangelical. Many of Emergent's original visionaries came out of the Willow Creek-inspired Leadership Network. They wanted to plant new churches but without a great-man figure in charge of thousands of anonymous worshipers. Each seeks a smaller communion, without hierarchy, with a return to beautiful and tactile worship. These young leaders are church planters, pastors, sometime-activists and serious Christian people but not academic theologians. They do know they are not satisfied with the theology they were given growing up or in evangelical seminaries. So they have gone hunting for something new: meeting with the likes of Miroslav Volf, Walter Brueggemann, Stanley Hauerwas, Nancey Murphy and N. T. Wright—the sorts of figures mainline churches have hailed for years. As a journalist I see more overlap between mainline and evangelical than is often thought. The developing theological allegiances of Emergent both show this overlap and take it farther.

Emergent or emerging churches have become a brand of sorts. Marcus Borg uses the term *Emerging* to advertise his events now—which is

---

[2]D. A. Carson, *Becoming Conversant with the Emerging Church* (Grand Rapids, Mich.: Zondervan, 2005). James K. A. Smith, *Who's Afraid of Postmodernism?* (Grand Rapids, Mich.: Baker, 2006) includes a trenchant critique of Carson, though Smith is not uncritical of Emergent.

enough to make me wish McLaren and friends had copyrighted the name. The "emerging church" is then a broad phenomenon; anyone can use the word, no one owns it. But the particular crowd I am referring to now often distinguishes itself online (where else?) as the Emergent Village—with Tony Jones as "national coordinator" and the only paid leader, Brian McLaren as worldwide spokesman, Doug Pagitt and dozens of other prolific authors as key members. Eddie Gibbs's and Ryan Bolger's *Emerging Churches* describes emerging churches as "communities that practice the way of Jesus within postmodern cultures."[3] Emergent Village's website does not even use the word *postmodern*, which is good, since the movement's philosophical emphases are not its strengths: Emergent is "a growing, generative friendship among missional Christians seeking to love our world in the Spirit of Jesus Christ"—an interestingly trinitarian description.[4]

It is very hard to talk about Emergent in a formal academic way because postmodern types like to avoid labels, and these figures are genuinely not all in agreement with each other. Emergent is serious when it describes itself as a "conversation." It may seem like more of a formal organization because the name is bandied about, there are publishing series associated with it and so on. But all of these folks are preaching on Sundays, and in quite different ecclesial traditions. There is no creed, no handbook, no seminaries, no denomination; one community insists it has no meetings and no members(!). They just like to "throw parties," as Andrew Jones from Emergent UK likes to say. That is, gatherings for conversation with theologians and one another, both in the flesh and on the Web. The best way to get to know churches aligned with Emergent Village is to spend time with them at one of these many gatherings around the country several times a year or at churches like Life on the Vine in Arlington Heights, Illinois, or Wicker Park Grace in Chicago. These are enormously talented church leaders, and their nose for faithful innovation often impresses me.

But I said I would criticize. To do so, I should say a word about what

---

[3]Eddie Gibbs and Ryan K. Bolger, *Emerging Churches* (Grand Rapids, Mich.: Baker, 2005).
[4]"About Emergent Village," Emergent Village <www.emergentvillage.com/about>.

Emergent is emerging from and what it is reacting to, theologically speaking. Mark Driscoll is founding pastor of Mars Hill Church in Seattle, one of America's fastest-growing congregations, with a church planting apparatus called Acts29 that is busily starting new churches elsewhere. He used to meet with his fellow young leaders in the Leadership Network in the early 1990s to talk about the then-buzzwords Generation X ministry and postmodern ministry. Driscoll shares with his fellow Emergent visionaries a love of popular culture, especially music, which he integrates into Mars Hill avidly. (This is, of course, quite a difference from fundamentalist reactionaries of yore.) But his theology is little different from classic fundamentalism either in substance or spirit. In Robert Webber's helpful collection *Listening to the Beliefs of Emerging Churches*,[5] Driscoll plays doctrine cop, excoriating his former comrades in the conversation, mostly with the theological form of the abstract list. Driscoll offers us long catalogs of "what Scripture says about Scripture," passages detailing the doctrine of atonement and rote detail on what the Bible says about hell. Theology here is scrubbed of any mystery. It is simply a dessicated inventory of beliefs culled from the Bible without attention to their context in the narrative. Driscoll also handily ignores passages that cut against the flow of his lists, such as Jesus' love for outcasts rather than religious people. Driscoll has Paul describe Jesus as "the second member of the Trinity," says Jesus accepts the "Old Testament Canon as it exists today, without any modifications" and has Scripture say clearly the "Jesus is called God throughout."[6] Never mind it took the church centuries to wade through Scripture and ponder its way toward the doctrine of the Trinity, the shape of the canon and the divine nature of Christ. It does not trouble Driscoll to say the Christian view of God is "superior to all others" and that Jesus "condemns all other religions."[7] I suppose Driscoll is alluding to the story in which the Buddhist monks appear to Jesus and he curses them. Driscoll oddly insists

[5]Robert Webber, ed., *Listening to the Beliefs of Emerging Churches* (Grand Rapids, Mich.: Zondervan, 2007).
[6]See Mark Driscoll's essay, "The Emerging Church and Biblicist Theology," in *Listening to the Beliefs of Emerging Churches,* ed. Robert Webber (Grand Rapids, Mich.: Zondervan, 2007), pp. 21, 23, 27.
[7]Ibid., pp. 27, 71.

"the gospel message . . . does not emanate in any way from the culture" and holds the "unredeemed people . . . are totally sinful in their every motive, word, deed and thought."[8] He means it too—he excludes one interlocutor's use of a liberal theologian because the man, Henry Churchill King, helped found *The New Republic,* and objects to a quotation from the poet Rainer Maria Rilke because his mom wished he was a girl—which everyone knows entails automatic disqualification from the canon of theological poetry.[9] When he gets around to telling Karen Ward of the Church of the Apostles that she has no authority to lead a church because she is a woman, it is one of the more charitable things he has said in the whole book.[10]

I take Emergent as a welcome reaction against this sort of theology, one in which God's mind is transparently open to the manly man pastor who builds an ecclesial empire by dispensing these facts about God to the rest of us. The Bible is treated here like an oracle, a totem, and not a witness to the living Word of God who is the resurrected Christ. There is no attention here to church history or to Christ's constant and radical grace extended to outsiders and call to repentance to insiders. There is also in Driscoll a Manichaean split between the good church and the totally unredeemed outsiders. Strikingly, for one so proud of resisting trendy theology, Driscoll picks up on the quite trendy view of the social Trinity: he argues the doctrine of the Trinity is essential to Christian faith since it "reveals a God who exists as a loving community."[11] No, it does not—it reveals a mystery of one God who is eternally three persons, not three people.[12] Driscoll shows here the importance of Augustine's teaching against pride: in supreme confidence of our sinlessness and superiority, we champion something that is in fact wrong. Augustine would not be surprised.

It is not surprising that Doug Pagitt, a longtime leader in Emergent, would react harshly to Driscoll. In fact, he overreacts. For Pagitt, the issues the church dealt with in the first or fourth or sixteenth century are simply

---

[8]Ibid., pp. 29, 33.
[9]Ibid., pp. 145, 184.
[10]Ibid., p. 184.
[11]Ibid., p. 28.
[12]The collections of essays in Sarah Coakley, *Rethinking Gregory of Nyssa* (Malden, Mass.: Blackwell, 2003), make this quite clear.

a misfit with the issues we deal with today: "the change from the Jewish sect struggling with the Jewish/Gentile question to the Hellenization [*sic*] and Christian empire is immeasurable."[13] He wants theology to believe in "progress, to get better," to be "far more humane."[14] He uses an example close to the heart of the Internet-savvy Emergent culture: in the late 1990s he needed an adapter card and a phone cord to get online, but now all he needs is a wireless card, no cord at all. "In my view, theology is like the adapter"—ever evolving, and fast.[15] This is a good thing, because the early church is an unmitigated disaster for Pagitt, especially in its Augustinian forms. Pelagius had a theology that fit his "Druid notions of the Northern Island region of his home," whereas Augustine "supported the Greek understanding of God taken primarily from the Greek Pantheon imagery."[16] The "Irish of Pelagius' land" sought to find "the goodness in creation and organize the church to live in harmony with the God of the earth. For the Greeks of Augustine's land, the dance was Roman spirituality. This called for an explanation of how one might appease the removed God living in an 'elsewhere heaven.' "[17] For Pagitt, the early church, except for Pelagius apparently, was intrinsically Gnostic, with a God "removed from creation and protected in an isolated heaven," the "removed mover." He concludes, "The need to have a more full gospel that jettisons as much as possible the tentacles of Gnosticism that have plagued Christian theology for centuries has, perhaps, never been more necessary."[18]

Where to start? Pelagius was British, not Irish; Augustine was Roman, not Greek; this took place in the fifth century, not the fourth; and Augustine drew on Platonic sources, not "plutonic."[19] More seriously and inter-

---

[13]Doug Pagitt's essay, "The Emerging Church and Embodied Theology," in *Listening to the Beliefs of Emerging Churches,* ed. Robert Webber (Grand Rapids, Mich.: Zondervan, 2007), p. 127.

[14]Ibid., pp. 138-39.

[15]Ibid., p. 122.

[16]Ibid., p. 128.

[17]Ibid., p. 129.

[18]Ibid., pp. 134-36. Pagitt never reveals any sources here, but if I had to guess it would be handbook introductions to "Celtic Christianity" that use Augustine as a whipping boy.

[19]Ibid., p. 134. The reference to "plutonic" sources could simply be a typographical error, and so this criticism should be directed at Zondervan and not at Pagitt. But Pagitt's misdescription of so much else in the early church leads me to wonder whether blame goes in both directions.

estingly, why does Pagitt get to call the early church "Gnostic"? We know the word *Gnostic* only because early church opponents to this Christian heresy, among them Irenaeus, denounced belief in salvation by gnosis, in disparagement of the body. It is a point of hardened dogma for Pagitt here that the early church was irredeemably vile. He even uses a Christian dogmatic category to brand it and excommunicate it. Fundamentalism is a hard habit to break.

More interesting still is Pagitt's confidence in modern progress. I know something about this—I work for a magazine called the *Christian Century* that meant for the twentieth century—not the twenty-first—to bring the ushering in of the kingdom by renewed Christian missionary, ecumenical and political efforts. Didn't quite work out that way, did it? Postmodernism has rightly pointed out that unbridled belief in modern progress has often brought us better and more efficient ways to kill people, not just to get on the Internet in coffee shops. Pagitt presents a surprisingly modern moment from a movement so keen to align with postmodern sensibilities.

Most important of all: Augustine. To say that God is removed from Augustine is to suggest one simply has not read *Confessions*. God is closer to Augustine than Augustine is to himself—more interior than his own self. Indeed, some scholars have criticized Augustine for a God too close to his own soul, for "inventing" the modern self.[20] The one who is far away from Augustine is Augustine—in a dissolute wasteland, wandering far from home, like the prodigal son, trying to evade a God who loves him lavishly. God's answer to Augustine's predicament is not a thunderbolt from a Greek pantheon. It is incarnation. Many philosophies and religions can give you a glimpse of God afar off; only in Christ does God come in flesh, as the crucified slave at our feet. Augustine reacts to his Manichaean past throughout his career with lyric praise of the very fleshiness of our God as the perfect remedy for the tumor of human pride.[21]

---

[20]The literature is vast, but Charles Taylor, *Sources of the Self* (Cambridge, Mass.: Harvard University Press, 1992), will always be worth reading. Michael Hanby, *Augustine and Modernity* (London: Routledge, 2003), is a welcome critique of Taylor.

[21]These emphases come from Augustine *Confessions*, bks. 2, 5 and 7, trans. Henry Chadwick (Oxford: Oxford University Press, 1992).

Both Driscoll and Pagitt evince the sort of pride Augustine sees as our condition under sin. The interesting thing about pride in *Confessions* is that it is not pure rebellion against God, running in the opposite direction. It is unintentional mimicry of God. The proud person imitates God unwittingly.[22] We humans all have to imitate God. We can try to imitate God's magnificence and end up as little tyrants, confident in ourselves and belittling of opponents. Or we can imitate the humility of God, enfleshed to save, poured out in love of others. In other words, pride is not thinking too highly of oneself. Humility is not beating oneself up. Pride is pathetically trying to imitate God's grandeur instead of becoming comfortable in God's flesh, the body of Christ, the church. The antidote to pride is something close to Emergent's heart: friendship. When Augustine tries to read the Bible by himself in *Confessions,* he is put off by it. It is nothing compared with the stately prose of Cicero. But then he meets Ambrose, who shows him how to read it. And Simplicianus, who tells him about the great philosopher Marius Victorinus's conversion to Christianity. And Ponticianus sees Augustine reading Paul and immediately tells him about Anthony, whose battles with demons in the desert show lust can be conquered. In other words, Scripture is not to be read by solitary individuals trying to cook up their own belief systems from scratch—that is pride; do not do that or you will wind up hating the flesh and denying the goodness of the world. Scripture is to be read with and through friends, both living friends, the church on pilgrimage, and dead friends, the church in glory. Augustine's great ire, like Jesus', is aimed at those who would be religiously good by their own resources—the Donatists who would have a better church, the Pelagians who can make their own way toward holiness, thanks very much. For Augustine, neither group needs Jesus or the ordinary church of humdrum sinners at the church down on the corner—and Augustine desperately needs both.

So how hard does my charge of pride hit the rest of Emergent? Driscoll is now on the outside firing back at his erstwhile friends. Pagitt is pastor of

---

[22]I draw here on James Wetzel, "Snares of Truth: Augustine on Free Will and Predestination," in *Augustine and His Critics,* ed. Robert Dodaro and George Lawless (London: Routledge, 2000), and on *Confessions* 2.

one church among hundreds in Emergent, though a visible one and a prolific author. Much of the conversation is much more interesting than what
Driscoll and Pagitt offer. For example, take Tony Jones's book on *lectio divina*.[23] Jones's work shows clearly that Emergent's reaction against evangelicalism can lead it to sink its roots deeper into the soil of the ancient Christian church. Jones does not apologize for using a twelfth-century master of
prayer, a certain Guigo II, to introduce the art of sacred reading of Scripture to his lay readers today. We should read Scripture not like we teach
our graduate students to read—as fast as possible, to have something to say
in seminar. Jones unforgettably compares these reading habits with a hot-
dog-eating contest.[24] No: we are to chew on Scripture, like a dog does a
bone or a lion does a carcass: slowly, meditatively, turning over the key
words in the text in our brain, reading them literally, figurally, for minutes,
even hours. To pray like the ancient church is to learn to slow down generally, and then to bathe all our lives in prayer, such that Jones and his wife
can learn to see child rearing, diaper changing, mac-and-cheese baking as
also prayerful. He gives specific instructions about posture and breathing.
And he shows us how he teaches this way of reading to children in his
church in Minnesota. This is Emergent at its best: practical, physical even
(sit up straight, have the lights dim but not too dim, do not be too full or
too hungry), recovering an ancient resource for a new day, showing us an
ancient-future way of being evangelical.

This is Emergent's genius, I think: its willingness to experiment litur-
gically and practically. I do not use the word *genius* lightly—these folks
have been steeped in the best practices of evangelicals, their christocen-
trism, their love of Scripture, their passion for worship and outreach and
activism. Now, in an experimental manner, they are deconstructing some
of the barricades evangelicals customarily place around the things they
cherish to see what happens. Emergent is evangelicalism with the guard-
rails off. And some of the results are simply brilliant. A church in Atlanta
that spends its Easter Sunday cleaning up a playground that had been filled

---

[23]Tony Jones, *Divine Intervention* (Colorado Springs, Colo.: Th1nk, 2006).
[24]Ibid., p. 59.

with syringes and crack vials. By the end, they stand in a circle around a civic space for children reborn and shout that "Jesus is Lord," with dirt on their Easter best.[25] A church called Communality that bought a house in a troubled part of Lexington, Kentucky, where they could affect the neighborhood, invite neighbors to join them and share a common purse. Now that is a response to modernity that is serious: giving up on suburbia, eschewing wealth and offering costly hospitality.[26] Another Emergent community in St. Louis, Levi's Table, has made a similar commitment to a common purse. There is no pastor and no staff, everyone tithes, and no one gets paid. So when the local food bank's truck broke down and they needed $11,000 to fix it, this church of twenty people could say, "Done; what else do you need?"[27] Several other Emergent communities here and in Europe are experimenting with monasticism, making vows of poverty, chastity and obedience that include space for marriage and children.[28] This strikes me as a fundamentally hopeful movement for the future of the church. I not only wish it success, I even think the future of the church depends on this sort of revival of monasticism. It is one of the great ironies of church history and economics that communities that pledge to poverty are marked by generosity of heart, while suburban spaces with mountains of cash like Wheaton are full of people who are stressed they do not have enough, with maxed credit cards and superficial relationships. This new-monastic sliver of Emergent has much to teach all of us.[29]

There are other ways this proudly postmodern group is pushing roots deeper into premodern soil. There is a marked enthusiasm among Emergents for ancient church liturgy. It is hard to find one of these communities that does not celebrate the Eucharist more frequently than do its evangel-

---

[25]Troy Bronsink, "The Art of Emergence: Being God's Handiwork," in *An Emergent Manifesto of Hope*, ed. Doug Pagitt and Tony Jones (Grand Rapids, Mich.: Baker, 2007), p. 71.

[26]Sherry Maddock and Geoff Maddock, "An Ever-Renewed Adventure of Faith: Notes from a Community," in *An Emergent Manifesto of Hope*, ed. Doug Pagitt and Tony Jones (Grand Rapids, Mich.: Baker, 2007), p. 84.

[27]Gibbs and Bolger, *Emerging Churches*, p. 151.

[28]Most notably Andrew Jones, <www.tallskinnykiwi.com>. See also Karen Sloan, *Flirting with Monasticism* (Downers Grove, Ill.: InterVarsity Press, 2006).

[29]I think here of Alasdair MacIntyre's hope for "another—doubtless very different—St. Benedict," in *After Virtue*, 2nd ed. (Notre Dame, Ind.: Notre Dame University Press, 1984), p. 263.

ical forebears. To put it in their language, "The liturgical thing is erupting everywhere."[30] So House of Mercy in St. Paul has not only regular confession, Eucharist and evening compline but also an appointed thurifer to swing the incense pot and an annual stations of the cross liturgy for Good Friday, with church members' artwork at each station.[31] Karen Ward of Church of the Apostles in Seattle speaks of herself not as priest of this Episcopal church but as abbess, presiding over a community of those who have made vows in the church, seeking God together. At Pagitt's Solomon's Porch in Minneapolis, one is likely to pray while making the sign of the cross. There are ways in which these churches are more Catholic than most post-Vatican II Catholic churches, which ironically look longingly at evangelical megachurches due to their shortage of priests.[32]

Now, this enthusiasm for practices in general, and ancient Christian ones at that, can be dangerous. They can be a sort of fetish in which icons and sacraments and vows become trinkets, things done for the sake of novelty rather than in order to pursue holiness in Christ. Doug Pagitt speaks of himself as "post-Protestant," and a key book on Emergent lists all the ways these churches "feel more Catholic than Protestant."[33] Icons, candles and so on. But "Catholic" is not something you can feel this way. It is a specific church, in submission to the bishop of Rome, trying to hold all that the church has taught in the one body from the apostles to now in every time and place. You cannot feel it any more than you can feel married without being married—it involves a particular people with whom one must join up.

How then can I be so hopeful about the renewal of these practices among Emergents? Because practices can outpace theory and leave room for the theoretical foundation to be built later. It is good for the church to celebrate the Eucharist as much as possible, even if we do not do it "right."

---

[30]Gibbs and Bolger, *Emerging Churches*, p. 225.

[31]Ibid., p. 226.

[32]See Brian Mitchell, "The American Catholic Merger-Church: A Too Small Answer," in *An Emergent Manifesto of Hope*, ed. Doug Pagitt and Tony Jones (Grand Rapids, Mich.: Baker, 2007), pp. 109-18. This chapter fits oddly with the rest of the book, and I remain dubious whether Roman Catholics will take much interest in Emergent.

[33]Gibbs and Bolger, *Emerging Churches*, p. 38.

I would wish for a Communion table open only to those who are baptized and confess the apostolic faith, and Emergent's many communion tables are open in a way I find careless. But the fact is they are practicing the Eucharist. To call a community a monastery or its leader an abbot or abbess can be an act of hubris. You probably have to be around a while, say, a few centuries, before you can claim it without blushing. All the same, they are pursuing a form of the life envisioned by saints like Anthony and Benedict and Bernard; who knows what good can come of a practice rushed into like this, however fool-hardily? Renewed efforts at ancient Christian practices may represent here the sort of foolishness for Christ that can make new things possible, things we cannot now foresee. The unity and catholicity of the church have been tragically broken at least since the Reformation, more likely since the split between East and West in the eleventh century, or even some of the mismanaged controversies of the ancient church, but it is a unity we still confess in our creeds and must pursue in risky ways with our lives. As a mainline Protestant, I mouth a commitment to a single catholic church that these folks are living out in fresh ways. Who knows how God will bless them?[34]

What I have called Emergent's genius for practical innovation in worship and church life should not be taken to mean they alone care about ancient-future innovation. Many of the things I have mentioned are also being pursued by evangelical churches that are not part of the Emerging church movement.[35] The new monasticism is made up of either Mennonites or those influenced by the Mennonites. They are much less interested in what is culturally relevant and much more interested in pursuing the form of life laid out for us in the New Testament, including Jesus' call to nonviolence, love of enemies and peacemaking. Some of the emphases on

---

[34]I'm thinking here of Walter Kasper's famous statement, "The ecumenical aim is not a simple return of the other into the fold of the Roman Catholic Church nor the conversion of individuals, even if this must obviously be mutually acknowledged when based on conscience. In the ecumenical movement the question is conversion to Christ. In him we move closer to one another." See Jason Byassee, "Going Catholic: Six Journeys to Rome," *Christian Century,* August 22, 2006.

[35]See Jason Byassee, "The New Monastics: Alternative Christian Communities," *Christian Century,* October 18, 2005; Jon Stock, Tim Otto and Jonathan Wilson-Hartgrove, *Inhabiting the Church* (Eugene, Ore.: Cascade, 2007).

hospitality and culturally relevant outreach have been practiced for years in quite modern churches like Willow Creek, the very mother church against which many Emergent leaders are reacting. Evangelicals are much less allergic to sacraments generally than they have been in centuries, and not only at Emergent, as Webber has shown and my students at Wheaton embodied. My friend Tim Conder, a leader in Emergent Village, worries that his fellow participants in the Emergent conversation may have "inappropriate respect for the existing church" and describes how he would return from early Emergent conferences with what he thought were fresh ideas, only to learn his Bible Church congregation had thought of it years before.[36]

The fact that Emergent does not have the market cornered on faithful innovation points to a problem in the conversation: it tends to overstate when it describes itself publicly. It is not uncommon for Emergent folks to speak of their interest in theology done relationally, rather than propositionally or doctrinally.[37] This is simply a false dichotomy. Surely propositions or doctrines do not exclude relationships. For Christians, they enhance them. The church needs both. Another common theme is that Christianity has been thought of as preparation for death or heaven in the afterlife, and in contrast, Emergent is interested in how we live.[38] This, again, oversimplifies and overshoots. Faith surely needs to be both, and if any culture needs wisdom on how to die well, surely ours does. There is a tendency to overstate the victory of postmodernism, since many of the church's ideas "simply are not viable in postmodern culture."[39] Or, even more boldly, Bolger and Gibbs write that to avoid the risk of engaging postmodernism simply is to "let the church exist without the kingdom, without Jesus, and thus without its proper identity as the people of

---

[36]Tim Conder, "The Existing Church/Emerging Church Matrix: Collision, Credibility, Missional Collaboration and Generative Friendship," in *An Emergent Manifesto of Hope*, ed. Doug Pagitt and Tony Jones (Grand Rapids, Mich.: Baker, 2007), pp. 105-6.

[37]John Burke, "Response to Mark Driscoll," in *Listening to the Beliefs of Emerging Churches*, ed. Robert Webber (Grand Rapids, Mich.: Zondervan), p. 37; and *An Emergent Manifesto*, p. 102.

[38]Gibbs and Bolger, *Emerging Churches*, p. 55; Spencer Burke, *A Heretic's Guide to Eternity* (San Francisco: Jossey-Bass, 2006), p. 82.

[39]Gibbs and Bolger, *Emerging Churches*, pp. 28-29; Pagitt's essay "The Emerging Church and Embodied Theology" in *Listening to the Beliefs of Emerging Churches*, p. 43.

God."[40] Perhaps they exaggerate for effect here, but surely postmodernism is not a point of dogma, without which we lose the kingdom, Jesus and the church!

My reading is that postmodernism is a form of modernity, one that shares modernity's emphases on tolerance regarding a religion relegated to one side of the dichotomy between public and private spheres.[41] Postmodernity tends breathlessly to announce some bold new future that the dusty old institutions of the past had better ready themselves for, lest they be left behind—just as its modern forebears tended to do. That is, the very rhetoric often employed by Emergents on behalf of postmodernity is itself modern rhetoric. We often hear this sort of thing in my mainline circles: the church had better acclimate to historical criticism or gay ordination or PowerPoint in worship or whatever, else it will vanish into the dustbin of history. This way of speaking is not an argument; it is a slogan, thrown like a grenade when what we need is a surgeon's careful scalpel. There are plenty of places where modernity is alive and well—my mainline liberal church, Gary Memorial United Methodist Church in Wheaton, carries on much as it did in the 1950s and is doing just fine. Mark Driscoll's neo-fundamentalism is incredibly modern out in Seattle and is clearly having no trouble growing. It seems to me Emergent can speak of itself as offering faithful new resources for Christians in some places, without tearing down the work being done quite differently. Surely *différance* is an emphasis of postmodernism that should overcome the modernist hubris of accusing someone else of missing the boat.

One tradition that has been wrestling with modernity and postmodernism for centuries now is the Roman Catholic, ironically enough. Emergent could use some theologians in dialogue with figures like Herbert McCabe. The great Dominican saw the limited but necessary place of creedal and doctrinal Christianity. He could write, "I don't know how they will be formulating Christianity in the twenty-fourth-century, but at least I know

---

[40]Gibbs and Bolger, *Emerging Churches*, p. 46.
[41]I borrow here from lectures and conversation with my friend Steve Long of Marquette University.

they won't be Arians or Nestorians."[42] Nicholas Lash is another Catholic
theologian from whom Emergent has much to learn.[43] Lash described a
theologian as one "who watches their language in the presence of God"
(see—one can be cheeky without alienating one's fellow evangelicals).
Lash means it: theology is a matter of care for words, in Scripture, the
creeds, in worship, for without vigilant attention to language we fall very
quickly into idolatry. For Lash, the first casualty of sin is carelessness with
language. I love Emergent's energy, its vision, its effort to renew not just
evangelical churches but the whole church of Jesus Christ. When it pur-
sues this, it ought not malign other churches, whether ancient, like Augustine's, or modern, like its fellow evangelicals. The blessing is that it need
not do so. It can look to Jesus, the pioneer and perfecter of our faith, without looking askance at those on its right or left. In doing so, it may remind
the rest of us to do the same. As it does so it can come out and articulate
enough theology for the rest of us to take part in the conversation as well.

---

[42]See Roger Owens, "Don't Talk Nonsense: Why Herbert McCabe Still Matters," *Christian Century*, January 25, 2005. See Herbert McCabe, *God Matters* (New York: Continuum, 2005), among many others.

[43]Among Nicholas Lash's many books, see *Theology on the Way to Emmaus* (London: SCM, 1986).

Contributors

Jason Byassee is assistant editor for the *Christian Century*. His publications include numerous articles and *Reading Augustine: A Guide to the Confessions, An Introduction to the Desert Fathers* and *Praise Seeking Understanding: Reading the Psalms with Augustine.*

Brian E. Daley, S.J., is Catherine F. Husking Professor of Theology at the University of Notre Dame. He is past president of the North American Patristic Society and is particularly known for his books *The Hope of the Early Church* and *Gregory of Nazianzus.*

Michael Graves is assistant professor of Old Testament at Wheaton College. He is the author of *Jerome's Hebrew Philology: A Study Based on His Commentary on Jeremiah.*

Jeffrey P. Greenman is associate dean of biblical and theological studies and professor of Christian ethics at Wheaton College. He is the coauthor of *Unwearied Praises* and editor of three books, including *Reading Romans Through the Centuries* and *The Sermon on the Mount Through the Centuries.*

Christopher A. Hall is provost, dean of Templeton Honors College, and professor of biblical studies and theology at Eastern University. His books include *Reading Scripture with the Church Fathers* and *Learning Theology with the Church Fathers.*

Mark Husbands is the Leonard and Marjorie Maas Associate Professor of Reformed Theology at Hope College. He has completed the monograph *Barth's Ethics of Prayer* and has edited six books, including *The Beauty of God* and *The Community of the Word.*

George Kalantzis is associate professor of theology at Wheaton College.

He is the author of numerous articles on patristic thought and the monograph *Theodore of Mopsuestia: Commentary on the Gospel of John.*

Paul I. Kim is a doctoral student and teaching fellow in the Religion Department at Baylor University. He also serves as pastor of First Korean Baptist Church in Waco, Texas.

Alan Kreider is associate professor of church history and mission at Associated Mennonite Biblical Seminary. He edited *The Origins of Christendom in the West* and is the author of *The Change of Conversion and the Origin of Christendom*

Peter J. Leithart is senior fellow of theology and literature, and dean of graduate studies at New Saint Andrews College. His books include a theological commentary on 1 and 2 Kings and *The Priesthood of the Plebs: A Theology of Baptism.*

D. Stephen Long is professor of theology at Marquette University. His recent books include *The Divine Economy, The Goodness of God* and *John Wesley's Moral Theology.*

Nicholas Perrin is associate professor of New Testament at Wheaton College. His recent books include *Thomas, The Other Gospel* and *Lost in Transmission: What We Can Know About the Words of Jesus.*

Christine D. Pohl is professor of church in society at Asbury Theological Seminary. She is the author of *Making Room: Recovering Hospitality as a Christian Tradition* and coauthor of two books: *Responding to Refugees: Christian Reflections on a Global Crisis* and *Living on the Boundaries: Evangelical Women, Feminism and the Theological Academy.*

John D. Witvliet is director of the Calvin Institute of Christian Worship and serves as associate professor of worship, theology and music at Calvin College and Calvin Theological Seminary. His publications include *Worship Seeking Understanding: Windows into Christian Practice* and *The Biblical Psalms in Christian Worship.*

D. H. Williams is professor of religion in patristics and historical theology at Baylor University. His books include *Evangelicals and Tradition: The Formative Influence of the Early Church, Retrieving the Tradition and Renewing Evangelicalism: A Primer for Suspicious Protestants* and *Ambrose of Milan and the End of the Nicene-Arian Conflicts.*

Name Index

Subject Index

Scripture Index